MW01279990

MOTORMEN & YACHTING

OTHER BOOKS BY MICHAEL M. DIXON

"LIFE AT THE FLATS, The Golden Era of the St. Clair River Delta," *Collectors Edition* is an edited and revised compilation of the three volume history of the area first published in 1985. During the late 19th century the area was known worldwide as America's Venice, one of the country's most unique resort destinations. It first became a resort destination in an era before automobiles and telephones were dreamed of and its fame peaked in an era when magnificent white passenger steamers arrived almost one after another to exchange passengers at the docks of palatial private clubs and public resorts as well as the popular Tashmoo Park. The 192 pages in this edition are lavishly illustrated with over 250 rare illustrations.

"WHEN DETROIT RODE THE WAVES, a summer cruise from Toledo to Port Huron aboard the excursion boats of the early 20th Century" retraces the South Channel of the St. Clair River so vividly detailed in the Mike's previous books and continues north to Port Huron and south to Toledo. In "When Detroit Rode the Waves" the reader boards the Steamers *Tashmoo* and *Greyhound* for a full day excursion from Toledo to Port Huron with stops in Detroit and many of the parks and resorts along the Detroit and St. Clair Rivers, in an era when Detroit was home to the nation's largest fleet of excursion and passenger ships. With 40 full-color pages illustrating the historic cruise and over 100 period post cards, the past doe not seem so remote. Among another 90+ illustrations are reproductions of advertisements for period hotels and products that help to capture a glimpse of the early 20th century and allow us to enjoy a bit of a grand era that many of us never knew.

For copies of these great books visit
www.MervuePublications.com, email the author
at MervuePublications@comcast.net or contact:

St. Clair Memories
49 Macomb Place
Mt. Clemens, MI 48043

www.StClairMemories.con
Email: info@StClairMemories.com

MOTORMEN
&
YACHTING

Volume I

THE WATERFRONT HERITAGE OF THE AUTOMOBILE INDUSTRY

By

Michael M. Dixon

Cover art by Camilo Pardo

Mervue Publications

© 2005 by Michael M. Dixon
ISBN-13: 978-0-97108-332-5
ISBN-10: 0-97108-332-0
Library of Congress Control Number: 2005931684

All rights reserved. No part of this book may be reproduced or transmitted in any form or
by any means, electronic or mechanical, including photocopying, recording, or by any
information storage and retrieval system, without permission in writing from the author.

PATRON'S DEDICATION

Publishing of this book could not have been possible without the financial support of Pre-publishing Subscribers. A Patron Special Edition is dedicated to the following:

Mr. & Mrs. George Hayes Bay
Chuck and Scotty Brockman
Paul & Judy Chauvin
Commodore Mushrat, a/k/a Bob Coulter
Barb & George Crown, Crown Studio & Gallery
Beverly & Geoffrey Mulford Dixon
Russell & Susan Dixon
Jane & Pete Dow
Charles T. Fisher III
David & Shelley Gagnon
Bill and Nancy Gard
George & Lori Gill
Gorton & Renata Greene
Bruce, Katherine and Geoffrey Greening
Robert J. Hafel
Ted Held
In Memory of Charlie Hubner
Jim and Nina Johnson
In Memory of Our Parents, Paul & Judy Krietsch
Tom & Annie Lockwood
Patrick M. McQueen
Peter W. Meek
Douglas R. Micknass
Ron & Gloria Moore
The NAHC & Friends of the Detroit Public Library
Rodo Padilla & Family
Kenneth E. Schramm
Mike and Sandy Skinner
Dr. Edwin and Patricia Soler
Gary & Holly Steward
Rev. Fr. Douglas Terrien
In Memory of Lloyd and Carmen Torres

About the Author

Michael M. Dixon is a descendant of early settlers who played active roles in Detroit's transformation from "Furs to Factories." Many of those same people were pioneers in the transformation of the nearby St. Clair River Delta, Harsens Island and the St. Clair Flats, into one of the nation's most desirable and unique summer retreats in the late 1800s. Michael has always enjoyed sailing and cruising the delta area and the other connecting waters from Lake Huron to Lake Erie. A natural interest in the history of the waterfront communities along the Detroit and St. Clair Rivers led to him detailing the history of the St. Clair Flats and Harsens Island in a series of books that have been compiled in the *Collectors' Edition of Life at the Flats.*

The author, above, with a once revolutionary *Naphtha* Engine.

When Detroit Rode the Waves, followed as a logical continuation of Michael's research of life and things around the Detroit and St. Clair River. In the 19th and early 20th century the only means of reaching "The Flats" was by boat, usually one of the many passenger ships that made Detroit the home port to the nation's largest fleet of excursion and passenger steamships. *When Detroit Rode the Waves* recreates a narrated summer cruise on one of the majestic excursion boats, illustrated with over190 illustrations, including 100 classic color post cards. The collection of images combined with descriptive text captures a rare glimps of that grand era.

Motormen & Yachting is yet another continuation of his interest in the history of the life and industry on the Detroit and St. Clair Rivers. Michael anticipates one more volume in the series that will conclude with the history of Gray Marine Motor Company.

COVER ART

Media: oil on canvas (72"x22")
by Camilo Pardo

The cover art depicts Michael's premise that the development of lightweight internal combustion engines suitable for personal transportation vehicles first took place on lakes and rivers.

Camilo has spent most of his career at Ford Motor Company Advance Studios and is currently chief designer in Ford's Living Legends Studio where he was responsible for the design and development of the new GT-40. He graduated from the College for Creative Studies (CCS) in Detroit and received the Industrial Design Society America Merit Award in 1985. Camilo is an accomplished artist whose work has been featured in galleries and shows worldwide. His paintings are found in private and corporate collections and, among many locations, have been exhibited at the Detroit Institute of Art, the Paris Motor Show and the Meadow Brook Concours d'Elegance.

ACKNOWLEDGEMENTS

Published works are acknowledged in the chapter references but, without the personal assistance of many individuals and special collections this manuscript would not have completed.

Above all, I must thank my mother, Joan Mulford Dixon, who in addition to being a loving and supportive mother, must be acknowledged for having been the one of her generation who had the interest to save boxes of miscellanea collected by prior generations. The hidden treasures they held provided my first clues to the relationship that early motormen had with both marine engines and pioneer automobiles. For some 20 years I have been adding to the information found in those boxes.

For bringing years of collecting to a logical conclusion, I must thank the staff and directors of the "Motor Cities" National Automotive Heritage Area for a grant that enabled me to research distant collections and forced me to set a completion date. The staff and collections of the Antique Boat Museum, Clayton, New York, and the Mystic Seaport, Mystic, Connecticut, provided valuable support and the perspective to make this more than just a Detroit story. Thanks also go to the staff and collections of The Henry Ford (Museum), whose archives go well beyond the history of everything Ford, and the Dossin Great Lakes Museum, Detroit History Department.

Without the collections and generous assistance from Mark Patrick, curator of the National Automotive History Collection, his staff and the staff of other departments of the Detroit Public Library this manuscript may never have been completed. The special resources of the Library's National Automotive History Collection, Burton Historical Collection and the Science and Technology Department together offered hundreds of hours of research opportunity. Their files and periodical collections made possible the large number of illustrations that bring this story to life.

Scott Peters at the Michigan History Museum in Lansing has spent years compiling a data bank on Michigan boat and engine manufacturers. His generous contribution provided the framework to consolidate my miscellaneous files into a substantially complete, illustrated reference guide to Michigan marine engine manufacturers operating before and during the formative years of the automobile industry.

At times this project became overwhelming and risked being put back into boxes. I am appreciative of the many friends who looked over drafts and provided technical oversight of the subject, constructive criticism and, most importantly, encouragement, including Arthur Mullen, Paul Duffy, Michael Skinner, Charles K. Hyde, John Polacsek and Matt Lee. Special thanks go to Carol Lynn, Al Warren and Jean Pomroy, whose review of early drafts made this final copy more readable.

Photos: Except as noted, most of the illustrations in this book have come from the author's collection, including digitally enhanced reproductions from period publications, including magazines, newspapers and catalogs. A special acknowledgement and thanks goes to the Detroit Public Library for the use of many rare photographs from its special collections.

Preface

The project that became this book began almost 20 years ago. At that time I intended to revise and illustrate the history of Gray Marine Motor Company written by my grandfather, John W. Mulford. The corporate biography written by my grandfather was limited to the corporate life of Gray Motor Company (1905-1926) and Gray Marine Motor Company (1923 to 1968). The founder of both companies, O. J. Mulford, clearly traced their origin back to the time of the Sintz Gas Engine Company, builders of marine gas engines since 1891.[1] A Sintz marine engine was prominently on display in the lobby of Gray Marine Motor Company.

Knowing that the oldest surviving American gas powered automobile is powered by a Sintz marine engine,[2] it seemed to me that background on that company deserved some additional investigation. Research revealed that the Sintz engine was the first commercially successful gas engine used on the Great Lakes and it significantly contributed to the popularization of power boating in the 1890s. Observing that both corporate and personal relationships associated with the men and machines from the Sintz and Gray enterprises carried into the early years of the automobile industry led me to believe the role of the marine engine in shaping Detroit's image as "The Motor City" has been significantly under rated by most historians.

The technical relationship was stated simply by Westin Farmer, naval architect and for 30 years the editor of Popular Mechanix magazine: *"the marine engine is the parent of the automobile engine."* Regarding the cultural lineage, early motormen developed lightweight internal combustion engines that introduced mechanically powered personal watercraft at a time when the horseless carriage was ridiculed and treated as a nuisance. In doing so, they built a profitable gas engine industry and opened men's minds to the possibilities of self-powered personal transportation vehicles. Some of the best remembered motormen who participated in the early days of the marine engine industry in Detroit include Charles B. King, Henry Leland (Cadillac and Lincoln), David Buick, Henry Ford, Henry B. Joy (Packard), and Ransom Olds.

Steam engines had powered the industrial revolution and had been the first to mechanically power ships. Some of the wealthiest Americans of the 19th century owned large steam yachts for personal recreation and commuting between their country homes and the major business centers. By the late 19th century the harbors of major cities were populated with small owner-operated powerboats using new types of small engines: Naphtha, Alco-Vapor, electric and a variety of internal combustion type engines. A growing number of middle-class observers desired powerboats and popular demand followed.

In researching early owner-operated powerboats, I came to appreciate the largely forgotten contribution of a then revolutionary external combustion vapor type engine, the patented "Naphtha" engine. The Naphtha engine was patented in 1883, before the existence of an internal combustion engine capable of operating with a liquid fuel. They operated on the familiar principles of the steam engine but, because its naphtha fueled burners also boiled

---

1. The Sintz Gas Engine Company (1891-1904) was acquired and moved to Detroit in 1900 as a subsidiary of the Michigan Yacht & Power Co. Its president, O.J. Mulford, was the company's Detroit agent and his boatbuilding business had become its largest customer.
2. Elwood Haynes built an automobile with a Sintz engine in 1894. That vehicle is in the collection of the Smithsonian Institute.

naphtha, a type of gasoline, it was not technically a steam engine and was not subject to the regulations of the Steamboat Inspection Act.[3]

By circumventing the Steamboat Inspection Act the "Naphtha" launch became the first commercially produced, mechanically powered, owner-operated "automobile" in America. It was also the first practical engine in the world to rely solely on a portable liquid fuel. Their use by the very wealthy quickly spread throughout America and foreign countries. Electric powerboats began to appear by 1890, and added another option for a growing demand among the very wealthy.

In the 1890s, when boiler explosions were still a frightening and all too common an experience, the sound of the strange "exploding" internal combustion engines must have terrorized not just the horses but the community at large. However, with few affordable alternatives, many people accepted the gas engine as the prime mover in owner-operated powerboats. By their example many people came to appreciate the advantages of internal combustion marine engines by the dawn of the 20th century.

In the East, vapor engines and electric motors were the leading prime movers but, pioneer motormen in the Great Lakes did not manufacturer the patented "Naphtha" or show much interest in electric motors. Instead they tinkered with gas engines. The area's industry was largely based on shipbuilding and marine steam engine manufacturing. The necessary talent and equipment was directly transferable to building internal combustion engines. Notably, by the mid-1890s, neither steam nor internal combustion engines were protected by general patents.

In addition to shipbuilding, the nation's carriage and rail car manufacturing industries were also concentrated in the Great Lakes area owing to the cheaper availability of raw materials, such as iron ore and lumber. By the time the Eastern elite had created the beginning of an automobile industry based on steam and electric motors,[4] the gas engine pioneers of the Great Lakes area were ready to build comparatively inexpensive automobiles powered by gas engines.

When the Olds Motor Works made the decision in 1901 to stop manufacturing stationary and marine engines[5], it went into production of a single model gas powered automobile at a popular price. Immediately it became the world's largest manufacture of gas powered road vehicles. On that success was founded a great industry in the City of Detroit and the steam and electric types began to lose market share and gradually disappeared from the market.

The marine gas engine business may not be recognized as a great industry when compared to the automobile. However, as late as 1910, *Gas Engine* magazine observed that while much attention was being given to impressive numbers of automobiles being produced, the largely invisible gasoline marine engine still outnumbered automobile engines in use by a factor of two to one. It was the impressive number of marine gas engines that prepared a generation of mechanics to establish Detroit's automobile industry.

---

3. All steamboats operating on Federal waterways were regulated by the Steamboat Inspection Act. Without exception, all steamboats required annual inspections and were required to be operated under control of a licensed steam engineer and captain.
4. Thousands of electric powered automobiles had been built and sold in Hartford, Connecticut before there was any commercial automobile manufacturing established in Detroit.
5. Commercial production of the "Curved Dashed Olds" began in March. The marine engine business was sold to Michigan Yacht and Power Company several months later.

In the near future I intend to return to the original project and more thoroughly explore one of the most important marine engine manufacturers, Gray Motor Company and its successor Gray Marine Motor Company. And, by its example, in some way illustrate how the marine engine and automobile industry continued to benefit from each other beyond the pioneer era. The story of Gray Marine, and many of the men associated with the company will illustrate the common development and growth of both the gasoline marine engine and the automobile engine businesses. It will also be shown, as history repeats, that Gray Marine played a leading role in field testing and promoting an acceptance of the two-cycle, high-speed Diesel in the era preceding and during World War II. In the end the economic factors brought by World War II and its aftermath led to the demise of the independent marine engine manufacturers. Most closed their doors over the following decade and Gray Marine was nearly alone when production ceased in 1968.

I hope that the information contained in the following pages will contribute to a better understanding of the pioneering days when steam, electric, "Naphtha," and gasoline engines were all debated as the prime mover of the future. Also I hope that this will create some interest in and appreciation for the long gone independent marine engine manufacturers.

Michael M. Dixon, 2005

TABLE OF CONTENTS

INTRODUCTION

"Historically, the marine engine was the parent of the automobile engine."
-Weston Farmer, Editor, Mechanix Illustrated, 1938 - 1984

This is a story about small engines before and during the early years of the automobile industry. Before the advent of reliable and affordable lightweight internal combustion engines, steam, Naphtha and electric engines had been a commercial success in power boats. The popularity of steam, Naphtha and electric launches led to increasing demand for affordable engines to use in small boats in the decade before Detroit became the manufacturing home of a production model automobile of any kind. In the mid-1890s, a thriving small gas engine and boat building industry with a national reputation was concentrated on the Grand River in Grand Rapids and Lansing, Michigan. By the late 1890s Detroit investors had relocated several of those businesses to Detroit where other talented machinists were already turning their attention to small gas engines. In that way Detroit became the "Motor City" before it became an automobile center.

To understand the evolution of personal transportation leading to early days of the automobile industry, this writer believes it is important to understand the development of not only the gas engine, but also the other types of engines that competed as prime movers in the formative years. Small boats provided a commercial opportunity for engine builders and in so doing provided the testing field for development of lightweight portable engine technology. By their example, power boating opened men's minds to the potential of personal motorized transportation.

To introduce a timeline, a trend towards the ownership of personal motorized transportation began shortly before the American Civil War. Before there were any significant experiments with horseless carriages there were steam yachts owned by the super wealthy for recreation and commuting between their country homes and the major urban centers. However, practical and regulatory constraints generally limited the use of steam engines to large boats. For the less wealthy a motorized vehicle that could be operated without hired hands, on the owners' personal schedules and on their particular routes would not be available until new technology made it possible, practical and affordable.

The 1883 patent for the *Naphtha* engine addressed both design and regulatory issues. The Naphtha engine was a compact vapor engine that stacked the boiler on top of the engine, thus freeing passenger space. It used a clean portable liquid fuel that could be stored in otherwise unused space below decks, thus freeing additional passenger space. Because it boiled naphtha, a type of gasoline, it was not a "steam" engine and so was not restricted by regulations governing the use of steam engines in boats. While still an expensive luxury item, the Naphtha engine popularized power boating by using a familiar technology that circumvented restrictive regulations. An internal combustion engine capable of operating with a liquid fuel supply was not commercially available anywhere until after Nicholas Otto developed the first workable carburetor in 1885. For that reason the Naphtha engine can be credited with providing the first commercially successful owner-operated, self-powered vehicle in America.

There had been only a few private steam yachts in Michigan when the Naphtha was patented. In the 1892 catalog from the manufacturer of the Naphtha engine, a referral list includes 31 owners in Michigan. A small number, yes, but they were remarkable vehicles that provided an example for thousands of observing steamboat passengers. Many of the observers who began to appreciate the possibilities of personal self-powered watercraft. Consequently, marketing demand was building for small affordable power boats, at a time when no such demand yet existed for a horseless carriage[1]. It was a time when horseless carriages were ridiculed and treated as nuisances.

By 1893 electric boats were available and enjoying a commercial success, most notably in rental fleets and as small passenger-boats. Fifty-five were used that year at the World's Columbian Exhibition in Chicago. By comparison there were only two gas powered boats at the fair, one powered by a Daimler engine built in New York and another built by the Sintz Gas Engine Company of Grand Rapids, Michigan.

Both the Naphtha and electric launches were affordable options only for the very wealthy. However, by 1903 a fully equipped gasoline powered launch manufactured in Detroit was available for $100 from C. H. Bloomstrom Mfg. Co.

The internal combustion engine provided an option that was affordable to a growing middle class and people who used boats to make living, such as fishermen and ferrymen. These people had reason to tolerate the frightful exploding "perfumed" engines that were abhorred by the upper class. A few stops and starts, while inconvenient, did not halt forward momentum in a small boat[2] as they would in a horseless carriage. By the late-1890s, owner-operated power boats were a common sight on navigable waterways and harbors everywhere.

The field testing of lightweight, reliable gas engines in small boats brought their manufacture to a reasonable level of technical maturity by the time there was any commercial interest in self-powered, owner-operated land vehicles. Apart from the technical advances learned from waterfront testing, widespread use of the internal combustion engine in boats significantly contributed to creating an acceptance of the "exploding" type of engines by the general public.

At the end of the 19th century a promising automobile industry was emerging on the east coast, concentrated in Hartford, Connecticut. At that time, eastern manufacturers were building complex steam carriages and simple, reliable, but expensive, electric automobiles. In New York, the exclusive manufacturer of the Naphtha engine had supplied thousands to owner-operated power boats throughout the country and overseas.

Pioneer motormen in the Great Lakes area did not manufacture the patented Naphtha and electric motors, but instead built on the area's heritage of shipbuilding and manufacturing of marine steam engines. The talent and equipment necessary to build and repair steam engines was directly transferable to building internal combustion engines. Like steam engines, internal combustion engines use pistons and valves and neither the steam engine nor most types of internal combustion engines were protected by general patents by the mid-1890s.

At the end of the 19th century there was already a number of Michigan motormen with

---

1. Even in Europe where automobile development was way ahead of American automobiles throughout the 1890s, nobody had built more than a couple of automobiles by 1892.
2. Even today any competent boat handler should be able to control the landing of a small sail or power boat after the engine is shut down.

national reputations for their gas marine engines, including the Sintz Gas Engine Company and the Sintz family's Wolverine Gas Engine Company. In addition, Ransom Olds, and Charles B. King[3] were nationally known Michigan marine engine manufacturers. Others such as David Buick and Henry Ford enjoyed a local reputation for marine engines that generated the sales that sustained their engine testing and development before the days of a Detroit based automobile industry. Before taking over the failed Henry Ford Company and transforming it into the Cadillac Motor Car Company in 1902, Henry Leland[4] built marine gas engines for others. Every automobile manufacturer in Detroit's formative years (up to 1903) had previously manufactured and/or serviced marine engines.

Forgotten Motormen

There were other gas engine pioneers in the MotorCity at the turn of the century who built both marine gas engines and automobiles. Many have been forgotten and lost to history, but a few can be identified. An extraordinary example is Carl H. Bloomstrom. He began building marine gas engines as early as 1891 and built his first automobile in 1897. After relocating to Detroit in 1901 he became well known as a manufacturer of marine engines, launches and automobiles. Max Dingfelder's automobile was well received in 1903, but after an impressive exhibit of his marine engines at the 1908 Detroit Motor Boat Show, his name seems to disappear. Stanley DuBrie is little remembered except by marine engine enthusiasts but, while he manufactured marine engines as a specialty, he built his first automobile in 1897. In 1904 the DuBrie-Caille Automobile received good reviews before the Caille family dropped that plan and instead manufactured a popular line of marine engines. DuBrie continued manufacturing marine engines under his name and in 1910 he built the Templeton-DuBrie automobile. Before building the great Kermath marine engines, James Kermath began building automobile parts and a complete automobile, the "Kermath Speed-Away," that received good reviews. Before building the Hammer-Sommer automobile, Henry Sommer was building marine engines. These men are briefly remembered in the appendix, "Metro Detroit Marine Engine Builders."

Owing to the cheaper availability of raw materials, such as iron ore and lumber, the nation's carriage and rail car industry were already concentrated in the Great Lakes area. Not surprisingly, by the time the Eastern elite had created an automobile industry based on steam and electric motors pioneer motormen in the Great Lakes area were ready to build practical gas powered vehicles cheaper and faster.

In March 1901, the Olds Motor Works made the decision to shift from manufacturing stationary and marine engines, to the production of a single model gas powered automobile at a popular price. That same year Olds Motor Works became the world's largest manufacture of that type of vehicle. On that successes was founded a great industry in the City of Detroit and the steam and electric type automobiles began to disappear from the market.

---

3. His partners in the Charles B. King Co., Henry B. Joy and John S. Newberry, Sere the leading investors who brought the Packard Motor Car Company to Detroit in 1902.
4. Reportedly his first internal combustion engines were small ones built for Frank J. Dimmer, who had a boat shop in Detroit and later larger marine engines were built for Charles Strelinger for the retail trade. He was also a manufacturer of blocks and other parts for many of Detroit's pioneer motormen.

This story begins with Section I, "Power Behind the Transportation Revolution." All of the major engine types that competed as prime movers in the late 19th century, steam, Naphtha, Alco-vapor, electric and both two and four-stroke internal combustion engines contributed to the process of opening men's minds to the possibility of mechanically powered personal transportation vehicles. It will be shown that they all had their first commercial success as prime movers in boats, long before there was any automobile industry.

It is this writer's opinion that if a gasoline engine that could operate on a portable liquid fuel had not come of age in the last years of the 19th century, an automobile industry would have developed without it. The industry would have been concentrated in the east and may have moved as far west as eastern Lake Erie, to take advantage of the cheaper movement of raw materials, iron ore, coal and lumber, by way of steamships. If a network of charging stations would have been built soon enough, electrics may have dominated. And if regulatory restrictions had been lifted on steam power in small boats, the advances in small steam engine technology developed for the turn of the century automobile might have been available sooner. Certainly, small boats with keel cooled condensing systems, utilizing available space below deck to carry a sufficient liquid fuel supply, would have operated very well, especially on the great fresh water lakes. Nevertheless, the faster more fuel efficient internal combustion engine would eventually have come along and become the dominate prime mover for all small vehicles. However, in either hypothetical scenario, Detroit may not have been the "Motor City." The early interest in internal combustion engine by Detroit motormen gave them a competitive advantage in the critical early years of the automobile industry. That the technological advancements of early small gas engines were field tested on the water before there was any commercial interest in horseless carriages is the main message of this story.

Section II, "Off to the Races, Part I," is the first part of a brief, two-part history of early power boat racing. The first part covers the years when power boat racing was local and included all the competing types of prime movers: vapor, electric and exploding gas engines. It was a newsworthy activity that attracted attention to possibilities of powered vehicles. In that era Detroit yachtsmen participated in races from western Lake Erie to southern Lake Huron. From the scarce available references to those early races it can be seen that Detroit motormen were leaders in putting the gas engine in the forefront. Sanctioned "Naphtha" launch races have been documented as early as 1895 around New York. The earliest powerboat races of importance to Detroit were held on Lake Erie in 1897. It is interesting to note that in July 1950 the first recorded power boat race sanctioned by a yacht club on the Detroit River was more than a year before the first automobile race in the Detroit area.

In "Trendsetters", Section III, the early gas engine years of six notable motormen are recalled. It will be shown by their examples that gas engine expertise was greatly advanced by their marine engine developments.

Section IV explores the second period of power boat racing, 1903-1912, and highlights the continued testing and innovative designs of marine engines that contributed to advancements for all lightweight, high-speed, internal combustion engines, both on and off the water.

As an aid for future reference, two appendices are included: Chapter 17, Detroit Area

Marine Engine Manufacturers and Chapter 18, Other Michigan Marine Engine Manufacturers. These last two chapters include mini-biographies of the companies that were manufacturing marine engines before World War I.

In concluding, in September 1913 the automobile industry was young, but well established, when the Detroit Board of Commerce's magazine, *The Detroiter,* published a review of the city's many industries. The reviews were written by leaders in their fields. O. J. Mulford was asked to contribute the review of the gasoline engine business. He was well suitable to the task as the founder and head of Gray Motor Company. He had been in the gas engine business since before the days of the automobile industry and had been on the Board of United States Motors (a predecessor of Chrysler Corporation), co-founded the King Motor Car Company and headed the advertising agency that represented both the Ford and Packard motor car companies from 1903-1910. As a well informed insider he wrote:

> *To a very great degree, no doubt, Detroit owes its dominance in the automobile world to its interest in the marine gasoline engine, before the days of the automobile.*

He cited Charles B. King, Henry B. Joy, A. E. Brush, William Kelly, David Buick and Henry Leland as leading automobile men that were first builders of marine motors. After citing impressive production numbers he went on to say:

> *. . . the marine gasoline engine business of itself, is not a great industry, as compared with the automobile, yet it can take to itself, to a great extent, the credit of having put Detroit on the automobile map in the eyes of the world, and at the same time of making Detroit the greatest producer of small marine motors of any city in the world.*

Personal Transportation in the 19th Century

A transportation revolution began when bicycles and power boats opened men's minds to new possibilities of personal transportation in the last decades of the 19th century. Mankind long ago envisioned flying machines, space travel and self-propelled vehicles. However, the visions of people like Leonardo da Vinci and Jules Vernes were ahead of not only the available technology but, they also preceded any perceived need or popular demand.

The transition from the centuries old form of land transportation by horse and carriage to one of automobiles was neither quick nor easy. For most of the 19th century the concept of personal transportation was very limited and certainly did not include a popular vision of individually owned and operated vehicles propelled by mechanical means.

There simply was no perceived need for personal transportation vehicles in the 19th century. In the larger cities, public transportation was generally adequate and distances between home and work were short. Street cars, first pulled by horses over iron capped wooden rails, were common by the mid 1800s. By the end of the century places such as Detroit were well served by motorized street cars in the city. Interurban light-rail passenger trains connected the city to neighboring communities in southeastern Michigan and beyond. At the turn of the century a leisurely ride in the country still meant a buggy ride or an excursion by rail or steamboat, many of which included bands or other entertainment.

In rural America the common farm wagon had long been adequate to provide necessary transportation for the family. By the end of the century an ordinary buggy was selling for just over one month's wage of an ordinary tradesman.

In 1893 the Wilber H. Murray Manufacturing Company advertised buggies for $55.95, about the same price as a bicycle.

The Bicycle and Good Roads

It is generally acknowledged that the evolution of the bicycle, from the athletically challenging "High Wheel" machine to the popular modern "safety" bike, contributed to advances in component technology that played a significant role in leading the way for lightweight carriages and the automobile. The advent of the safety bicycle also contributed to changing men's perceptions of personal transportation by introducing the possibilities

21

of independent travel over ordinary highways. Perhaps most importantly, the bicycle movement led the way in promoting the cause for building good roads and securing the right of access to public roads for mechanically propelled vehicles. As early as 1891, *Outing,* the magazine of the American Wheelmen, called upon all Wheelmen to refuse to vote for any candidate to support good roads.

The first popular bicycles were the High Wheeled, so-called "ordinary" bicycles, in the 1870s. They quickly became a fad and competitive bicycling attracted the era's daredevils

By 1880 gears and chains came into use permitting the design of the modern, so-called "safety" bicycles that have the same size wheels front and back. However, it was not until 1892 that improvements in weight, strength and reliability led to "safety" style bikes beating the High Wheelers on the race track. Air filled tuves and tires did not come into common use until the early 1890s and coaster brakes did not come about until the late 1890s. Each improvement made it possible for more people to get involved. When improved bicycles expanded the market beyond sporting daredevils to include gentlemen and ladies, a far reaching social revolution was underway.

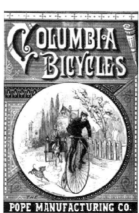

Bicycles were not necessarily well received when they first began to appear on public streets Many people feared being run over by wild wheelmen and it was reported that horses reared in fright. In 1880 New York City banned bicycling in Central Park!

Col. Albert Pope, the leading bicycle manufacturer in America, feared that if cities banned bicycles from public spaces, interest in the bicycle would die. He staged a challenge to the ban and financed the defense fund. It was a long seven-year fight but, after several setbacks, in 1887 the New York state legislature passed a law giving bicycles the same rights as horses and carriages. That decision was an important precedent that led the way for the right to use automobiles on public roadways.

The growing number of vehicles forced advances in traffic control regulations that brought more order to the chaos that controlled the nation's streets. When New York City required bicycles to have brakes, the cyclists protested claiming it would promote less safety by removing the incentive for riders to learn how to properly jump off!

The fledgling automakers had the most to gain from good roads but, they were not ready to join Pope in the fight. For the most part, automakers at the turn of the century consisted of small garages turning out a limited number of vehicles for a local market. Rather than making time to support a national movement for paved streets, they concentrated on building cars that could travel the muddy, rutted roads.

Author Stephen Goodard points out that it was the railroad industry, and not automakers, that came to Pope's aid in promoting good roads. Up to that time such produce as beef, milk and eggs were semi-seasonal commodities where impassable roads kept the items out of the market place. Railroad owners saw that an interlinking system of good roads would enable farmers to deliver their goods over the entire twelve months of the year, thus allowing more cargo to be carried per train and thereby eliminating chronic seasonal shortages of railcars. In the spring of 1901 Stuyvesant Fish, president of the Illinois Central Railroad, and Pope's friend, sent eight railcars full of road building equipment from Chicago to New Orleans. The train stopped at communities in five states to give instruction and demonstrations to county road supervisors. At each stop they left short strips of paved roads. By 1905 the "Good Roads Trains" had covered thirty-six states. What the railroad companies did not envision was that they had created the infrastructure to support a new form of competition.

The bicycle movement was also instrumental in bringing on a profound social change in fashion trends. Garments designed for bicycling initiated a welcome departure from the more formal dress requirements of the Victorian Era. Reportedly, Susan B. Anthony said that the changes in fashion brought about by the bicycle did more to advance woman's liberation than anything else in the world.

The American Waterways

Beasts of burden was not a satisfactory substitution to power personal transportation vehicles across open water.[1] However, America's excellent system of waterways provided a natural highway for all types of mechanically powered boats. Experiments to provide personal transportation over the waves had existed ever since man first tried to cross a river. New types of power were always welcome experiments in process to find ways to replace wind and muscle power for all types of watercraft, large and small. Naturally a transportation system based on steamships preceded railroads by decades.

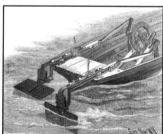

Pedal Power was not just for bicycles

All types of mechanical power were employed in boats, including pedal power. As prime movers, steam, vapor, electric and gasoline engines first achieved commercial success as marine engines. Due to practical limitations on the use of steam to power

---

1. There were actually some horse powered ferries in the first decades of the 19th century. The horses powered paddle wheels by running on treadmills or operating turnstiles.

launches and regulatory restrictions on the use of steam engines on Federal waterways, other non-steam options were eagerly sought to power small (16 to 35 foot) boats. Small, simple power plants called "naphtha" engines began to appear in the mid-1880s and were readily accepted as prime movers in ferryboats and yacht tenders which stimulated an interest in power boating for pleasure.

By the 1890s, the popularity of "Naphtha" and electric powered launches created a market demand they could not fully supply. About the same time, small internal combustion engines were reaching a nominal level of performance that made them acceptable alternatives. Earlier, "exploding" type engines had been found only in remote areas or behind factory walls, so the public was not very familiar with them. Compared to the quiet, familiar steam and electric motors, gas engines frightened both men and horses. On the water, however, they provided transportation and recreation while avoiding confrontation with a fearful public. By the end of the decade advances in the design of the lightweight "exploding" marine engines were creating possibilities for personal transportation that could not have been imagined earlier.

To better understand the advent and acceptance of self-powered, personal transportation vehicles, it is necessary to explore development of the alternative types of power that were adopted for use in transportation vehicles on land and over water. The following chapters explore the evolution and adaptation of the steam, vapor, electric and internal combustion engines in the chronological order of their development and public acceptance.

References:

Berkebile, Don H., editor, "American Carriages, Sleighs, Sulkies, and Carts," Dover Publications, Mineola, NY, 1977

Goddard, Stephen B., "Colonel Albert Pope and His American Dream Machines," McFarlan & Co., Jefferson, NC, 2000

Maxim, Hiram Percy, "Horseless Carriage Days," Harper & Brothers, New York, NY 1937

The Automobile's Bicycle Heritage, The Society of Automotive Historians, Automotive History Review, Fall 1902

www.bicyclemuseum.com, the web site of the Bicycle Museum of America, New Breman, Ohio.

www.columbiabikes.com, the web site of Columbia Manufacturing, Inc., Westfield, Massachusetts, successor to Pope's Columbia Manufacturing Company.

www.pedalinghistory.com, the web site of the Bicycle Museum, Buffalo, New York

Steam Power

The Familiar Force of the Industrial Revolution

Mechanical devices harnessed the powers of wind, water and muscles for ages. The technology for the "Industrial Revolution" began in the early 1700s when the power of steam was harnessed and power plants could be built where they were needed, even when distant from rivers or when the air was still, and without a crew of men or animals to provide muscle power. The history of mechanically powered transportation began with steam engines. In a pattern of development that will repeat itself, steampower would become commercially successful powering boats long before success was noteable on land vehicles. As early as 1707 Denis Papin is reported to have run a primitive steamboat on the Fulda River in Germany.[1]

Steam engines became the pride and symbol of prosperity, productivity and progress. Nowhere was that more true than in America. In his book about James Watt, steel magnate Andrew Carnegie estimated that in 1840 the world had engines in use totaling 1,650,000 horsepower, of which Britain had 620,000 (37.5%) and the United States had 760,000 (46%). By 1888 The United States alone had 14,400,000 horsepower; Britain had 9,200,000 and another 7,120,000 were in use in the British colonies and dependencies. In total horsepower in use, for all purposes combined, steam led all other power sources into the mid 20th century.

Steamships and Railroads

In the United States the visionary John Fitch was unprofitably operating steamboats along the American East Coast as early as 1790. Robert Fulton, however, has the honor of making steam-powered navigation a commercial success. In 1807 Fulton fitted the 133-foot "Clermont" with a Boulton & Watt steam engine and ran the 150 miles from New York to Albany in an unprecedented 32 hours, returning in 30. Soon after, he was advertising regularly scheduled passenger service, and the next year he commissioned two new steamboats.

The first steamship on the Upper Great Lakes was the *Walk-In-The-Water*, launched in Buffalo in 1817. It was an immediate commercial success with twice-weekly round trips between Buffalo and Detroit. The opening of the Erie Canal in October 1825 launched a massive migration by steamship to and through Detroit that would shape that city's future in shipbuilding and in both the manufacturing and servicing of marine steam engines.[2]

Walk-in –the-Water, Courtesy Dossin Great Lakes Museum

In England, Richard Trevithick built his first steam carriage by 1801. However, he

1. Cummings, Lyle, *Internal Fire*, p 3.
2 An example of earlier technologies providing the infrastructure for the new, the tow-path alongside the Erie Canal was built for horses to pull barges and it became the first highway for automobiles traveling between New York and the Great Lakes states.

determined that the biggest obstacle to their acceptance, and economic success, was the combination of their awkwardness and the generally unsatisfactory road conditions. So, he redirected his efforts and in 1804 became the first to operate a steam carriage on rails. The first locomotive carried 10 tons of iron and 70 passengers for 10 miles. This was the first example of a mechanically powered vehicle traveling on rails anywhere in the world. It is interesting to note that his experiments with a horseless carriage did not so much lead to more horseless carriages as it led to building the railroads. Trevithick, a pioneer horseless carriage builder, was the father of the railroad industry.

In the United States the first railroads were built in response to the opening of the Erie Canal. The Erie Canal gave New York an economic advantage over other eastern seaboard port cities by providing a navigable route directly to the Great Lake ports. At about the same time Philadelphia developed an extensive canal system connecting to the Ohio River. Baltimore did not have that option. The land to the west of Baltimore was unsuitable for canals and freight rates over land could not compete with the canals. So the civic leaders in Baltimore responded by laying the cornerstone of the Baltimore & Ohio Railroad on July 4, 1828.[3] The seaports of Boston and Charleston quickly followed with railroad lines of their own.

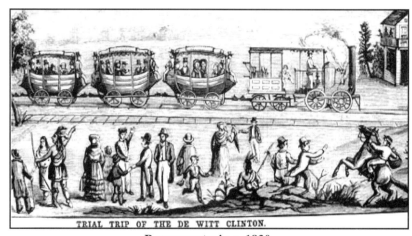

TRIAL TRIP OF THE DE WITT CLINTON.

Passenger train c. 1830

In a situation that would be familiar to the early bicycle and automobile enthusiasts, the National Railroad Museum's website recalls community opposition to the first railroads:

> *"...there was a great deal of opposition surrounding early railroad development. Skeptics, vested interests, tavern keepers, turnpike and toll bridge operators, stagecoach lines, teamsters, canal operators, and local governments all tried to hinder rail development. Railroads that paralleled canals had to pay special taxes. One New York town required the railroad to stop at one end of town and forced passengers to walk to the other end to board the next train. An Ohio school board labeled the railroad 'a device of Satan to lead immortal souls to hell,' but the railroad was an idea whose time had come."*

The first track in the state of Michigan was laid in 1836, only eleven years after the opening of the Erie Canal and eight years after the start the Baltimore & Ohio Railroad. In 1853 track ran west from Detroit to Chicago and east from Detroit through Canada to New York.

---

3. The honor of laying the cornerstone went to Charles Carroll, the last surviving signer of the Declaration of Independence.

Detroit Riverfront c. 1890

By the time the first transcontinental rails were connected in 1869, steam engines were carrying people and commerce over rails and water throughout the nation's interior. Travel that had previously taken days or weeks could be completed in hours or days. No longer did mere distance present a barrier to travel, commerce or the dissemination of information.

By the close of the 19th century every city on navigable waters had a railroad station and a fleet of steamboats. Many steam boats combined cargo hauling and postal service with inter-city passenger travel that offered entertainment both on-board and at company parks established along the routes.

Nowhere was that more notable than in Detroit. At the close of the 19th century Detroit was connected by rail to both Chicago and New York and had the largest fleet of passenger ships in the nation. Between 1897 and 1914 Detroit's fleet is known to have carried ten times the number of passengers as ships using the port of Chicago.[4]

In an article titled "No One Lost" the Cleveland Leader, February 14, 1898, reported:

> *"...Detroit as usual heads all other ports in the district, which includes Lake Michigan, Huron and Superior, in the arrival and clearance of passengers for 1897. 5,303,119 people were carried in and out of this city by passenger steamers and this surpasses all records. Chicago can show only 500,238... Buffalo and Cleveland, which are both in another district, probably cannot show more than*

Detroit Riverfront c. 1910

─────────

4. For 1914 the US Steamboat Inspection Service reported that the number of steamship passengers in Detroit was 5,303,119 compared to 500,238 in Chicago. For 1914 the numbers were 10,368,258 and 1,260,713, respectively..

> *400,000, and this is a liberal estimate, particularly for Cleveland. This vast army of people was transported from point to point without the loss of a life..."*

Millions of passengers viewed Detroit's port and river scene from the decks of a steamboat. The activity of pioneer power boaters did not go unnoticed. Steamship passengers saw a group of people who could go where they wanted, on their own time schedule. They must have been the envy of millions of spectators. The noise, smell, smoke and other negatives of developing other engine technologies on the river went unchallenged by frightened pedestrians and horses.

Motor Yachts

Private power boating was not generally considered as a transportation option in the 19th century. However, in the mid-1800s there were a few private steamboats, all employing domestic staff and ship's crew, including the licensed steam engineer required by the US Steamboat Inspection Service. The extremely wealthy were accustomed to maintaining large staffs, so this did not present an obstacle for them. However, the burden of maintaining a licensed engineer on staff, in addition to the initial costs of ownership, limited private power boating to only the extremely wealthy.

The first known motor yacht in the world is believed to have been the 120-foot steam boat *Mania*, built for Englishmen Thomas Acheron-Smith by Robert Napier[5] in 1830. The innovation was not met with enthusiasm by the English aristocracy and the Royal Yacht Squadron responded by enacting strict rules against the ownership of steam-powered yachts. Unconcerned by the social setback, Acheron-Smith resigned from the Royal Yacht Squadron and went on to commission eight more steam powered motor yachts by 1850.

In 1842 Queen Victoria commissioned the 225-foot paddle-wheeled steamer *Victoria and Albert*. In 1853 she commissioned a second royal motor yacht. By then aristocrats seemed more agreeable to accepting motor yachts.

In America the first known motor yacht was the 270-foot side-wheeled Steamboat *North Star* built for railroad baron Cornelius Vanderbilt in 1852. The next year the Vanderbilt family completed a 15,000-mile world cruise in an unprecedented four months.

While it was no longer possible to dismiss the advantages of motor yachts, few others appeared until after the Civil War. In 1864 there were two steam yachts registered in the New York Yacht Club's yearbook. For 1882 it listed twenty-three steam yachts owned by its members.

By the 1880s it became fashionable for a number of steam yacht owners to commute from their country homes to the financial districts of New York, Detroit, Boston and Philadelphia, among other cities. In May 1886 the New York Yacht Club obtained the use of a city pier exclusively for its commuting members.

A few Detroiters were also commuting between their city offices and summer homes along Lake St. Clair. Steam yachts such as *Leila*, co-owned by a dozen commuters, and *May Lily*, owned by A. E. Brush, were used to commute between the city and summer

---

5. A 40-foot Napier boat and engine won the first Harmsworth International Trophy race in 1903.

Steam Yacht *May Lily* passing by twin summer homes in Detroit's suburban neighborhood of Grosse Pointe c. 1884

homes in Grosse Pointe. Reliable steam boat passenger service enabled commuting between summer homes on the St. Clair River delta and the commercial center of Detroit from the 1870s until the 1920s.

High Speed Steam Engines

American motor yachts were generally built with an emphasis on speed. Consequently, the development of high-speed steam engines in the 1880s launched an intense, and expensive, quest for speed.

In 1885 the 300-foot Hudson River passenger boat *Mary Powell* was reported to travel as fast as 25 miles per hour. It was recognized as the fastest steamboat in the United States. That year noted yacht designer Nathaniel Herreshoff built an 86-foot demonstration yacht named *Stiletto* that reportedly made an 8-hour run at 26.5 miles per hour. In *Yachts in a Hurry* C. Philip Moore told the popular story of *Mary Powell's* encounter with *Stiletto*:

> *"On June 10, 1885, Nat Herreshoff, designer of Stiletto's hull and all her machinery, ran his creation alongside the big side-wheeler for a few miles, then in a burst of speed swept ahead and crossed the bow of the fired-up Mary Powell, then slowed to let her pass, then opened up again and overhauled and shot past her. This was a convincing demonstration, and one that won enduring fame for the Herreshoff brothers. As a result, Stiletto was sold to the U. S. Navy in 1887 to be used as a torpedo boat."*

When *Stiletto* was sold to the U. S. Navy, *Then Now,* another Herreshoff built yacht, may have been the country's fastest private vessel. The 85-foot long yacht was used by New York publisher Norman L. Munro to commute from his home on the New Jersey coast to his offices on Manhattan Island.

In 1887, Lord & Taylor's President Edward P. Hatch commissioned Charles Mosher to build a fast 50-foot steam yacht that he named *Buzz*, for use at his summer home on Lake Champlain. *Buzz* reportedly maintained a speed of almost 27 mph.

Fast steam yachts and their official speed records attracted considerable attention but, efforts to promote steam yacht racing were unsuccessful. In 1891 the American Yacht Club announced plans for a spectacular race. The event was promoted as the race of the century and a large field of fast yachts was anticipated.

When it came down to race day the only two boats willing and able to compete in the Amerian Yacht Club's regatta were Norman Munro's 63-foot, Mosher designed *Norwood* and William Randolph Hearst's 112-foot Herreshoff creation *Vamoose*. However, on the way to the starting line, *Norwood* ran aground. As a consolation event for the spectators the American Yacht Club arranged for Hearst to exhibit *Vamoose* on a measured course. Three runs were made at an impressive 24 mph.

A proposed rematch attracted a large degree of public interest. The following illustrations appeared with a *Scientific American* journal review of both boats in October 1891.

The 112-foot *Vamoose*, was powered by an 800-hp Herreshoff steam engine with five cylinders, totaling over 1,400 cubic inches. The boiler measured 8-feet 4-inches long and 8.5-feet in diameter. Together the equipment weighed 13.5 tons, what for that time was an impressively low 34-pounds per horsepower.

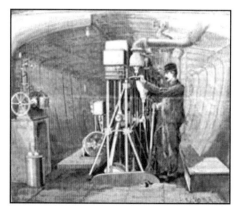 *Vamoose's* engine, left, Boiler, right

30

Norwood with Vamoose **in the background**

The 63-foot *Norwood* was powered by a 400-hp Mosher steam engine. After repairing the equipment damage sustained on the way to the American Yacht Club race, "Norwood" ran a measured mile at 27.2 mph. That time it was recorded under the auspices of the Atlantic Yacht Club and was recognized as an official world record. Her semi-circular hull shape was revolutionary, and became the standard for racing displacement hulls for the next ten years. A similar design was used for *Standard*, winner of the American Power Boat Association's first Gold Cup race in 1904.

In 1896 the Mosher designed, 80-foot *Ellide* was recorded at 40 mph. The owner, Burgess Warren, used her as a luxury day boat for many years on Lake George, New York. *Ellide's* accommodations included a dining room, galley, head and a commodious cockpit where Warren fished the lake.

The steam-turbine engine, first patented by Englishmen Charles Parsons in 1884, reached a significant level of development in the 1890s. On June 27, 1897, Parson and his 100-foot razor thin *Turbinia* burst upon the Naval Review honoring Queen Victoria's Diamond Jubilee. Picket boats, whose duty it was to keep the area clear, could not catch the intruding ship. *Turbinia* was powered by three revolutionary 2,000-hp steam turbines. Steam turbines became the standard for fast ocean liners such as the *Mauretania*, and *Lusitania*. In 1931 the British passenger ship *Queen Mary I* made a transatlantic trip with an average speed of over 35 mph.

The pinnacle of steamboat speed was the beginning of a long tradition of powering fast boats with war surplus engines. Charles Randell Flint commissioned Charles Mosher to design two 4,000 hp steam engines that he planned on using to power a torpedo boat for use in the Spanish-American War. The short-lived war left Flint with two partially completed "super engines," so he commissioned the 132-foot *Arrow*. Launched in 1900, *Arrow* did not have a public trial until 1902. Without pushing the engines, lightening the hull's load or cleaning the bottom, *Arrow* shattered the water speed records by running a measured mile at 44.13 mph.

The extravagant yacht was actually a sound investment that led to an order for ten torpedo boats and eight submarines from the Russian Navy. Subsequently Flint removed one of the engines to make space for entertaining. In 1906 the yacht was sold[6] to E. F. Whitney who continued to use it for commuting and entertaining for many years.

---

6. The yacht was reported to be for sale for $110,000 in *Sail and Sweep*, April 1903

Arrow's speed record was not eclipsed until 1911, and then it was by an all-out unlimited race boat, *Dixie IV*. No commuter yacht broke *Arrow's* record for 20 years, until L. Gordon Hamersley's 70-foot *Cigarette*, built by Gar Wood and powered by four-400 hp WWI surplus Liberty V-12 aircraft engines, traveled 50 mph.

The Steam Launch

While the sport of high-speed steam-driven power boating was being pushed to its technological limits by a few of the daring and very wealthy, others wanted to enjoy the more sedate pleasures of power boating. Until the mid-1880s the only choice was a steam powered launch.

Steam engines were quiet, familiar, and reliable in operation. Based on the expectations of the time, there had been no compelling reason to use anything else for most applications. However, a small steam boat left much to be desired. In the book *Speedboat*, author D.W Fostle described a "light" power vessel of the mid 1880s:

> *"a 30' steam launch with the ability to cruise at 7 knots, burning 1-1/2 tons of coal to run 100 miles, and requiring machinery that filled the middle third of the hull."*

After installing the equipment, fuel bunkers and professional crew, only about one third of the hull was available for the owner and guests. The equipment involved to operate them was a complex system of pumps, valves and gauges, and high pressure superheated water. Writing for *The Rudder* magazine in 1896, Edward T. Birdsall, M.E. described the experience of an outing in a small steam launch as follows:

> *"They are hot, dirty, liable to disastrous explosions, and expensive to run and keep in repair. . . One who has never been off for a day's pleasure in a small steam launch cannot imagine the amount of misery that one of these craft is capable of creating. The trip is usually extended beyond the capacity of the supply of fuel, with the result that the boat arrives home minus seats, lockers and floor boards."*

Steamboats were expensive to operate, not only for the equipment maintenance and fuel, but because they often employed large crews that included the licensed engineer required by the Steamboat Inspection Service. Along with the licensed steam engineer, the crew usually included a stoker, deck hands and a licensed pilot. In addition, when the owner decided to go out he had to allow up to an hour to stoke the boiler and bring it up to operating temperatures from a cold start. At the end, everyone was likely to be dirtied by a fine deposit of soot.

Steam Powered Outboard

When asked why his 1907 outboard motor patent had not protected him from competition, Cameron D. Waterman explained: *"I never had a basic patent because way back in 1883, a fellow whose name I forgot, stuck a small steam boiler on the back of a boat, used a propeller, and was given a U. S. patent on what he called an outboard motor."*

The Steamboat Inspection Service

In 1838 the US Congress first acted to protect the public with law to "provide better security of the lives of passengers on vessels propelled in whole or in part by stem." Oversight increased with the Staemboat Act of May 30, 1852, but not until the creation of the Steamboat Inspection Service were steam vessels of all types and purposes, without exception, on federal waterways, subject to the licensing and inspection requirements. The Steamboat Inspection Service was created in 1871 as a reaction to the public outcry to tragic boiler explosions. There were probably more explosions on land, but most explosions on the water occurred within view of horrified onlookers and very often involved serious injury and loss of life. As a consequence, steamboats on federal waterways required inspection, licensed pilots and only licensed engineers were allowed to operate the boilers (these regulations did not apply on land or inland lakes). The regulation made no distinction between the small equipment of a 20-foot launch and the large ones of an ocean liner.

In addition to the cost of acquisition, fueling and maintenance, the cost of professional crew must be added to the expense of operating a steamboat of any size on federal waters. Consequently, there were many disadvantages to steam engines that became noticeable as other options became available and small boat operators led the way in supporting pioneer motormen building alternative power plants suitable for small boats.

Steam Powered Road Vehicles

A practical steam powered automobile did not come on the market until the late 1890s, but as early as 1805 Oliver Evans operated a steam powered "automobile" on an American street. In the 1770s, Oliver Evans designed, patented and built the first continuous-flow production lines that became standard equipment in U.S. mills. By the early 1800s Evans turned his attention to steam power. In 1805 he was contracted by the City of Philadelphia to build a dredge for use in maintaining the harbor. Evans baptized the vehicle *Oructur Amphibolos*. To transport the 17-ton craft to the river he connected the dredge's steam engine to a set of wheels. After several test runs and a demonstration at the Town Square, the craft rolled under its own power to the bank of the Schuylkill River, where it slid into the water and scurried along dredging up mud. Evans went on to build about fifty steam engines and boilers for mills, steamboats and factories. He was never able to secure financing to produce another automotive road vehicle.

In Britain, where roads were substantially better than in America, there was a boom in steam carriage activity between 1832 and 1840. A number of companies formed to operate steam carriages for public transportation; the London and Birmingham Steam Carriage Company, 1832; the Paddington and London Steam Carriage Company, 1832; Heaton's Steam Carriage Company, 1833; the London, Holyhead and Liverpool Steam Carriage Company of Scotland, 1834; the Hibernian Steam Coach Company, 1834; and the Steam Carriage and Wagon Company, 1838. However, between 1840 and 1896 they were effectively run off the roads by restrictive rules and excessive tolls. In 1896 the British "Locomotive on the Highway Act" finally did away with the requirement to have three men in attendance. One assistant was required to walk in front of the vehicle waiving a red flag. The speed limit was raised to 14 mph.

The Standard Catalog of American Cars documents that John Kenrick Fisher built a steam powered vehicle in 1840. In 1853 he established the American Steam Carriage Company in New York City, the first American company organized to build automobiles. There is no record that any were sold by the company. It is known however, that Fisher built other vehicles and is believed to have built his sixth in 1869.

Perhaps the most well known among the early American experimenters was Sylvester H. Roper of Roxbury, Massachusetts, who built ten steam passenger vehicles between 1859 and 1895. In 1868 one of Roper's horseless carriages was purchased by W. W. Austin and taken on tour to exhibit at county fairs. During his thirty years of building automobiles public interest never amounted to more than curiosity that supported side-shows at carnivals and county fairs.

Steam Powered Motorcycle

In 1869 Sylvester H. Roper built a steam powered bicycle that he demonstrated at circuses and fairs. This steam powered motorcycle is in the collection of the Smithsonian Institute. In 1896, Roper died of a heart attack while driving one of his improved steam powered motorcycles 40-mph on a bicycle track in Boston

There was nothing new about self-propelled road vehicles when Henry Ford saw his first steam powered wagon in summer of 1876. Shortly before his thirteenth birthday, Henry Ford was riding toward Detroit in a horse drawn wagon with his father. *In Young Henry Ford*, Sidney Olson reprinted part of a memo written by Ford in 1923:

> *"I can remember that engine as though I had seen it only yesterday . . .I was off the wagon and talking to the engineer before my father knew what I was up to. It was simply a portable engine and boiler mounted on wheels with a water tank and a coal cart trailing behind."*

In 1878 the State of Wisconsin hosted the nation's first automobile race, offering $10,000 to the inventor of a practical machine that could travel 130 miles from Green Bay to Madison under its own power. Alexander Gallagher and his steam machine won the race with an average speed of six miles per hour, but could not claim to have demonstrated a "practical" machine.

In Michigan, the experiments of Ransom Olds were the earliest of any importance. On August 5, 1886, a Lansing newspaper, *State Republican*, announced that Olds had built his first steam carriage:

> *"The junior member of the firm P.F. Olds & Son has invented an ingenious steam wagon that runs easily and smoothly on the streets and is liable to cause the long expected revolution in road vehicles."*

In 1892, the second Olds steam-powered carriage was sold to an English company and shipped to Bombay, India. It was lost at sea, but it has the distinction of being the first known export of a Michigan automobile.

Steam Powered Lawn Mower

A functional steam powered lawn mower was built by James Sumner of Leland, England in 1893. One surviving example is in the collection of the University of Reading. Sumner's company was named the Leland Steam Motor Company. Later the company became the motor-car manufacturer British Leland.

At the close of the 19th century over 400 enterprises built steam-powered automobiles in America. Many of them were experimental vehicles that did not go into commercial production. Some companies continued to manufacturer "steamers" until the 1920s.

In "America Adopts the Automobile, James J. Flink noted, *The American steam car ... became popular once it had been improved in the closing years of the nineteenth century with the introduction of liquid fuel and the flash boiler, which allowed instantaneous starts provided the pilot light had been left on.*

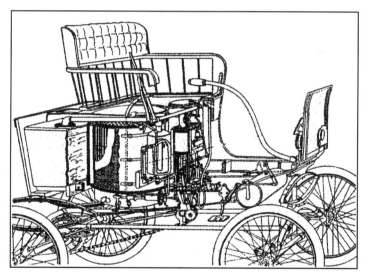

This diagram of a steam car layout indicates the challenge of containing the burner, boiler, water and fuel tanks as well as the engine, within the confines of a lightweight passenger vehicle.

In the context of the then available technology, steam powered automobiles offered many advantages. First, the engines operated on the familiar principles of the steam engines that the "Industrial Revolution" had proven to be so reliable. Second, they could operate on just about any combustible such as wood, coal, kerosene, natural gas or gasoline. Third, steam engines operated under con-tinuous pressure that provided almost instantaneous torque and smooth transmission of power to the wheels, precluding the challenge of shifting unsynchronized transmissions. Fourth, steam engines were powerful enough to drive up steeper grades than possible with the alternative engine choices.

By the dawn of the 20th century the steamer had reached a technological plateau. High-pressured boilers and double-acting engines were driving automobiles to record breaking speeds. In 1906 a Stanley Steamer held the world speed record of 127.66 mph.

On the other hand, steam power has some serious disadvantages. Most steam-powered automobiles at the beginning of the 20th century were dirty, dangerous, and required so much attention that it was almost impractical for one man to run a steam wagon through the busy streets of a city. Even as they reached a technological plateau the steam carriage's consumption of water required frequent stops and the rate of fuel consumption was greater than that required by a comparable gasoline engine powered carriage.

Business Automobiles

TO THE TRADE:

We supply automobile manufacturers, carriage makers, and others with our seven and eighteen horse-power compound engines (marine type), also all steel boilers, and kerosene burners. We are the originators of the idea of supplying convertible outfits for transforming any horse vehicle into an automobile at small cost, furnishing them with drawings and instructions so that any blacksmith or carriage maker can do the work.

PEERLESS LONG DISTANCE STEAM CARRIAGE CO.
WASHINGTON, D. C.
Motor vehicles and supplies of all kinds and special types to order.

LIBERAL REDUCTION IN PRICES.

With a view to extending the field for our perfected Business Automobiles and introducing them to firms who are contemplating the adoption of horseless vehicles, we are prepared to make the following special offer:

For a limited time only we will receive orders on the basis of a 50 per cent. reduction on current market prices, and will sell our best types of delivery wagons, heavy trucks and omnibusses as follows:

Delivery Wagons $750.00
Heavy Trucks 900.00
Omnibusses 1500.00

These are thoroughly practical automobiles, and have been tested under all conditions. The wagons have been adopted by business houses generally, and also the trucks, which are suitable for breweries, packing houses, factories, lumber yards, wholesale firms and other establishments hauling heavy loads.

The power used is steam, the only absolutely reliable motive power for this class of work. Any rate of speed may be assumed to suit all conditions of traffic and roads. Can be easily operated by any ordinary workman possessing "horse sense." The purchaser of every one of our automobiles receives a written guarantee from The Hartford Steam Boiler Inspection and Insurance Company.

HOW TO ORDER

Orders will be filled according as they are received, but in each case must be accompanied by the customary deposit of $200, as a guarantee payment, irrespective of the financial standing of the purchaser. The American Savings Bank, of Washington, D. C., will receive all deposits in the nature of guarantee payments, and checks and money orders may be made payable to the above bank. Address all communications to the company's office.

Peerless Long Distance Steam Carriage Co.

Catalogues and Information Furnished on Request.   727 14th St., N.W., WASHINGTON, D. C.

In 1901 the Peerless Long Distance Steam Carriage Company offered complete steam carriages and kits to convert any horse carriage into an automobile. Their seven and eighteen horsepower compound engines were noted as being of the marine type.

Despite the long history of experiments with steam-powered vehicles, practical use of a steam car was a late development and its popularity declined quickly. The decline in popularity of the steam car was arguably due to the rapid and continued advancements in the performance of internal combustion engines. Combined with reduction in weight to power ratios and improvements of drive train components the gas car builders were able to resolve many of the basic design issues. Soon the steam car had little practical advantage and several serious disadvantages. This is why "steamers" quickly began to disappear from the roads in the early 20th century.

**Steam enthusiasts contine to build new steam launches and restore old ones.
Their presence is always welcomed at antique and classic boating events**

References:

Carnegie, Andrew, "James Watt," Double Day & Do. New York,1905.

Cummins, Lyle, Internal Fire, C. Lyle Cummins d/b/a Casnot Press, 7976, 2000

Fostle, D.W, "Speedboat," Published jointly by United States Historical Society and Mystic Seaport Museum Stores, CN, 1988

Greenhill, Basil, "The Rise of the Ocean-Going Merchant Steamship," Maritime Life and Traditions, No. 9, 2000

http:www.grosseile.com/community/history/outboard.hmtl

http:www.dself.dsl.pipex.com/MUSEUM/TRANSPORT

Interview with George King III, steam and naphtha engine historian and licensed steam engineer, in Mystic, Connecticut, August 19, 2002

MacTaggart, Ross, "The Golden Century, Classic Motor Yachts 1830 – 1930", W.W.Norton & Company, Inc., New York, 2001

Moore, C. Philip, "Yachts in a Hurry, An Illustrated History of the Great Commuter Yachts," W. W. Norton & Company, New York, 1994

Olson, Sidney, "Young Henry Ford, a picture history of the first forty years," Wayne State University Press, Detroit, MI, 1963

Naphtha Vapor

The power behind America's first production, owner-operated "automobile."

The advent of small owner-operated powerboats expanded the concept of personal transportation beyond the horse-drawn carriage, sail boats and man-powered row boats and bicycles to include mechanically powered vehicles. In the mid-1880s the patented Naphtha engine brought Americans a prime mover that was lighter, more compact and less complex than the steam engine. Before there were any practical self-powered land vehicles on the market and while gasoline was still a little-used waste product of petroleum distillation, the Naphtha engine, was popularly used for the propulsion of small boats. To the Naphtha engine goes the distinction of being the first to power a practical, commercially successful, mechanically powered, owner-operated transportation vehicle. For nearly two decades, engines, powered by vapors other than steam, dominated the market for owner-operated vehicles.

In 1883 Frank Ofeldt patented his design for a marine engine that circumvented the restrictive regulations of the Steamship Inspection Act (see page 33). The Naphtha engines and steam engines both operated on the familiar principle of expanding a gas under pressure. However, instead of water the Offelt's engine vaporized naphtha, a low grade gasoline then being used as a solvent for dry cleaning, thinning paint and fueling gas stoves. By definition, it was not a "steam" engine and, therefore, not covered by the Steamship Inspection Act. Conveniently, naphtha was also used as the fuel to heat the boiler.

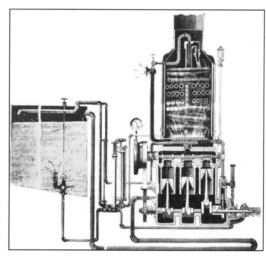

Naphtha engine installed, left, and cut-away view, right

Note, the whistle, in the top of the cut-away illustration, blew with naphtha vapor.
(Hopefully nobody nearby in the downwind direction was smoking.)

Noted yacht designer Clinton Crane described the Naphtha launch as follows:

> "... the first motorboat that could be used without hiring a licensed steam engineer. For power it had a little, three-cylinder, single-acting engine driven by naphtha vapor, naphtha being what we would probably now call gasoline although, as I remember it, rather more volatile. The naphtha was carried in a copper tank in a bow compartment, separated from the rest of the launch by a watertight bulkhead and ventilated and scuperd so that if the tank leaked the naphtha went overboard.

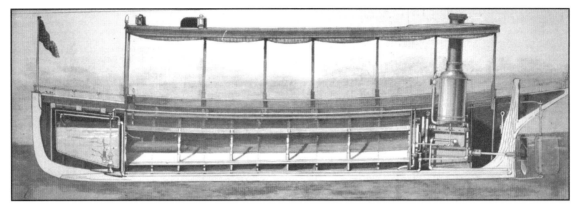

Cut-away view of a typical Naphtha launch

"The naphtha ran back through a pipe under the boat and was pumped into the boiler, which consisted of a coil of copper pipe in a round, insulated drum with a chimney. From the boiler, a pipe led to the burner and another to the engine. When running, the pump was driven by the engine, but a hand pump was used for starting. The burner was primed much as you prime a vapor stove. The exhaust led back under the boat through another pipe which condensed the vapor and returned it to a tank forward. "This was supposed to be a safe arrangement, and no licensed engineer was required by law. Most of the larger yachts had naphtha launches, some small enough to be carried aboard an 80 foot schooner. Surprisingly enough, fires were rare."*

Equipment, including the boiler, engine and coal boxes, occupied most of the center of a typical steam launch. However in a typical Naphtha launch, the rear placement of the unitized naphtha boiler and engine, supplied by a liquid fuel from a tank under the deck, freed most of the cockpit space to allow room for passengers.

Compare the passenger space in the 25-foot Naphtha Launch *Anita*, left, and the 25-foot Steam Launch *Ariel*, right. *Ariel's* cockpit lost space comparable to a Naphtha for its boiler. Aft of the boiler is a box containing coal and behind that is the engine. What the Naphtha launch could not install beneath the deck was stacked with the boiler.

Circumvention of regulations requiring a licensed engineer proved to be the most significant of several innovations included in Ofeldt's design. For the first time an owner could operate his own power launch and leave the dock on his own schedule, at any hour. Additionally, compared to steam engines, the Naphtha engine weighed one-fourth as much, used about one-fourth the space, was nearly twice as efficient at converting heat

THE NAPHTHA LAUNCH.

EVERY MAN HIS OWN ENGINEER.

Combining Safety and Economy with Durability.

☞ The above cut is an exact reproduction of our 25-foot Launch, 4 H. P. Engine.

40 Launches, from 16 to 35 feet in length, in our Show Rooms to-day, and inspection is cordially invited. Send stamp for our new Illustrated Catalogue.

GAS ENGINE & POWER CO.,

131st St. and Brook Ave., New York City.

Extract from Letter.   *   *   *   I have built more than thirty Launches for my own use, but have seen nothing to compare with your NAPHTHA ENGINE for compactness, convenience, or safety and I gladly recommend them as preferable to anything ever produced for the purpose.

JACOB LORILLARD.

As advertised in 1887 in *The American Yachtsman*. Mr. Lorillard was a prominent yachtsman. In 1889 Outing Magazine reported he was having designs made for his 50th yacht.

into work, required significantly reduced warm-up time, and was simpler and safer to operate. The manufacturer, Gas Engine and Power Company, described four major benefits in their 1896 catalog as follows:

> "*First. The small space taken up by our engine, in the stern of the boat, gives more room, enabling the boat to seat twice as many persons as a boat of the same size fitted with any other [steam] engine.*

> "*Second. The weight of our engine is much less than any other make – 1 horse-power weighing only 150 pounds, 2 horse-power only 200 pounds, 4 horse-power 300 pounds, 6 horse-power 500 pounds, 8 horse-power 600 pounds, 10 horse-power, 700 pounds, 12 and 16 horse-power 800 to 1000 pounds, or less than one-fifth the weight of other engines and boilers of same power.*

> "*Third. It takes only two to five minutes to get under headway, and can be stopped, when running at full speed, within the length of the boat. The reverse motion is instantaneous and effective.*

"Fourth. It is clean. No coal or oil being used, there is neither dirt, dust, ashes nor smell, and as steam is not used, no water, is required. We expand naphtha for power and use the same vapor, in part, for fuel. The elastic power of naphtha is greater than that of steam.

"And this is the only engine in the world that actually embodies the true principle and all the essential points of superiority. Others are advertising Improved Naphtha Launches, which use steam for power and naphtha for fuel only, or the naphtha explosively, and are therefore no more like the Naphtha Motor than is an ordinary oil or coal-burning engine."

The Gas Engine & Power Company was organized in 1885 with the primary objective of building pleasure boats powered by Ofeldt's Naphtha engine. The financial backing came from Clement Gould and Jabez A. Bostwick. Bostwick, an executive of the Standard Oil Co., may have been looking for other uses for his company's principal product. The domestic market for kerosene had sharply decreased since the advance of electric lighting and the export market had not yet grown to absorb the excess.

The Gas Engine & Power Company and Charles L. Seabury & Co., Consolidated

The Gas Engine & Power Company (GEPC) began modest operations at 131st Street in New York City. Due to the overwhelming demand for the product, by 1891 they moved to new facilities in Morris Heights with ¼ mile of frontage on the Harlem River.

In 1905 GEPC was still building and marketing the Naphtha launches, but by that time a line of gasoline engines bearing the trademark "Speedway" was also being built and marketed by the company. A few years later GEPC merged with noted yacht builder Charles L. Seabury & Company. The long and cumbersome name of The Gas Engine & Power Company & Charles L. Seabury & Co., Consolidated was used until 1919 when they adopted the name Consolidated Shipbuilding Corporation. The firm continued to operate for many years as an important shipbuilder. According to author C. Philip Moore, from roughly 1900 to 1930 Consolidated was possibly the largest custom yacht building operation in the world.

Naphtha engines were reliable, inexpensive to maintain and both familiar and simple to operate. They were immediately popular for boats used to tend yachts ("yacht owned by the super-wealthy. Resorts and hunting lodges soon found them useful as shuttles to ferry guests from waterfront railroad stops.

Most significantly, enthusiasm for power boating grew throughout the country and created a demand for small, lightweight engines. The independence provided by the vapor engines, and their ease of operation, appealed not only to wealthy yacht owners and ferry operators, but also to a larger number of not-so-wealthy individuals. There were recreational opportunities for all those who wanted self-powered watercraft.

L. Francis Herreshoff, a member of the family of noted naval architects and yacht builders and editor of *The Rudder* magazine, reminisced about Naphtha launches in a 1965 article. He dismissed the fact of frequent fires as merely annoyances that rarely caused any real

The Only Naphtha Launch.

Over 2,000 built and sold in nine years. Unequalled as a Pleasure Craft. Owners and users report complete satisfaction. No licensed Engineer, or Pilot, or Government inspection. Used by Government in Quarantine, Light House, Customs and Engineering Departments. A large assortment of finished boats carried in stock for immediate delivery. Send 10 cents in stamps for New Illustrated Catalogue.

Electric Launches

manufactured conjointly with Electric Launch Company of World's Fair Fame.

GAS ENGINE AND POWER COMPANY,
Morris Heights on the Harlem, New York City.

This 1895 advertisement in *Field & Stream* magazine appeared on the same page with ads for electric, steam and gasoline launches. However, no other marine engine manufacturer at that time could boast that over 2,000 units had been bought and sold in nine years.

problems as a precaution the engine wells were lined with copper. He praised Ofeldt as a genius not only because he designed a steam-type expansion engine that got around the law requiring licensed engineers but also because it resulted in launches that had few serious accidents. The Naphtha engine was smaller, lighter and much quicker to start than a steam engine of similar power. Herreshoff went on to say, *They sold like hot cakes right up to around 1900 when the internal combustion engine began to be reliable and lighter than the naphtha ones."*

The typical Naphtha launch was between 16 to 35 feet and powered by a 1 to 6-hp engine. The company's catalog for 1896 also offered 8 to 16-hp engines on production cruising launches up to 42-feet. A 53-foot yacht was available and drawings of custom twin-screw Naphtha yachts of 64, 67 and 76 feet were also shown.

Yacht clubs began hosting Naphtha launch races in the early 1890s

In 1896 *The Rudder* magazine reviewed a 76-foot Naphtha yacht being built for Mr. Alfred Van Santvoord, the owner of the Albany Day Line, a New York steamship company. The magazine concluded the review suggesting that the size of the yacht tended to strengthen the *"often made prediction"* that steam power for propulsion of larger craft would soon be superseded by naphtha or electrical power. Interestingly for the discussion ignored internal combustion engines.

Catalogs for the Gas Engine and Power Company provide referral lists of over 1,300 owners in 1892 and 1,600 in 1896. The Naphtha launch owners were concentrated in the company's home state of New York, but owners were also represented throughout the United States and foreign countries. Detroit and other Great Lakes cities were well represented. Among the wealthy owners to be found in Detroit are; Cameron D. Waterman, father of Cameron B. Waterman, who is often credited as being the inventor of the outboard motor,[1] Fred E. Butler whose father, William A. Butler, is credited with being the first wealthy Detroiter to build a summer home on the St. Clair River Delta (Harsens Island & The St. Clair Flats)[2], and J. W. Westcott, who began mid-river mail delivery to passing ships on the Detroit River in 1895[3]. Another notable name is James W. Packard, of Warren, Ohio. His automobile company was renamed the Packard Motor Car Company after relocating to Detroit in 1903. Following is the complete 1896 referral list of owners in Chicago, Illinois, Detroit, Michigan, and Cleveland, Sandusky, Toledo and Warren, Ohio:

CHICAGO, Illinois:

George A. Seaverns	W. H. Aldrich	Edwin Norton
I. N. Camp	Geo. G. Parker	George R. Davis
E. R. Gilman	Montgomery Ward & Co.	C. N. Fay
Phil. Armour, Jr	Alonzo G. Fisher	T. A. Kochs
Watson F. Blair	C. W. Leeming	General Jos. T. Torrance
R. Hall McCormick	Mrs. W. H. Thompson	
W. W. Cheney	Montgomery Ward	

CLEVELAND, Ohio:

S. H. Chisholm	C. W. Harkness	Henry W. Corning
W. R. Huntington	D. E. Stone	John Corrigan
William DeMooy	John P. Broghan	C. E. Burke(3 Launches)
L. McBride	G. B. Pettingill	Samuel Mather
L. L. Leggett	Johh Huntington	W. S. Root
C. W. Bingham	George H. Worthington	

DETROIT, Michigan:

H. B. Scott	Ford H. Rogers	Albert Ives
James R. McKay	Traugott Schmidt & Sons	George Beck
Cullen Brown	C. D. Waterman	Collins B. Hubbard
Hermann Dey	T. H. Newberry	George H. Lothrop

---

1. It is a common misconception that Waterman invented the outboard motor. An electric outboard was exhibited on the Seine River during the Paris World Exhibition in 1881. In 1883 a steam powered outboard motor was patented in the US and by 1896 an outboard internal combustion motor was commercially available from the American Motor Co., of Long Island, New York. About 25 of those motors were built, which for that era was certainly enough to qualify as a production motor. Waterman may rightfully be credited with independently designing and building the first commercially successful outboard motor. He built his first working model in 1905. In 1906 Waterman built 25 and incorporated in November.
2. Visitors to his summer home founded the Old Club in 1872. When he died in 1891 he was reported to have been the largest landowner in Detroit.
3. The J. W. Westcott Company delivered 175,000 letters to more than 19,000 ships passing Detroit in 1896. The company continues to provide the service today to ships passing on the only body of water to have its own zip code, 48222.

F. E. Butler	Gilbert Hart	R. Henkel
H. A. Strassburg	Dr. Edwin Lodge	M. M. Stanton
J. W. Westcott	Com. M. B. Mills	

SANDUSKY, Ohio
| J. O. Moss | F. A. Hubbard |
| C. G. Neilsen | E. H. Marsh |

TOLEDO, Ohio:
| H. P. Tobey | John Weber(3 Launches) | George Van Vleck |
| F. B. Shoemaker | William Bretsch | |

WARREN, Ohio:
J. W. Packard

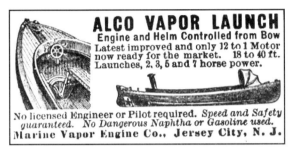 

Advertising for the Alco Vapor launch noted that no licensed engineer or pilot was required and that no dangerous naphtha or gasoline was used.

Ofeldt left the Gas Engine & Power Company and in 1895, he introduced the Alco-Vapor engine. This time Ofeldt's engine used a mixture of water and alcohol. He persuaded the regulators that the primary expansion agent was alcohol which when heated created vapor and not steam, which by definition is created only by heating water. The financial backer in the new company was Commodore E. C. Benedict, a Connecticut millionaire best remembered for the way he served eggs to guests on his yacht *Oneida*.

Few details are known about the company(s) that manufactured the Alco-Vapor Engine. In 1897 the manufacturer is advertised as The Marine Vapor Engine Company, with J. B. M. Showell as president and Chas. A. Wright as Secretary-Treasurer. In 1903 the manufacturer is found listed as The Marine Engine & Machine Company with E. C. Benedict as president and J. B. M. Showell as Secretary.

Alco-Vapor engines operated under higher pressure than Naphtha engines. This made them more powerful, and probably provided a better weight to horsepower ratio. Their speeds were also greater, driving launches 10-12 mph, and reportedly their smell was more pleasant. Another benefit claimed in their advertisements was "No dangerous Naphtha or Gasoline Used." The Alco-Vapor launches quickly became a feature on the up-to-date yachts. Ignoring the internal combustion engine, Edward T. Birdsall, M.E., wrote in 1896 that the only rival to the Naphtha launch to have appeared up to that time was Ofeldt's Alco-Vapor launch.

Naphtha and Alco-Vapor launches dominated the market until the late-1890s. As weight reduction and advancements of carburetion and electrical components improved the performance and reliability of the internal combustion engine, they became suitable for

President Grover Cleveland's Alco-Vapor Launch *Esther.*
**The casing around the boiler of Alco-Vapor engines was usually rectangular,
differing them from the Naphtha's barrel shaped casing.**

use by an amateur operator. In a *Detroit Free Press* feature story "Growth of Power Boating on Fresh Water, In the Past Ten Years," July 9, 1905, Commodore Otto F. Barthel wrote, *"In the early days of power boating the New York naphtha and alco-vapor launches had entire sway and the gasoline launch was the exception."*

Only two years before becoming an investor and officer of the Packard Motor Car Company, Richard P. Joy's choice for a power boat was a fine crafted hull powered by a quiet Naphtha engine. In August 1900, he made the first entry in the logbook of the Naphtha launch *Doris*:

Doris's **graceful "swallow-tail" transom was typical of many launches of the era**

"Doris, built by the Gas Engine & Power Company, Morris Heights, New York City, 30 feet long overall, 6 foot 6 inches beam, draft 2 feet, - 6 horsepower, speed 8 miles per hour.

Launched [at] Letts Coal Dock Detroit August 20th 1900

Engine turns 295 rotations [per minute] at 78 pounds pressure

Engine turns 300 rotations [per minute] at 80 pounds pressure"

At the end of three seasons Joy noted in the log book that the boat had traveled a total of 3,566 miles. He also noted that ten barrels (550 gallons) of naphtha ran the launch 1,547 miles, about 2.8 miles per gallon. An invoice records that the price for Naphtha at that time was $.05 per gallon.

Joy's purchase of a Naphtha launch in 1900 may be a prime example of a class aversion to the "exploding" type of propulsion. The 30 year-old Richard P. Joy had been brought

46

up in an age that appreciated the elegance of a fine carriage and he may have had an aversion to the idea of an oily exploding source of power beneath the seat of a carriage or cradled beside him in a launch. It was not unfamiliarity with the device. Richard's brother, Henry B. Joy, had for several years been a partner in the gasoline engine business of Charles B. King. Consequently, Richard Joy probably already knew much about the capabilities of internal combustion engines, but simply did not like them.

While the operating cost of a Naphtha launch could be much less than a comparable steam launch, a Naphtha engine had poor fuel economy compared to an internal combustion engine. We can compare actual relative costs using the example recorded by Richard Joy in his logbook. The 30-foot, 6-hp Naphtha launch cruised at eight miles per hour and got about 2.8 miles per gallon. At $0.50 a gallon, a one hundred mile cruise in the Naphtha launch cost about $1.79. In *Speedboat*, Don Fostle gave the example of a similar 30-foot steam launch that used one and one-half tons of coal cruising one hundred miles at seven knots. Based on the cost of coal reported by the Scientific American, March 21, 1891, the operating cost would be about $9.00, before considering the additional cost of wages for the required licensed steam engineer. According to Fostle, a comparable internal combustion engine consumed about one pint of fuel per horse-power per hour, or about 10.67 miles per gallon at eight miles per hour, cost of about $0.56 for the same one hundred mile cruise.

The ultimate weakness of the vapor engines was probably their speed. Joy's engine turned about three hundred revolutions per minute, one-half the speed of Daimler's first high-speed internal combustion engine in 1885. The typical Naphtha Launch attained speeds of about 8-mph and the Alco-Vapor launches reportedly attained speeds up to 12-

A typical Naphth launch moored in front of a summer home on Harsens Island, near Detroit, circa 1900. Across the river, in Algonac, Chris Smith began putting engines in his boats about that same time. From the Collection of the Prints & Photograph Division, Library of Congress.

mph. The advent of powerboat racing increased performance expectations to a level that only the latest internal combustion engines could provide.

By 1900, internal combustion engines had improved their power to weight ratios and performed with acceptable reliability. They also sold for much less than comparable vapor engines. Vapor engines were still more familiar and reliable than the cheaper "exploding" engines, but at the dawn of the 20th century the number of small boat-owners willing to pay the higher price for the slower, vapor engines was declining rapidly.

"Many People are still Recommending"
In 1907 the Naphtha was advertised as the *Old Reliable*

As late as 1907 The Gas Engine and Power Company was taking out half page advertisements for the Naphtha engines inside the front cover of *The Rudder*, the leading yachting magazine of the time. However, at the dawn of the 20th century, more powerful, faster and fuel-efficient internal combustion engines were rapidly replacing the gentle, reliable Naphtha and Alco-Vapor Engines. The fashionable yachting fad for Naphtha and Alco-Vapor launches had lasted twenty years.

L. Francis Herreshoff, cited earlier, recalled that the last Naphtha launch built in his family's shipyard was not until 1915. Many were still being used up to the time of World War I, but due to their brass and copper content, most of them were scrapped for shell casings. Today there are only some six to eight complete naphtha engines known to exist.

While briefly on the world stage and long forgotten, Ofeldt's engines had an incalculable effect on opening men's minds to the wider possibilities of personal, self-propelled vehicles, and a horseless carriage no longer seemed so far fetched. By eliminating the mess of storing and stoking coal and disposing of ashes Ofeldt's engines made power boating an appealing recreational activity. Ofeldt engines allowed the gentleman yachter to operate a power boat free from the regulatory burden and expense of a licensed steam engineer. By circumventing the requirement of maintaining a professional crew, Ofeldt's engines also made it affordable for the not-so-wealthy to get out on the water at convenient times and go to places of their own choosing without having to row, learn to sail or acquire a steam engineer's license. Many inventors and competitors wanting to avoid violating the Ofeldt patents were directed to the electric and internal combustion gas engines as solutions.

The legacy of Frank Ofeldt's revolutionary vapor engines is that their use created a demand for lightweight power plants using a clean portable fuel. Ofeldt was the man who ushered in the transportation revolution of the 19th century as the inventor of the first owner-operated self-propelled vehicle to be widely used in America.

References:

Barthel, Com. Otto F., "The Growth of Power Boating on Fresh Water in the Past Ten Years," Detroit Free Press, July 9, 1905

Birdsall, Edward T., M. E., "Gas and Vapor Marine Engines," The Rudder, New York, 1896

Catalogs, Gas Engine & Power Company, New York, NY, 1892, 1896 and 1906

Catalog, The Marine Vapor Engine Company, 1897

Catalog, The Marine Engine & Machine Company, 1903

Crane, Clinton, "Clinton Crane's Yachting Memories," D. Van Nostrand Co., New York 1952

Farmer, Weston, "Those Wonderful Naphtha Launches," Yachting, August, 1973

Farmer, Westin, "Halcyon Days," Yachting, January, 1975

Fostle, D.W, "Speedboat," Published jointly by United States Historical Society and Mystic Seaport Museum Stores, CN, 1988

Hall, Robert, "Where the Industry Began," Motor Boating, New York, 1924

Herreshoff, L. Francis, "Naphtha Launches," The Rudder, New York, 1965

http:www.grosseile.com/community/history

Interviews with Jim Wright, Naphtha engine historian - owner, and George King III, Naphtha historian and licensed steam engineer, Mystic, Connecticut, August 19, 2002

Loweree, H. W, "The Pioneer Power Boat Builders," Power Boating, New York, 1914

Moore, C. Philip, "Yachts in a Hurray," W. W. Norton & Company, NY

Obituary for Frank W. Ofeldt, Brooklyn Standard Union, New York, October 1, 1904

Outing Magazine, February, 1889, Vol. XIII No. 5

"The Naphtha Launch of the Gas Engine and Power Company of New York City," Scientific American, Munn & Co., New York, NY, March 16, 1895

"The Naphtha Launch," Steamboats and Modern Steam Launches, March-April, 1961

Electric Power

The Elegant Choice for Personal Transportation

Electric power burst forth at the 1893 World's Columbian Exhibition in Chicago as the wonder of the age. Until then, waterwheels, sails and steam had powered the Industrial Revolution without much help from other types of engines. On opening day there was 22,000 horse-power of electrical generating capacity, hundreds of thousands of arc and incandescent lights, moving sidewalks, an electric railway, and motors powering equipment all over the fairgrounds.

***Electra* was the prototype for 55 electric launches built for the 1893 Columbian Exhibition in Chaicago**

To some observers, no electric feature of the fair scored so instant a success as the electric launch. Fifty-five electric-launches carried more than a million visitors on over 66,000 recorded trips. By comparison, there were only two gasoline launches, one powered by a Sintz engine and the other by a Daimler. The only gasoline powered automobile was a Daimler, and it went largely unnoticed. More notice was given to the one electric carriage on display, an uncomfortable machine that was present only as a novel form of promoting the electric storage batteries manufactured by its owner.

During the industry's early years, when the electric motor appeared to be the most promising type of motive power for the coming transportation revolution, two men, Isaac Leopold Rice and Albert Pope, dominated the industry. The end of the 19th century was an era that preceded anti-trust legislation, and monopolistic titans of industry set their sights on electric power. Albert Pope's early gamble on the electric vehicle may have brought about the end of his business empire but, Rice's Electric Boat Company adapted to the whirlwind technological changes and successfully evolved into what today is General Dynamics.

The Electric Launch

The possibilities of launches powered by electric motors was of interested for some time before the Chicago exhibition. In 1881 a workable electric outboard motor was run on the river Seine by its French inventor Gustave Trouve, as a demonstration during the Paris World Exposition.

By the mid-1880's Anthony Reckenzaun and others were writing scientific papers and promoting the economic feasibility of electric launches in Europe. Electric boats were used at many European exhibitions and were promoted by operators of rental and excursion fleets. For example, the Immisch Launch Company, a British firm, had a fleet of about 50 electric launches. They ranged in size between 20 and 65 feet and were rented for recreational excursions on the Thames River as early as 1890.

Gustave Trouve's 1881 electric outboard

Anthony Reckenzaun and his brother Frederic immigrated to the United States and in 1888 built the 28-foot launch *Magnet*, which may be credited as the first electric boat in America. One of the first electric launches commercially available in the United States appeared in an 1889 catalog of sporting boats published by J. R. Rushton, Canton, N.Y. A stock 18-foot launch was offered with a 1-hp electric engine and the recommended 60 storage batteries for a price of $490. By comparison, Rushton offered the same boat with a 1-hp steam engine for $375. To dispel the disadvantages of greater initial cost and the necessity of having a base for charging, Rushton noted that there was no requirement for a licensed engineer as one of the following advantages:

"You can apply it to smaller boats than you can steam; it is noiseless and clean; no smoke, no fuel, no dirt, no grease, no danger. Your power is always ready (if your batteries are charged). You can start and stop at a moment's notice – turn a button and off you go. Your batteries are charged to run so many hours, and you can spend that power at one time, or you can take an hour's run each day for a week. In a small boat your batteries are placed under the seats, out of the way, and, being low down, act as so much ballast. You can run fast or slow, and according to speed, do you expend your power.

Do you go to a summer resort and pay $3 per day for a boat and oarsman? Take an ELECTRIC BOAT, and save a man's wages and board. Take an ELECTRIC BOAT and take your friend along and feel free to discuss the political situation – your oarsman will not gossip. The cost of charging the batteries is merely nominal, and you will soon save the cost of your outfit.

Do you want a large craft? Take an ELECTRIC BOAT and save government inspection (if on any public waters) and expense of engineer and pilot. You will soon save the extra cost of your outfit."

The contract to provide the fleet of electric launches for the 1893 World's Columbian Exhibition in Chicago was awarded to the Electric Launch and Navigation Company. The company did not have its own boatyard until 1900, so the prototype, named *Electra*, was built by the Gas Engine and Power Company, the exclusive manufacturer of Naphtha engines and builder of yachts and launches.

The Electric Launch and Navigation Company, later known as the Electric Launch Company (Elco), supplied some 55 identical launches for the fair. Each boat was 35 feet 10 inches overall length with a 6 feet 2.5 inch beam, powered by 4-hp Reckenzaun motors built by the General Electric Company and fitted with batteries supplied by the Consolidated Electric Storage Company. Because Elco did not have its own boatyard the building of the boats was subcontracted to both the Racine Boat Works and the Detroit Boat Works at a delivered cost of about $3,000 each.

55 identical electric boats provided transportation and tours at the 1893 World's Fair in Chicago

At the close of the fair the launches were sold and later used in different parts of the country for both private use and for public hire. In the Smithsonian Magazine, July 2003, Lance Morrow wrote about the boat his family has continuously maintained and enjoyed since his grandfather purchased it from the Chicago fleet for $1,736.

Electric launches provided a solution to nearly every objection to the steam and Naphtha engines: complete freedom from noise, heat, smoke, gas, cinders, ashes, and no wait to preheat boilers or mess to clean up when the trip is over. The electric engine and the batteries can be tucked under the seats or under the floorboards, both increasing the passenger carrying capacity, and by lowering the center of gravity, the added weight increased the boat's stability.

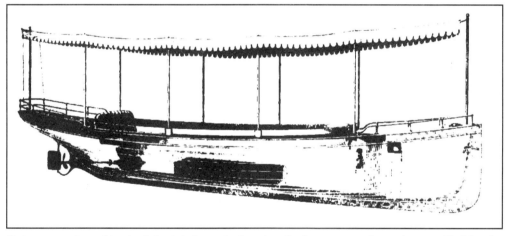

Cut-a-way view of typical electric launch showing the low center of gravity provided by the placement of the storage batteries below the floor boards

Drawbacks of the quiet, odorless, smooth running electric launch were its initial price and the necessity of staying with-in range of a charging station. Owners of Naphtha and gas engine launches could store reserves of fuel at remote locations, but remote charging stations were rare, so the range of an electric was limited. Regarding the initial cost, author D.W. Fostle provided an example of the comparative costs in 1896: a 21-foot launch with a 1¼-hp electric motor cost $1,225 while similar Naphtha launches cost $850 and a similar launch powered by one of Steinway's Daimler gas engines cost about $800. Ultimately the limited speed attainable by electric launches may have been the final blow.

So, while the possibilities of electric launches introduced many to the pleasures of power boating, ownership was largely limited to operators of rental and excursion fleets. Ultimately widespread use of the electric launch was doomed by the advances in the performance and reliability of cheap internal combustion engines.

General Dynamics and the Electric Boat Company

By the time of the Chicago "Columbian World Exhibition" in 1893 several nations were already exploring the possibilities of electric powered submarines. In 1887 the U. S. Navy first issued require-ments for bidding on a proposed submarine. The Spanish and French navies had working prototypes by 1888. In 1892 the Detroit Boat Works built a prototype for George C. Baker of Chicago. He submitted it as one of three

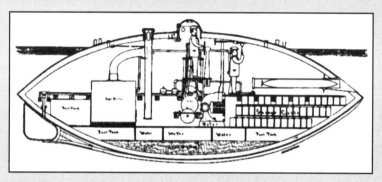

proposals received by the U. S. Navy during the summer of 1893. Another proposal was submitted by the Holland Torpedo Boat Company headed by John Holland. Holland, who had already produced more than four prototype electric submarines, is the one many consider as the father of modern submarines. In 1900, his sixth became the "USS Holland," the US Navy's first commissioned submarine.

The *USS Holland* was the first submarine in the world to use both internal combustion and electric motors. Electric motors were used for underwater propulsion and an internal combustion engine was used for surface propulsion, recharging the storage batteries, and to compress air reserves. By the time Holland's submarine was modified to meet the demands of the Navy, the company was part of Isaac Leopold Rice's conglomerate, the Electric Boat Company.

Historical records seem to have lost the details of how and precisely who founded the Electric Launch and Navigation Company. Henry R. Sutpher was closely associated with the ownership and management of the company as early as 1892. He ran the operation until the Elco division of the Electric Boat Company was closed in 1949.

Until 1900, Elco acted as a marketing company contracting the components and assembly of electric launches. For many years the engines were built by Electric Dynamic and the storage batteries were built by the Electric Storage Battery Company, later known as Exide, both owned by Isaac Leopold Rice. In 1897, Rice added the Electric Carriage and Wagon Company to his collection of companies and reorganized it as the Electric Vehicle Company. The next year he sold the battery and vehicle company to a group of wealthy investors who merged them with the automobile division of the Pope Manufacturing Company. Flush with cash, Rice purchased Elco and the Holland Torpedo Boat Company, built a manufacturing facility and merged them all into the Electric Boat Company.

Rice had envisioned a great future for electric launches and submarines. He also adapted well to technological change. Elco continued to build pleasure boats and submarines using whatever propulsion systems were best indicated. The building of pleasure boats was just a small branch of the Electric Boat Company when the company diversified by acquiring Canadair in 1947. In 1949 the pleasure boat operation was closed, but the shipbuilding business has continued to thrive.

In 1952 the Electric Boat Company reorganized and assumed the name it uses today, General Dynamics. While it was still the Electric Boat Company, in 1951 the company signed a contract to build the world's first nuclear submarine. The "USS Nautilis" was christened in 1954. Today General Dynamics and its 70,000 employees are the US Navy's leading supplier of combat vessels. The conglomerate's products also include aircraft, missiles and tanks.

Electric Automobiles

Electric boats were not new but, there were not any significant electric road vehicles in America at the time of the Columbian World Exhibition at Chicago in 1893. However, by that time William Morrison of Des Moines, Iowa, had built an awkward electric carriage that was capable of running for thirteen consecutive hours at 14 mph. The 4-hp motor was energized by twenty-four storage batteries. However, that vehicle was originally built only as a way to promote batteries and not to advance the development of a practical road vehicle.

Harold Sturgis purchased the Morrison carriage to use as a promotional stunt to demonstrate the products of the American Battery Company of Chicago at the Columbian World's Exhibition. Later he exhibited the carriage at fairs around the country and in 1895 entered it in the Chicago Times Herald race, the first automobile race of any importance in the United States.

The publisher of *Cosmopolitan* magazine, John Brisben Walker, personally reported from both the 1893 and 1904 world fairs. In a September 1904 article comparing the technology exhibited at the two fairs, he said that he was unaware of any automobile at the 1893 fair with the exception of a small, uncomfortable electric carriage that was giving demonstration rides in the technology hall. In his opinion the novelty of the carriage attracted attention to Sturges's batteries without stimulating any public interest in electric automobiles. Walker may be considered to have been a keen observer of the early automobile industry: in 1899 he was a co-founder of Locomobile, the first commercially successful manufacturer of a steam powered automobile in the United States.

Sturges and William Morrison were not really interested in automobiles. According to the *Standard Catalog of American Cars*, in 1907 Morrison told an interviewer from the Des Moines "Register & Leader", *"I wouldn't give ten cents for an automobile for my own use. But, of course, by this I'm not belittling their usefulness by any means."*

Reportedly Morrison's other inventions included the first motorboat on the Des Moines River.

After the Morrison/Sturgis electric vehicle, the next electric of any note was the *Electrobat* designed by Henry Morris and Pedro Salom. Morris and Salom organized the Electric Carriage and Wagon Company in 1896. The next year they ran a fleet of twelve electric cabs in the City of New York before selling the company to Isaac Leopold Rice, president of the Electric Storage Battery Company. Rice reorganized the business as the Electric Vehicle Company and expanded the New York electric taxicab fleet from thirteen to about one-hundred. By then Rice already owned companies to supply the engines and batteries, so integrating the manufacturing of vehicles, and operating fleets of electric cabs created a conglomerate with unlimited potential.

The Pope Manufacturing Company conglomerate added an electric vehicle division in 1896. By 1899 the company built some 2,000 electric vehicles in Hartford, Connecticut; two years before Detroit had any company producing more than a few experimental automobiles. At the time it looked as if Pope would dominate both the American bicycle industry and the emerging automobile industry, and that New England would be its home.

In 1898 Rice sold both the Electric Vehicle Company and the Electric Storage Battery Company to a group of wealthy investors. The companies were consolidated and the next year the company merged with the automobile division of the Pope Manufacturing Company. The investors had big plans to monopolize the automobile industry and were betting on the future of electric vehicles. To hedge their bet they also controlled the Selden patent that would plague gasoline powered automobile manufacturers for another dozen years.

Mr. and Mrs. Thomas A. Edison in one of Walter C. Baker's first electric carriages. Circa 1898
Courtesy NAHC

Thomas A. Edison is known to have encouraged Henry Ford but, he also worked closely with Walter C. Baker, and was Baker's first buyer. Reportedly Edison once said to Baker, *"If you continue making your present caliber of automobile and I my quality of battery – the gasoline buggy will be out of existence in no time at all."*

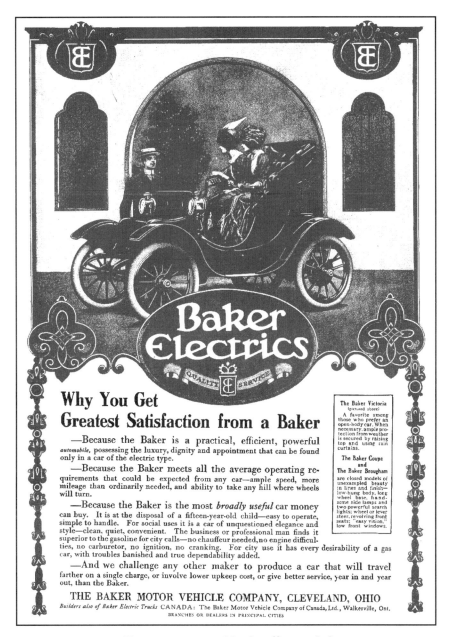

Easy to operate – No chauffer needed
**…possessing the luxury, dignity and appointment that can be found only
in a car of the electric type…**

In Cleveland, Ohio, Walter Baker[1] began experimenting with an electric vehicle in 1897 and the next year he organized the Baker Motor Vehicle Company. The electrical wizard

---

1. Walter Charles Baker, born in Cleveland, Ohio, 1868, was a prolific inventor. When he was only 18 he designed and supervised construction of a railway bridge. In 1895 he formed the American Ball Bearing Company and pioneered using ball-bearing axles for horse-drawn vehicles. In 1900, at the first national auto show he displayed the first shaft-driven automobile. In 1915 the Baker Motor Vehicle Company merged with the Rauch and Lang Carriage Company to form the Baker, Rauch & Lang Company. The company stopped making passenger automobiles during WWI but, continued making electric industrial vehicles. In 1953 Otis Elevator Company purchased the company and it became the Baker Division. The name was not entirely discontinued until 1999 when Linde Corporation dropped the name.

Thomas A. Edison purchased the first "Baker", a 550-pound buggy with a 3/4 – hp motor and 10 battery cells capable of traveling some 20 miles. Baker vehicles increased in sophistication of design and performance. With Edison's commitment to develop a better battery, the future looked bright for electric vehicles.

The gentle electrics enjoyed an advantage over the hard to start, noisy, smelly gas vehicles that required wrestling with complicated gear shifters and manual starters. They also enjoyed advantages over the steamers that required long start-up times, delicate engine and boiler adjustments and frequent stops for water and fuel.[2] If a network of charging stations had been in place, the electrics would have had an advantage on all the practical aspects of the early automobiles.

Electrics could also be built to go fast. A Jeantaud electric automobile from Belgium was the fastest car in the world in 1898 at 39.25 mph. In 1899 the *Jamais Contnete*, another Belgium electric, raised the land speed record to 65.79 mph. That was the world record until a steamer raised the official world's speed record to 75.06 mph in 1902. However, unofficially, that same year, Walter Baker reportedly drove his electric "Torpedo" 104 mph at Ormond Breach, Florida.[3]

Oil Gushers and Electric Starters

At the turn of the century electric vehicles were more reliable and easier to operate than alternative types of automobiles. They were more expensive to acquire but, the electricity needed to charge the batteries was less expensive than the fuel required to operate steam or gasoline powered automobiles comparable distances. Until 1901.

In January 1901, America's first "oil gusher," erupted at Beaumont, Texas, and the relative operating costs changed dramatically. Gasoline prices plummeted just as lightweight, internal combustion engines and related components were beginning to be widely recognized as manageable, reliable options for motive power on land and sea. To make matters worse for the electrics, just as the price of gasoline plummeted, the cost of electricity was on the rise.

It was not long before electric launches and automobiles could no longer compete with the cost and performance of vehicles powered by the improved internal combustion engines. Edison's improved batteries[4] finally arrived, about 1910, but it was already to late to regain market share. Electric car production peaked in 1912, the year the first electric starter was offered on a production model gas powered automobiles.

Many observers have noted that the final blow for the electric automobile was when a small electric motor was applied to gas engines. Self-starting equipment reduced the risks from the starting cranks that often resulted in broken arms and sprained wrists. More importantly the electric starter broadened the market by reducing the physical

---

2. Complaints were also made of the smell from the fuel used for their flash boilers, gasoline.
3. The Official world's land speed record did not break 100 mph until 1904 when France claimed the record with an internal combustion engine.3. Clara Ford's Detroit Electric is in the collection of the Henry Ford (Museu) and Helen Newberry Joy's Detroit Electric is in the colletion of the Detroit Historical Museum and on loan to the Henry Ford Estate – Fairlane.
4. Automobile collector and *Tonight Show* host Jay Leno has a 1909 Baker with the original Edison batteries that goes 110 miles on a single charge.

strength required to start the engine. For some time, electrics continued to enjoy a niche as an elegant "Lady's car." Notably, Mrs. Henry B. Joy (Packard Motor Car Company) and Mrs. Henry Ford almost never publicly operated the gas-powered automobiles that their husbands manufactured.[5] Mrs. Joy was particularly well known as one of the last matrons to drive her electric regularly around the streets of Grosse Pointe in the 1940's.

By 1930, the once common sight of an electric car was a novelty. By that time the Detroit Electric Car Company, the last of the electric car manufacturers, was building vehicles only on an as-ordered basis. In 1942 the Detroit Electric Car Company manufactured its last car.

The Legacy of Col. Albert Pope

Col. Albert Pope was the father of the American bicycle industry and the outspoken leader of a national movement for good roads. He also established an automobile industry in Hartford, Connecticut, years before anything comparable began in Detroit.

Pope's *Columbia* bicycle empire began in 1878, shortly after bicycles were introduced to America at the Philadelphia Centennial Exposition in 1876. By the 1890's the Pope Manufacturing Company was New England's largest manufacturer and, with some 15,000 Columbia bicycle agencies worldwide, there were few cities of any size without one.

The Pope Manufacturing Co led the nation in the use of mass production processes and precision manufacturing. It was also a model of an integrated conglomerate. It was organized to manufacture, market, advertise, sell and maintain wheeled vehicles. At its height as a bicycle manufacturer in the early-1890s, the organization of Pope companies included the following:

Bicycle Department – Manufacture of Columbia and Hartford brand bicycles.
　　Hartford Tube Works, a manufacture of hollow steel tubes (acquired by Shelby Steel Tube Co. in 1900).
　　Hartford Rubber Works, a manufacturer of bicycle tires (acquired by United State Rubber, predecessor of Uniroyal, in 1905).
　　Columbia Steel Co., a manufacturer of sheet metal located in Elyria, Ohio.
　　Metallurgical Department, a manufacturer of ball bearings as well as a researcher and developer of new methods for pressing metal, testing & quality control of parts. Publicity/Advertising/Publishing Department, including the publishing of *Wheelman* and *Outing* magazines. It also financed the publishing of *The American Bicycle*

By the mid-1890s bicycle sales were declining. The market for new sales was saturated, a victim of their own business success, and Pope found himself with excess production capacity. In 1896 Pope decided to add a motor carriage division. Hiram Percy Maxim, an early proponent of internal combustion powered vehicles, was hired to develop a marketable automobile.

---

5. Clara Ford's Detroit Electric is in the collection of the Henry Ford (Museum) and Mrs. Joy's Detroit Electric is in the colletion of the Detroit Historical Museum and on loan to the Henry Ford Estate – Fairlane. Henry B. Joy led a group of investors to acquire the Ohio Automobile Company and relocated it in Detroit as the Packard Motor Car Company.

Like so many of his peers, Pope was a man who had been brought up appreciating the elegance and perfection of fine carriages. He found incredible the notion that people would want a vehicle with messy grease-slathered parts and an exploding machine tucked under its seats. The versatile Maxim was directed to develop an electric automobile.

On May 13, 1897 Pope ceremoniously unveiled the Mark III Stanhope, the world's first public demonstration of a production model automobile. Engineers and reporters from all over the world were given the opportunity to operate one and they were given photographs to take to their hometown newspapers. In 1898 Pope Manufacturing Co. produced 500 electric and 40 gas powered automobiles. By 1899 they produced a total of 2,000 electric vehicles.

With bicycle sales in decline and automobile sales on the rise, the visionary Pope organized the American Bicycle Company in 1899, to combine his bicycle operation with 44 other manufacturers. Some of the other bicycle manufacturers, such as Harry A. Lozier, Sr., in Toledo and his brother-in-law, Edwin Ross Thomas, in Buffalo, took their buy-out money and invested in the gas engine business. The American Bicycle Company had an $80 million capitalization,

At the same time, Pope merged his automobile division with the Electric Vehicle Company with a capitalization of $3 million. Assets of the company included the Seldon Patent that would plague the gasoline powered automobile manufacturers for another decade.

Sales for the bicycle industry continued to decline, but the Electric Vehicle Company's sales were on the rise and an 8% dividend was paid the first year. Pope had good reason to believe he had hedged his bets well.

In 1900, Pope sold his interest in the Electric Vehicle Company, placed his son in charge of the American Bicycle Company, and for the next three years committed himself to the cause of building good roads in America. During that time, he was nearly alone among the auto pioneers in working for legislation to pave roads, the critical infrastructure necessary for the future of the entire automobile industry.

Reversals of fortune can come quickly, and in 1903 the American Bicycle Company went into receivership. Alexander Pope reincorporated the Pope Manufacturing Co. and bought the remaining production facilities of the bankrupt bicycle business. He next created four automobile subsidiaries. Because Pope recognized that the automobile industry's future was going to be the gasoline engine, the four new automobile companies included only one producing electric vehicles. Pope could see the future, but the industry's former leader had lost momentum. The recreated Pope Manufacturing Company was short lived:

    Pope-Toledo, a luxury car, 1903-1909
    Pope-Hartford, a mid priced car, 1903-1914
    Pope-Tribune, in Hagerstown, MD, a compact economy car 1903-1907
    Pope-Waverly Electric, Indianapolis, In, 1903-15

The Electric Vehicle Company went into receivership in 1907, then reorganized in 1909 as the Columbia Motor Car Co. In 1910 it was absorbed into Benjamin Briscoe's conglomerate, the United States Motors. United States Motors went through bankruptcy in 1913 and reorganized as the Maxwell. (The only other survivor was the Gray Motor Company that was repurchased by that company's founder.) The next time the Maxwell company was reorganized, the name was changed to capitalize on the goodwill of its new owner, Walter P. Chrysler.

Pope Alumnae

After the Pope Manufacturing Companies faded from the scene, the automobile industry continued to benefit from the participation of such notable Pope Alumnae as the following:

George Day was long associated with Pope, beginning in the bicycle days. He was president of the Electric Vehicle Company until 1903. At that time he left to head the American League of Automobile Manufacturers (ALAM) as General Manager. He held that position from the time of its inception in 1903 until retiring in 1907.

Milton Budlong succeeded Day as president of the Electrical Vehicle Company in 1903 and again as head of the ALAM in 1907.

Henry Souther, an MIT graduate engineer, began working with Pope in the pre-automobile days. It was on his recommendation that Maxim was hired to start the motor carriage division. Souther later headed the Standard Roller Bearing Co. and at one time was the head of the Standards Committee of the Society of Automobile Engineers.

Harold Hayden Eames managed Pope's tube division and later served as the General Manager of Studebaker.

Herbert H. Rice was a key Pope employee from 1892 to 1907 when he purchased the assets of the Waverly electric. He continued to produce the Waverly until 1915 and at that time joined Cadillac Motor Car Company, where from 1921 to 1925 he was the General Manager.

Hiram Percy Maxim

Hiram Percy Maxim, an engineering genius who graduated MIT at age 17, was the most notable Pope alumnus. He was an early proponent of internal combustion powered vehicles and built his first gasoline vehicle in 1895. From 1896-1907 he was the chief auto engineer for Pope Manufacturing Company and its successor, the Electric Vehicle Co.

After the bankruptcy of the Electric Vehicle Company, Maxim built a prototype electric vehicle with T.W. Goodridge, formerly the General Manager of Studebaker (then the country's largest carriage maker), but the partnership dissolved before they went into production. Maxim then experimented with gliders and automobile mufflers. In 1909 he incorporated the Maxim Silencer Co. to manufacture silencers for firearms, a product that grew from his experiments to quiet automobiles.

Maxim received 49 patents. In addition to automobiles and silencers he also made contributions in other distinct areas such as founding the Radio Relay League, 1914, the International Radio Union, 1925, and the Amateur Cinema League, 1926. He also wrote the scenario for "Virgin Paradise," a motion picture produced in 1921, and three books including his memoirs of the early automobile industry, "Horseless Carriage Days."

References:

"Baker Sub-Marine Torpedo Boat," Marine Review, Cleveland, Ohio, May 19, 1892

Electric Launch Co, 1902 catalog, reprinted with introduction and notes by William C. Swanson, Swanson Marine Enterprises, 1984

Flink, James J., "America Adopt the Automobile," The Massachusetts Institute of Technology, Cambridge, Massachusetts, 1970

Goddard, Stephen B., "Colonel Albert Pope and his Dream Machines," McFarland & Co., Jefferson, NC 2000

Kimes, Beverly Rae and Henry Austin Clark, Jr., "Standard Catalog of American Cars 1805-1942 3rd Edition," Krause Publications, Iola, WI 1996

Leno, Jay, "Driving Fuelishly", Popular Mechanics, April 16, 2002.

Linde Corporation, "A Journey Through the Pioneering Origins and History of Linde Material Handling", www.lindelifttruci.com?history.htm

Steelhorst, Mary, "U. S. got a charge out of Cleveland's electric cars", The Plain Dealer, Cleveland, Ohio, February 27, 2005

Martin, Thomas Commerford, and Joseph Sachs, "Electrical Boats and Navigation," Charles C. Shelly, Publisher, New York, 1984, reprinted 2001, the Boat House, Portland, OR, with new Introduction by William C. Swanson and an Afterword by Bill Durham

Maxim, Hiram Percy, "Horseless Carriage Days," Harper & Brothers Publishers, New York, 1936

Park.org/Pavilions/WorldExpositions/Chicago2.text.hmtl

Rushton, J. H., "Rushton's Portable Sporting Boats," 1889 catalog, reprinted by the Boat House, Portland, OR, 2002

Walker, John Brisben, "Transportation in 1904," Cosmopolitan, New York, NY, 1904

Internal Combustion

Frightful Exploding Machines

Internal combustion (IC) engines share fundamental design elements with steam and other vapor type engines: inject an expanding element through a port or valve into a sealed chamber with a movable piston, expel the expanded element through another port or valve and repeat. Nevertheless, after the steam engine started powering the Industrial Revolution and made mechanically powered ships and railroads possible, it took an additional 100 years of continuous experimenting to develop reliable IC engines that were both light enough and powerful enough to successfully participate in the Transportation Revolution. An internal combustion engine capable of operating with a portable liquid fuel was not commercially availlable until 1886.

A cannon powered the first known IC engine. In 1673, Dutch astronomer, mathematician and inventor, Christiaan Huygens, designed an engine employing gunpowder to pump water. However, as it required a fresh charge of gunpowder to be placed in the cylinder before each firing, it did not prove to be very practical. There were many other reported experiments but the first marketable IC engine did not appear until 1860, and that engine, like the cannon, did not employ compression. A practical IC engine that compressed a fuel-air mixture before ignition became available in 1876.

While fundamentally similar in mechanical design to a steam engine, the technical requirements of IC engines can be more demanding. For example, in addition to injecting an expandable vapor into the working chamber, an IC engine must absorb the shock of sudden expansion within the cylinder. It also requires a system to ignite the vapor at a precise moment. To free the "gas" engine from dependency on city pipes it was necessary to create a system to vaporize a portable liquid fuel on an as-needed basis and mix it with the correct amount of air to enable an explosion. IC engine theories were often far ahead of the component technology. As engine speed and compression ratios increased, a primitive engine tended to self-destruct from the vibration, heat and pressure the engine was subjected to. This tendency was often made worse by the builder's inability to control the combustion process.

In the Beginning: The double-acting atmospheric internal combustion engine.

In 1860 Jean Joseph Etienne Lenoir, a Belgian earlier known for his electric-plating and other electrical inventions, designed and built a marketable internal combustion engine. Its construction was not much different from a double acting steam engine. Lenoir's engine did not compress the gas, but simply relied on the expansion caused when ordinary city illuminating gas is ignited. It also employed an explosion at each end of the piston.

Aside from some industrial applications, one of the engine's first uses was in a boat in 1861. According to author Lyle Cummings, Lenoir called attention to his engine by putting a 1-hp engine and bottled gas in a 16.5-foot boat and taking passengers for demonstration rides on the Seine River in Paris, France. Another boat owned by the Marquis d'Nare d'Aubais used a 2-hp Lenoir engine with bottled gas and ran on the Seine River from Paris to Charenton several times a week for two years. In 1863 Lenoir rigged an engine of this type to a carriage and reportedly made a three-hour round trip excursion out of Paris. It was a start, and his modest success attracted the attention of others.

Revolutionary IC developments began when Nicholas Otto set out to improve the efficiency of Lenoir's design. Otto entered the stage in 1861 when he first built a fuel guzzling Lenoir-type engine. In 1864, Otto and his business partner, Eugene Langen, formed N.A. Otto & Cie. to manufacture non-compression engines that used only one-third as much fuel as a similar Lenoir. However, it took three years of experiments before bringing the engine to market in 1867.

The market for the early IC engines was unenthusiastic and limited to urban commercial applications that wanted quick starting mechanical power for short periods between long periods of idleness. For extended use, the cost of ordinary illuminating gas was too expensive when compared to the cheap coal used by a steam engine. Consider the following example using details provided by *Scientific American*, March 21, 1891:

At that time a ton of coal generating 26,000,000 units of heat cost $6.00. The same heat units from illuminating gas cost $37.00. Fuel costs for a 100-mile cruise that required one and one-half tons of coal was $9.00, while the same cruise, using gas to heat the boiler would have cost $55.50.

On the other hand, to boil 2 quarts of water from a cold start requires not less than 5 pounds of coal, for what then would have cost 1.5 cents. However, using illuminating gas the task could be done quicker, cleaner and with less labor for a cost of 0.2 cents. So, for quick short term uses there was a clear advantage with gas, but the economies of scale gave coal a huge advantage for all other uses.

After the introduction of systems using portable liquid fuels, farmers and others who lived distant from public gas works were able to use IC engines. By the late-1880s IC engines were reasonably reliable and simple enough to be maintained by self-reliant rural Americans. These labor saving devices could be started quickly to pump water, grind feed, cut wood and perform a number of other uses that increased productivity with less manual labor. However, as one of the early one-horsepower engines could weigh as much as 1,000 pounds, they were as portable as a piano. But they could be set up practically anywhere a strong base could be provided.

The IC engine's widespread acceptance by rural Americans is one explanation for why mid-western motormen developed their early expertise. By comparison, at that time New England was more urban, so the people there had less need for the remote operating feature. New Englanders of the late 19th century tended to view the IC engine as a crude option that was best left to the western settlers. In the Great Lakes area, motormen were quick to adapt the region's marine steam engine building experience and to apply it to the new type of gas engine.

Until the IC engine began powering small boats and carriages, the technical demands on the engine were comparatively simple. Early engineers addressed the most basic concern – did combustion occur? The goal was simply to get the engine started and keep it running. Weight was not a serious concern when the engines were bolted down to industrial foundations. For portable uses on land, small engines could be mounted on solid platforms and pulled from site to site by horses or steam powered tractors. Strong foundations, combined with the weight of the engine, were generally sufficient to absorb the inherent vibrations of a machine that operated on the principles of containing powerful explosions several hundred time a minute. However, for use in a small boat, weight had to be minimal and vibrations needed to be eliminated as nearly as possible. Also, ignition systems requiring external flames could be reliably sheltered from the wind and rain on land, but were troublesome on the water.

In 1887 *The American Yachtsman* magazine reported on one of the first gasoline powered launches seen in America. There brief and unenthusiastic report had the following to say::

> *"One of the queerest little craft that have ever been seen around Bay Ridge is now lying in the Atlantic Basin. It is a petroleum launch, 28 feet 6 inches long, and belonging to Mr. H. L. Willoghby, of Newport. Mr. Willoghby had her built in Philadelphia for a cruising launch, and has appropriately named Midge."*

It was not until the late 1890s that IC engines became acceptable options for large numbers of power boats in America. For many, there seemed to be little future in IC engines. Daimler's American licensee, William Steinway, died in 1896, regretting the large investment he had made in establishing the Daimler Motor Company in America. Reportedly his estate appraiser wrote the entire investment off as worthless.

Compression and the 4-cycle engine

In 1872 future automobile pioneers Gottlieb Daimler and Wilhelm Maybach were hired by Nicholas Otto to help develop his ideas for a 4-cycle engine that would compress the fuel-air mixture before combustion. At the time everyone was familiar with double acting engines that utilized a power stroke of expanding steam or exploding gas at each end of the piston stroke. To Otto's contemporaries, the idea of wasting three strokes of the piston to create one power stroke was sheer folly. It is accepted history that Daimler himself had little faith in the plan and thought it would be a waste of time. Instead, it was one of the most significant developments in the history of IC engines and Daimler became one of its leading proponents.

While experimental development of the 4-cycle engine was in progress, Otto continued building a reputation for his atmospheric engines and established an international network

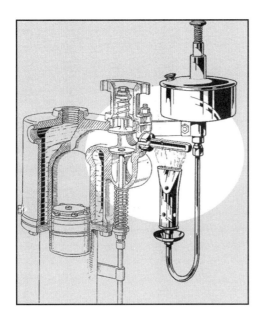

Hot Tube and Flame Ignition

Hot tube and flame ignition were commonly used in the formative years.

With the hot tube ignition system, a rod, functioning like a glow-plug, was kept hot by an external burner. When there was sufficient compression the heat of the internal tip was sufficient to affect ignition. The example to the left is the type used by Daimler in the 1890s.

With the flame ignition system, a squirt of fuel shot through an external flame directly into the charged cylinder, by way of a small port that opened at the precise moment required.

of licensees and subsidiaries. In 1869 the Crossley brothers acquired the British patent right to Otto's designs. In France the predecessor of the Panhard & Levassor Company manufactured Otto engines.

Otto's original representatives in the United States were James and Adolph Schleicher, two nephews of Otto's financial backer, Eugene Langen. In 1876 they lived in Philadelphia and were able to exhibit Otto's atmospheric engine at the Centennial International Exposition. IC engines made no notable impression on the general public, but it was a beginning. Some visitors took notes, including Clark Sintz and Henry Ford's father.

That same year, 1876, the team of Otto, Maybach and Daimler built the first practical, production IC engine that combined mixture, compression, combustion and expansion in the same cylinder. It was by far the most important single event in the evolution of the IC engine. The four-cycle, two-cycle, Diesel and rotary engines we know today are only variations on Otto's revolutionary theme of compression and ignition.

The Otto Company and its licensees diligently protected their patent on the 4-cycle design. An example is found in the following warning letter from the English licensee to the Editor of "Engineering" magazine dated April 19, 1883:

> *"Sir – It may be of more than passing interest to some of your readers to know that Mr. Otto has been obliged again to take action against several firms for infringing his patent. It is well that the public should know, that after the action of Otto v. Linford (in which Linford was defeated and ordered to pay costs and cease to manufacture), purchasers and users of the Linford engine were obliged to pay royalty to Mr. Otto. The Otto patent has now been upheld in three countries.*
>
> *Yours truly,*
> *Crossley Bros., Ltd*
> *Robert Wilson, London Mgr.*
>
> *London, April 19, 1883"*

In 1896, *The Rudder* magazine reviewed the 8 & 25-hp, 4-cycle marine engines from the Otto Gas Engine Works. The 8-hp model stood 39" tall and measured 36" x 24" at the base. Weight was not given for the 8-hp model, but the 25-hp model weighed in at one and a half tons, or one hundred and twenty pounds per horse-power. For a stationary engine, weight can be considered a virtue by appearing to be stronger and therefore, by implication, more reliable, but it was not a virtue in a small boat. The overweight Otto marine engines were generally limited to use as auxiliary engines to power generators and other equipment on large boats propelled by steam engines.

In 1881 Daimler and Maybach left Otto to set up their own firm. Up to that time IC engines weighed as much as one-thousand pounds per horsepower and operated at speeds of less than two-hundred revolutions per minute. For the next five years Daimler and Maybach labored to develop Daimler's vision of a smaller, lighter and higher speed engine.

Both Otto and Daimler, among others, worked to design a means to free the IC engine from city gas pipelines. Otto was again first with another "Quantum Leap." In 1885 Otto successfully controlled the vaporization of a liquid fuel within a self-contained IC engine. With this innovation the IC engine could move to the country. Otto did not patent the process, so Daimler and others were quick to follow up on the technology.

That same year, 1885, Daimler and Maybach developed a <u>one-half </u>hp air-cooled engine that weighed less than 200 pounds and developed 600 rpm. Although heavy and slow by later standards, 400 pounds per horsepower and engine speed of 600 rpm were great improvements over anything that had previously been built by anyone. Free from the city gas pipes, Daimler's "lightweight, high-speed" engine was used to propel an awkward, four-wheeled, wooden motorcycle. Reportedly, people were frightened by exploding engines and Daimler found it more prudent to field test engines in boats. In addition, marine engines initially generated more commercial interest than horseless carriages. In 1887 Prince Otto von Bismark purchased an 18-foot launch powered by a Daimler engine. Two years later Daimler took a launch to London for demonstrations on the Thames River and developed a significant market for marine IC engines in England.

The Daimler Motor Launches were *Steinway's*, a mark of quality then as now.

The absence of a stack and a coal-shoveling stoker on the Daimler launches made a lasting impression on early spectators. When asked about the early days of his engine's development Daimler reportedly said that it was power boating that did the most to quash prejudice against exploding engines using gasoline as a fuel.[1]

Two-cycle compression engine

Otto's patent protection of the 4-cycle design acted as a stimulus to developers of other types of compression type IC engines, including rotary and even a 6-cycle design. However, the most important alternative of the day was the 2-cycle engine. The first public demonstration of a 2-cycle engine may have been in June 1879 when an engine designed

---

1. Grayson, Stan, Engines Afloat, Volume I, Devereux Books, page 7.

by Dugald Clerk was exhibited in England at the Kilburn Royal Agriculture Show.[2] Automobile pioneer Karl Benz built his first engine that same year, using the 2-cycle principal.

The first commercially produced 2-cycle engines used a separate cylinder to mix and compress the gas and air mixture before forcing it into the working chamber just before ignition. The early igniter typically worked by shooting a tiny ball of gasoline through an external burner and then through a small port that opened briefly to allow the charge to enter the working chamber.

For the coming transportation revolution the 2-cycle engine possessed some appealing characteristics. A power stroke for every revolution of the flywheel provides a decided power to weight advantage over a similarly powered engine with a power stroke for every other revolution. Consequently, a two-cycle engine can be built smaller and lighter than a 4-cycle engine of similar power. By the end of the 19th century, a 2-cycle engine weighed as little as 30 pounds per horsepower.

By eliminating valves, camshafts and pushrods, 2-cycle engines could not only be built lighter, but cheaper. The initial cost to purchase was less and they were both simpler and less expensive to maintain. In his book *Old Marine Engines*, Stan Grayson explained:

> "Compared with the four-cycle, the two-cycle marine engine had one overwhelming virtue. It was simplicity. Valves and their mechanisms were dispensed with, replaced by intake and exhaust ports within the cylinder that were alternately covered and uncovered as the piston moved up and down... It did not mean that the two-cycle was trouble-free, only that its problems were usually quickly reparable, even in an open boat at sea. It was commonly said of the two-cycle that it could be repaired with a piece of baling wire and pliers."

Reliability is the primary consideration for any marine engine, followed closely by steadiness of operation and weight. With regards to the steadiness of operation, the greater frequency of ignition in each cylinder tended to balance the vibration of a two-cycle engine when compared to a four-cycle engine of similar power per cylinder. To be of comparable steadiness a 4-cycle engine required more cylinders, which then raised the weight, complexity, and cost.

In the early years of gas engine development simple one cylinder 2-cycle engine was the ideal choice for small launches. Two cycle engines dominated the markets for work and pleasure boats well into the 20th century. However, the continuous quest for greater speed and power required larger faster engines and the technical characteristics of the 4-cycle system eventually became critically important. Most notably, the speed of a 2-cycle IC engine is theoretically limited to half that of the 4-cycle by the rate of ignition and the time available for intake and exhaust functions. Using more cylinders addressed the steadiness of operation of the 4-cycle engines and improved valve mechanisms increased power to weight ratios. The 2-cycle design and development stopped at a reasonable stage of perfection but, the 4-cycle design continued to improve and eventually dominated almost all uses for the IC engine.

---

2. For many years 2-cycle engines were called Clerk-cycle engines in England. The first Clerk engine demonstrated in 1879 ran at a speed of 300-rpm, more than double the speed of Otto's 4-cycle engines.

Acceptance and Use

At the beginning of the 1890s, the only compelling technical advantage of an IC engine of any type was the ability to start quickly, although that was true more often in theory than in practice. The most important practical considerations were the comparatively low cost of acquisition, economical use of a clean portable fuel, and freedom from regulations governing steamboats.

Significant disadvantages of the early IC engines, commonly known as "exploding" engines, were that they were smelly, noisy, generally unreliable and largely feared by the public and horses. On land, any other option was generally preferable.

For small watercraft, an affordable, lightweight engine using a compact, portable fuel supply had tremendous advantages and few popularly affordable alternatives. As a marine engine, most of the associated noise and smell of an IC engine could be expelled underwater and disapproving pedestrians and horses were kept a safe distance from the offending explosions.

On the water, a one cylinder marine engine can be forgiven the occasional misfire as momentum continues to move the boat through the water. However, a lightweight experimental road vehicle might come to an immediate stop if, at the time of a misfire, the vehicle is on a slight incline or passing over an obstruction.

There were many reasons why internal combustion engines developed slowly and did not quickly capture the public's imagination until the last years of the 19th century. Compared to electrics, steam and other vapor type engines, the complexity of IC engines meant they were far more liable to stoppages and weaknesses for reasons that often appeared mysterious. While steam and other vapor engines are almost purely mechanical devices and the electric motor is almost purely electrical, the internal combustion engine is partly mechanical, partly chemical and partly electrical in its functions. The chemical and electrical parts may go wrong through causes not connected to any visible mechanism and mechanical disruption may be so slight as to escape notice.

A pent up demand was waiting for an affordable, reliable, lightweight, portable power plant. Market niches existed where quick starts and short-term use was required between long periods of rest, for use in remote locations were remote, and as a marine engine to power small boats.

The gentle Naphtha and electric engines continued to dominate the market for wealthy recreational power boaters until the dawn of the 20th century. However, fishermen and ferrymen, among others, needed a cheaper alternative and could accept the difficult starts and oily handling of early IC engines. Others were simply thrilled by the exploding engine and delighted in experimenting with them.

By the mid-1890s, pioneer motormen experimenting with the design and construction of lightweight engines could recover their developmental expenses by selling the test engines along the waterfront. There was always someone who was eager to install one in a boat previously powered only by wind and muscle. Small engine works began to appear in nearly every town bordering the American waterways.

Beeson's Marine Directory for the 1901 season of navigation reported on "A Gasoline Launch on the Yukon River" saying:

"We know of nothing that shows the wonderful advancement in the building of Marine Gasoline Engines more than the recent achievement of the Michigan Yacht & Power Company, in building a boat last season to run the White Horse Rapids and for use on the Yukon River."

As the performance of IC engines improved they found an almost unlimited market supplying engines to power boats. At the turn of the century the initial cost of a small boat and engine was within the reach of an expansive market. In 1901 the Michigan Yacht & Power Company offered a 20-foot family launch, with a 5.5-foot beam, equipped with a two and one-half horse power Sintz engine for $375. In 1903, a 16-foor launch powered by a 3/4-hp Bloomstrom engine was available for $100.

Melrose **was built in the Spring of 1900 for the Lewis River Mining and Dredging Company for use on the Yukon River in Alaska. Reliability and a portable fuel supply were critical as they often operated 5,000 miles from a base of supplies.**

In 1905 the Detroit Gas Engine & Machinery Company was advertising, "Convert your rowboat to a Launch" with a 1-hp engine complete with propeller and all hardware for $37.00. In 1906 the Gray Motor Company's first catalog offered one of their engines with a 16-foot launch, complete for $96. Comparably, that year the basic Oldsmobile and Ford automobiles cost $650-850.

At the end of the 19th century there had only been about a dozen automobiles of any kind known to have been built in Michigan. However, by that time there were many motormen around the Great Lakes States building stationary and marine IC engines. Area motormen were finding thrills on the waterways with small IC engines and a few visionaries/thrill seekers began strapping those engines on lightweight homemade carriages. Suddenly, in March 1901, the Olds Motor Works stopped making stationary and marine engines at its Detroit plant and began full time production of the world's first mass-produced IC powered automobiles.

It would be more than another decade before the number of IC engines used in road vehicles was greater than the number used in boats. In July, 1910, *The Gas Engine* magazine noted the marine gas engine was still the silent majority in the following assessment:

> *"This or that manufacturer announces 5,000 or 10,000 cars for 1910 and people wonder how so many cars can be used. The marine motor, on the other hand, is not apparently so popular or used to the same extent; but the facts contradict appearances, and those who are in a position to judge state that there are two marine motors in use for every one in an automobile. A little thought and a few trips along the waterways of the country would easily demonstrate the truth of these assertions; in the first place, the marine motor is older in point of usage than the automobile. Every little town bordering on a waterway has its motor factory, some to be sure, turning out only twenty or thirty a year, but all tending to swell the total."*

References:

Barthel, Com. Otto F., "The Growth of Power Boating on Fresh Water in the Past Ten Years," Detroit Free Press, July 9, 1905

Beeson's Marine Directory of the Northwestern Lakes, 20th Century Edition, Harvey C. Beeson Publisher, Chicago, Illinois, 1901

Birdsell, Edward T., M.E., "Gas and Vapor Marine Engines," The Rudder, New York, 1896

Catalog, Michigan Yacht & Power, Detroit, MI 1901

"Coal and Gas as Fuels," Scientific American, Munn & Co., New York, NY, March 21, 1891

Cummings, C. Lyle, Jr., "Internal Fire," C. Lyle Cummins, Jr., d/b/a Carnot Press, 2000

Farmer, Westin, "Halcyon Days," MotorBoat, January, 1975

Farmer, Westin, "From My Old Boat Shop; One-Lung Engines, Fantail Launches & Other Marine Delights," Boat House, Portland, OR 1996

Field & Stream, an advertisement, December 7, 1895.

Grayson, Stan, "Old Marine Engines, 3rd Edition" Devereux Books, Marblehead, Massachusetts, 1998

Miller, Gordon H., P. E., "The Heritage of Early Marine Engines," Classic Boating, May/June, 1995

The Gas Engine, The Gas Engine Publishing Company, Cincinnati, Ohio

Off To The Races

The Prototype Era, 1851-1903

At the dawn of the 20th century all types of engines, including steam, vapor, electric and gas, were powering boats and competing in regattas, often in the same races. Sailboat regattas still dominated the yachting scene and steam boats were the undisputed high speed champions. But with handicapping rules, or by out-and-out banning the steam boats, the other engines could compete and attracted some media attention. Powerboat racing was a newsworthy activity that attracted attention to the possibilities of powered vehicles. At the end of this era most automobile pioneers were competing to promote their engine technology.

The defining event that elevated boat racing to front page news in America was an unscheduled regatta during England's *Great Exhibition* of 1851. The exhibition was organized to celebrate Britain's supremacy in industry and naval power, and halls were built to house the world's greatest spectacles.

Five confident members of the New York Yacht Club joined in a syndicate to finance the building of the 101-foot yacht *America* with the objective of luring the Brits into a challenge race, bet heavily and pocket the winnings. But no one was willing to take the Americans up on the challenge until the editorials of the *London Times* belittled the British yachtsmen for not picking up the gauntlet. Bowing to public opinion, the Royal Yacht Squadron reluctantly arranged for the world's first international regatta.

The rules of yacht racing were still rather vague at that time. Had there been a handicap system, or if protests were considered, *America* would have been beaten by the smaller boats or disqualified for an inadvertent short-cut. Nevertheless, the American yacht was first to cross the finish line in a showcase regatta linked to the *Great Exhibition*. That was big news. It was a defining event that brought overnight recognition of America's technological prowess, affirmed the emergence of the United States as a world power, and hooked Americans on yacht racing.

About the same time, over the objections of the established yachtsmen, motor yachting began with a few professionally crewed, private, steam powered yachts. In 1883 the American Yacht Club of New York was founded exclusively for motoring yachtsmen. Contests of speed between steamers were common, but steamboat regattas were never successful. In 1891 the American Yacht Club announced plans for what was to be a spectacular invitational motor yacht race. A large field of entries was anticipated but, when it came to race day all that could be offered up was an impressive speed demonstration by Publisher William Randolph Hearst's 112-foot steamer *Vamoose*. The 800-hp quadruple expansion, Herreshoff steam engine propelled the yacht to a then impressive 24-mph.

By the mid-1890s the established yachtsman accepted *Naphtha* and *Electric* launches as respectable vehicles. However, they were still reluctant to accept the oily "exploding" engines. During the Naphtha launch races held at the Larchmont Yacht Club in 1895, one of William Steinway's launches powered by a Daimler engine was refused official entry. Reportedly the launch ran the course unofficially and beat all the Naphtha boats.

Moving to the Great Lakes, in 1884 some ten yacht clubs from Buffalo to Detroit associated

73

**The first known sanctioned race for boats using power other than steam was
held by the Larchmont Yacht on Long Island Sound in 1894.**

themselves as the Inter Lakes Yachting Association (ILYA). In 1894 they held the first of
the weeklong inter-club regattas that continuing to be held annually at Put-In-Bay, Lake
Erie. In 1896 *The Rudder* reported that the Put-in-Bay races were attended with as much
interest as any in the United States. In 1897 they included races for powerboats.

The ILYA Regatta race on July 7, 1897 included 8 powerboats. Gus Webber's small
open launch *Restless*, from Toledo, and Commodore William Huntington's cabin launch
Dearest, from Cleveland, both Naphthas, won in their classes.

At the ILYA regatta in 1898 six powerboats competed. Most of them were Naphthas but
at least one was a "gasoline" launch. Detroiter O. J. Mulford's 45-foot launch *Otsekita*
was powered by a 16-hp Sintz gasoline engine and won with a long lead over *Dearest*,
the previous year's winner. That same year future automobile pioneer David D. Buick

won the race for 27-
foot sailboats in his
sloop *Carrie B.* (The
next year Buick sold
his plumbing supply
business and began
m a n u f a c t u r i n g
marine   engines
under the   name
*Buick Auto-Vim &
Power Co.*)

Otsekita, **winner of the 1898 ILYA Powerboat Race**

In 1899 an Alco-
Vapor powered launch finished an eight-mile course 15 minutes ahead of the next competitor
at cup races on Lake George, New York, according to the testimonials reported in that
company's 1903 catalog. The same Alco-Vapor launch catalog reported that their launches
were easy winners in the races of the yacht tenders at a Larchmont Yacht Club regatta.

On July 7, 1900 the Detroit Yacht Club (DYC) hosted the first of many sanctioned power
boat races to be run on the Detroit River. Prominent bicycle, launch and engine dealer
William G. Metzger was the promoter and race committee chairman. The press release

stated: *"These races are confined to boats using power other than steam and the naphtha launches will naturally be in the majority."* The course was two times around a five mile circuit, starting in front of the clubhouse.[1]

William G. Metzger

In July 1900 Metzger promoted the first speedboat regatta on the Detroit River. That fall he added electric, steam and gas automobiles to his boat and engine showroom, creating the first independent automobile dealership in America. The following year he was the promoter of the first automobile race of any importance in the Detroit area, the famous race between Henry Ford and Alexander Winton at the Grosse Pointe Race Track in October, 1901.

The unlimited class in the first DYC race was won by O. J. Mulford in *Bab*, a 57-foot launch powered by a 20-hp Sintz two-cycle gasoline engine. Another contestant was entered by the "Dean of the Automobile Pioneers," Charles Brady King. King's 30-foot *Neptune* was powered by a four-cycle gasoline engine of his design, similar to the one he used in 1896 on the first gasoline powered horseless carriage to appear on the streets of Detroit.

On July 8, 1900, the Detroit Free Press noted, *"The power boat race of yesterday certainly demonstrated that the craft were jumping into favor with many yachtsmen... It was hard to realize that there were so many of the craft owned in the city as turned out for the races yesterday... Of course there will always be a big discussion which cannot be satisfactory to many as to the better type of (power) boat – whether it should be the gasoline[2], gas engine or electric craft."*

Bab won the first organized powerboat race on the Detroit River, July 7, 1900.
From the builder's 1901 catalog: *"The Bab was built to show what we could produce in a fast, sea-worthy, handsome gasoline launch, and at the same time, comfortable and roomy...."*

1. With only slight modification over the last one-hundred years it remains basically the same course that has seen more "Gold Cup" races than any other.
2. By "gasoline" Engine the writer was referring to the Naphtha engine.

On the east coast, the race committee for the Larchmont Yacht Club's Race Week in July, 1900, excluded gas (IC) powered launches, but there were two classes for gasoline (Naphtha) launches and one for Alco-Vapor launches. In another report, a New York Yacht Club regatta allowed gas engine launches to race in a class of their own, but only three competed, *Acadia, Janette* and *Racine*.

The Rudder magazine reported on the powerboat races of the Lake George Regatta Association held at Hague, N. Y. on August 21 1901. There were six contestants, including two "Naphtha" launches. The other four boats in the fleet of launches were powered by internal combustion engines that included both two and four-cycle engines from Sintz, Daimler and Lozier. It was noted that one of the entries, *Annette*, was modeled very much after *Beth*, a previous cup winner powered by a 5-hp Alco-Vapor motor that reached speeds of over 10 mph. The 29-foot *Annette* powered by a 4-hp Lozier gasoline engine was the fastest boat in the 1901 fleet, but the 17-foot *Ariel* powered by a 2-hp naphtha engine was the winner on corrected time by a narrow margin of 3 seconds. Visitors to the lake also witnessed a speed trial by E. Burgess Warren's 80-foot steamer *Ellide*. Capable of speeds reaching 35 mph, she was officially the fastest yacht in American waters.

In 1902 the Detroit Yacht Club's third powerboat regatta had 29 entries. William Metzger was again in charge of the race and also the donor of the silver cup prize for the first place. The main interest centered on the race between Captain John B. Ford's 60-foot *Titania*, Captain J. O. Teagan's 36-foot *Roxene* and O. J. Mulford's 54-foot *Little Lady*. Both *Titania* and *Little Lady* were built by Michigan Yacht & Power Company and powered by Sintz two-cycle engines. *Little Lady* had been launched only the day before and the steering gear had not yet been installed, so Mulford steered standing perched on the transom with an iron bar thrust in the rudderpost.

Another top finisher in the DYC regatta was Albert Stegmeyer's 20-foot *German Village*. Based on a testimonial letter from Stegmeyer that appeared in the 1902 Buick Motor Company catalog, it is believed that *German Village* was powered by one of David Buick's marine engines. (See page 131.)

Little Lady, **left center, narrowly edged out** *Roxene* **to the finish, but lost on corrected time in the Detroit Yacht Club's regatta in 1902.**

The New York Times reported on July 13, 1902 that the Columbian Yacht Club hosted a powerboat race for Electric and Naphtha launches. C. A. Starbuck's launch *Carmen* won the prize for the Electric class. Harry S. Elliot's *Alpha* and a jointly owned entry *Ardea* won the silver cups in the two "Naphtha" classes.

While Naphtha, Alco-vapor, electric and both two and four-cycle gasoline powered launches were competing in local and regional regattas, steam yachts continued tearing up the water with impressive speed trials. On July 16, 1902 Charles R. Flint's twin-screw 130-foot steamer *Arrow* ran an officially measured course on the Hudson River and beat all records. At 44.13 mph she claimed the world's speed record over the water until 1911, when an all-out gasoline powered hydroplane racer, *Dixie IV*, narrowly eclipsed that speed, making a new speed record at 45 mph.

By the early 20th century, power boat racing was accepted sport at yacht clubs around the country. All types of hulls and engine designs were present and each had their own proponents. Open and closed launches and cabin cruisers competed in designated classes. Power choices included the quiet steamers and electrics, the simple, reliable Naphthas and Alco-Vapor engines and the temperamental high speed fuel efficient "exploding" gasoline engines.

During this experimental era the guidance and direction of the sport of power boating was largely in the hands of enthusiastic yachtsmen. They were generally established yachtsmen who first acquired motor launches either as tenders for their sail or steam yachts, for comfortable recreation that was not dependent on the wind and hired crew, or because they were simply thrilled by the new technology.

There were still those not willing to give up on high speed steam engines. A few diehard steam-boaters continued to compete using high-speed steam launches from time to time with respectable results.

During the formative period the racing rules began to be defined. At first it was simply a free-for-all and then it was only a matter of dividing the participants by hull type and length. The first power boat regatta on the Detroit River on July 7, 1900, included five classes defined by the length of their water line – all boats under 20 feet, all boats over 40 feet, and three divisions in between.

In 1902 William Metzgar, Race Chairman for the Detroit Yacht Club (DYC), announced that they were going to eliminate the class system, reportedly for the first time on any water. Instead the DYC Regatta employed a handicap, time allowance system. They claimed there would be no partiality, as the handicapping committee would not know the identity of the boats when they figured the ratings and only the race committee knew the identity of the handicapping committee. With their entry, each captain furnished the dimensions of the boat by draft, cylinder head area and size of the propeller wheel, among other dimensions.

On August 10, 1902 the Detroit Free Press reported, *"Yesterday's trial was in the main successful and beyond question the largest and best-managed powerboat race ever held in the west,"* but they also noted, *"its defects were prominent. . . small boats had all the better of it in every way."* There was much controversy and in a follow-up report on *August 17 the Detroit Free Press wrote, "Perhaps no test ever showed the merits and defects of an innovation more plainly at the same time. . . The good points of the idea, however, were so obvious that it proved just as clearly that with a number of important modifications the system can be brought to a point of perfection. . ."*

A year later, following the ILYA Race Week of 1903 it was reported that there was something radically wrong with the system of handicapping then employed. A news-clipping claimed there was too much mathematics:

The races at Put-in-Bay might just as well have been held in a hall where there were plenty of black-boards for apparently the speed of the boats had nothing to do with the results of the event. . .It might be better in the future if the Put-in-Bay power boat races are to be run according to the system employed last week to leave the boats tied at the dock, assemble the owners on board the flagship and let them fight it out with pencil and paper. The first man able to evolve an original equation from the mean average of his horsepower plus the square root of half his displacement, divided by one-tenth the engineer's age, over two, might then be declared the winner."

It was also announced in 1903 that another experiment was to be tried on the Detroit River. An undated news-clipping titled "New Mulford Flyer" reported on the following innovation:

"In his new 60-foot gasoline yacht O. J. Mulford of Detroit, an enthusiastic power boat man will be his own steersman and engineer at the same time. . . Steering and running an engine at the same time has been done many times in smaller boats, say of 30 or 35 feet, but it is the first time on the lakes that such an experiment has been tried in a big boat of this kind. It will be watched with interest as it is not only a good idea, but a money saver, and more may take advantage of it. . . The boat is now in the frame shop of the Michigan Yacht and Power Co. . .She will probably be one of the fleet of Detroit power boats at the Canada cup races at Toronto."

1903 can be said to be the year that marks the end of an experimental era dominated by "yachtsmen" racing cruisers and ordinary launches. In *The Rudder*, January 1903, "The Advent of the Speed Launch," E. W. Graef made the following predictions:

"One thing in particular is bound to result from the advent of the speed launch, and that is, it will have the tendency to classify launches; that is, the "racer" and "cruiser" and the "ordinary" launch, and will do away with the highly powered ordinary types, which create such a disturbance in the water and lead the uninitiated observer to believe that she is doing it at a three minute gait, whereupon a real "racer," with the same power, could cut circles around her without disturbing the water enough to know she was on hand.

The real pleasure in owning a racer will be when they all get together and have it out, boat for boat, when the good qualities of the engineer and steersmen will play as an important part as the boat [and engine] itself. . ."

---

2 French resident J. Gordon Bennett was publisher of the New York Herald and past commodore of the New York Yacht Club. He sponsored the races from 1900 to 1905, using rules similar to those governing the races for the "America's Cup."

Repeating history, fifty-two years after the first international sailing yacht races, the Brits introduced international powerboat racing. In 1902 publisher Alfred Harmsworth offered a perpetual trophy for international competition of any type of motor boat not exceeding 40-feet overall. The first international power boat race for the trophy was to be held the following year as part of a race week in which Great Britain would also defend the Bennett Cup[2], the prize for international automobile races they captured in France. The first race for the Harmsworth Trophy was won by the 40-foot *Napier* using the marine engine version of the Napier automobile that ran in the 1900 Paris to Berlin race.

Prior to the Harmsworth trophy, powerboat racing was a local or regional event with little national following. This was especially so in America. About the time of the first international Harmsworth Trophy race the American Power Boat Association (APBA) was organized in an effort to standardize racing rules and elevate the emerging sport to one of national interest in America. Late that year they announced plans for the first APBA Gold Cup Race to be held in 1904. Unlike the Harmsworth Trophy races, the fist APBA Gold Cup races employed handicapping rules regarding the type of power used did not then the overall length of the boat.

The prototype era of power boat racing may have begun informally with a couple of pioneer power boaters out for a ride. No special hull designs dominated, but as engines became more powerful, builders borrowed hull designs from the fast steam powered torpedo boats. What little organized power boat racing existed in the 1890s was usually only a side show to traditional sailboat regattas, with divisions and handicapping generally based only on boat type and length. The early participants were generally traditional yachtsmen having fun with the new technology. Naphtha and Alco-Vapor engines often raced alongside electric and exploding (IC)gas engines.

During the prototype era race boats were the same boats the owners used for recreation the rest of the season. In 1903 boats built for speed and boats built for pleasure were separated into distinct classes for the fist time.

Marking the passing of the prototype era of power boat racing, well known yacht designer W. P. Stephens wrote in *The Rudder,* December 1905, that power boat racing had been taken over by men largely ignorant of the elements of practical boating. He went on to say,

> *". . .the guidance and direction of this newest form of power boating has been largely in the hands of a class best described as automoboatists, men who assume that because they know something about automobiles they also know everything about launches... many of the leaders are out first and foremost... for free advertising, and as a class are utterly ignorant of practical boating and yachting as well as the elemental principals of naval architecture...*

> *Looking on the bright side... where the designed speed has been moderate from an auto-boat standpoint, a fair amount of success has been obtained...a comparatively moderate speed has shown a high degree of reliability and regularity of performance."*

References:

Catalog, Michigan Yacht & Power Company, Detroit, MI, 2001

Calkins, Greg, "Racing Retrospectives," http:www.lesliefield.com/other_history/racing_retrospectives.htm, 2000

Fostle, Don, "Speedboat," Published jointly by United States Historical Society and Mystic Seaport Museum Stores, CN, 1988

Graef, W. W., "The Advent of the Power Launch," The Rudder, The Rudder Publishing Company, January, 1903.

The Rudder, The Rudder Publishing Company, New York, NY October 1901; January 1903; December 1905

Miscellaneous newspaper clippings including:

    Barthel, Com. Otto E. "Growth of Power Boating on Fresh Water in the last Fifteen Years," Detroit Tribune, July 9, 1905

    "Crack Races," Cleveland Leader, Cleveland, OH, July 27, 1898

    "D.Y.C Power Boat Races a Novel Attraction," Detroit Tribune, July 24, 1898

    "Inter-Lake Regatta at Put-in-Bay," Detroit Free Press, July 4, 1897

    "Innovation in Power Racing," Detroit Free Press, August 10, 1902

    "Prizes for Power Boats," New York Times, New York, NY, July 13, 1902

Gottleib Daimler and William Steinway

A Marketing Success for Internal Combustion in America

Gottlieb Daimler, 1893

William Steinway was the first North American licensee for Daimler engines. His story as a pioneer American motorman began in 1876 when William Maybach, then an agent for Nicolas Otto, introduced him to the internal combustion gas engine. In 1888 Steinway signed the license agreement with Maybach and Gottleib Daimler.

It is generally accepted history that Gottlieb Daimler was the first man to produce an internal combustion engine suitable for road vehicles and watercraft. However, he did not invent the internal combustion engine. In 1864, Nicholas Otto developed the first commercially successful internal combustion engine. Like its less successful predecessors, early Otto engines were fueled by gas supplied through the city lighting system. They were heavy, slow speed, "atmospheric" devices best suited to stationary industrial applications.

In 1872 Gottleib Daimler and his inseparable protégé and engineering genius, Wilhelm Maybach, were hired by Nicholas Otto to assist in the development of a revolutionary idea: an engine employing mixture, compression, combustion and expansion in the same cylinder. The breakthrough came in 1876. Much credit is due Otto as the creative thinker who independently applied one of the most significant concepts in the history of engines.

In 1882 Daimler and Maybach left Otto to research and develop Daimler's own ideas for an improved, high-speed engine. By 1883 they developed the "hot tube" ignition system in which an externally heated platinum tube ignited the compressed charge in the combustion chamber. The new system addressed ignition

The first Daimler motorized vehicle, 1885, was a rigid motorcylce with training wheels. Between the rider's legs was an open flame ignition system and an oily "exploding" machine.

timing issues and allowed engine speed to increase from 200 to 600 rpm. However, internal combustion engines were still dependent for fuel on gas supplied by the city gas lighting system.

In 1885 Otto was again on the leading edge of engine design as the first to develop a practical vaporizer that allowed the use of a liquid fuel. The design was not patented so Daimler and others were quick to utilize it.

In 1885 Daimler was able to produce a one-half hp engine capable of 900 rpm. Maybach placed it in a four-wheeled motorcycle. Later that winter a larger engine was installed in a carriage that they operated around Daimler's property in Connstatt, Germany.

Daimler, the man who is generally credited with pioneering the modern automobile, reportedly did not like to drive and may never have driven an automobile. Daimler was first an engineer and a "workaholic." His core competency was engines and he did not care whether they were powering industrial equipment, automobiles, trams, airships or boats.

This illustration of Daimler motor boat *DasBoot* accompanied the *Connstatt News* article in October 1888.

During the summer of 1886 Daimler and Maybach launched a motor boat. The first known newspaper article about Daimler's motor boats appeared in the *Connstatt News* in October 1888 reporting that Daimler operated his first boat on the Rhine, Main and Elbe rivers and on lakes in the summer of 1886. It was said that the trips were kept quiet because "some people had a strong fear of gasoline." To avoid scrutiny, a workman would secretly put the engine in the boat at 2:30 am. They reported that by October 1888, Daimler engines were in both small boats and boats carrying up to 20 passengers.

Daimler's first launch was powered by a single cylinder, 1-hp engine and carried eleven passengers for a voyage on the lake at Cannstatt. Later launches had two-cylinder, 4-hp engines that are believed to be the first "V" type engines.

About the same time they made their first "purpose-built" automobile. Both the Daimler launch and automobile were demonstrated at the Paris Universal Exhibition in 1889.

About 1889, Daimler took a launch to London for demonstrations on the

The first "V" type engines was installed in an 18-foot motor launch owned by German Prince Von Bismark in 1887.

Thames River. The spacious passenger area and the absence of soot and smoke attracted much attention and a significant market opened in England for the early Daimler marine engines. According to marine engine historian Stan Grayson, when asked about the early days of his engine's development, Daimler said the motorboat was the vehicle that did the most to overcome prejudice against using gasoline engines.

Writing for the British publication, *Journal of the Society of Arts*, in 1906, Bernard B. Redwood said that he well remembered the "many exciting flare-ups" that invariably accompanied a pleasant afternoon in an early Daimler launch. The flare-ups were caused by the use of the external flame, hot-tube ignition. As he described it, the main gasoline line fed a large surface-carburetor and an auxiliary tank supplied burners to heat the ignition tubes. To maintain air pressure in the main fuel line it was necessary to operate a small hand pump at short intervals. With two fuel lines, surface gasoline vaporizers, and external flames there were many opportunities for the "exciting flare-ups" to occur. However, for that era, it was more important that a lightweight, portable, high-speed engine started and kept running. After that, everything else was merely a desirable refinement.

The illustration, left, shows the widow of Daimler's French licensee Madame Sarazin in the Daimler launch waving to the gentleman in the Daimler road vehicle. This scene took place as an exhibition during the 1889 Universal Exhibition in Paris.

The relationship between the American industrialist of piano fame and the German engine pioneers began in 1876, when Maybach visited the Philadelphia Centennial International Exhibition as a representative of the Otto Engine Works. He spent three months studying American industrial methods. During that time he visited his brother, an executive with William Steinway's New York piano manufacturing company. On that visit he met William Steinway who was very interested in what Maybach had to say about internal combustion engines.

They agreed to stay in contact regarding future engine developments. Steinway undoubtedly followed developments with a keen interest but, it was a dozen years before he decided to act. During those intervening years Daimler continued to be a manufacturer of engines. Boats and automobiles were still experimental vehicles that served to promote his advancements in engine technology. By the time Steinway became the North American licensee all indications are that the primary market for Daimler engines was still for stationary and marine applications, not for horseless carriages.

William Steinway

William Steinway, the third of four sons, was considered the marketing genius behind the family business. He became the company's first president when Steinway & Sons incorporated in 1876. He was the first of the leading industrialists in America to make a significant investment to manufacture and promote the internal combustion engine as an option for motive power.

If the Steinway family had only made pianos, the name would still be one of the most well known brand names in America. But William was a "workaholic" and could well be called a 19th century Renaissance man. His business interests were progressive and embraced a wide range of activities, including street railways, ferry lines, gas works, real estate, and banking. He was also an early powerboat enthusiast.

In 1858 the family's 175,000 square foot factory was the first in New York City to incorporate steam power tools. In 1866 William laid the cornerstone for Steinway Hall, the premier performing arts center in New York for the next thirty years.

In 1870 William began purchasing real estate on Long Island, including an estate with 4,000 feet of waterfront. The family steam yacht *Mozart* took its maiden voyage that year.

The next year the company began building a new factory along with a progressive factory town. Housing for the benefit of Steinway factory workers was built but, residency was not limited to Steinway employees. The Steinway village was open to anyone who wanted to live there and the Steinway workers could choose to live elsewhere. The company built a sawmill, iron and brass foundries, and metal works. The Steinway transit company also began here.

Steinway began planning for a bridge over the East River as early as 1872 and by 1887 planned the first tunnels into Manhattan. When he died in 1896 he was head of the Rapid Transit Commission of New York and had begun building the Steinway Tunnels that are still used to connect New York's Grand Central Station with Long Island.

Steinway also built an amusement park on the island to keep the transit lines active on weekend and holidays. The park grounds were subsequently redeveloped as LaGuardia airport.

As a practical industrialist with imagination and vision, the strategic possibilities of the internal combustion engine must have seemed limitless to William Steinway. Not only could they could be used to power his streetcars and ferry boats, they could use gas produced by Steinway's gas works. The prestige of the Steinway name, a guaranty of quality, would certainly have been an asset to any enterprise. It could only have helped to create acceptance of the new gasoline engines.

Steinway's Daimler Motor Company

By the mid-1880s development of the internal combustion engine had advanced far enough to rekindle Steinway's interest.

In 1888 Steinway visited Daimler and Maybach in Cannstatt. He later wrote in his diary that he had been driven "across the country" in one of Daimler's motorized quadricycles. The visit concluded with Steinway contracting for the rights to manufacture Daimler products in the United States and Canada.

Steinway returned to America with the contract, a stationary engine and a trolley powered by one of the new engines. However, it was not until April 1891 that the first American Daimler engines were produced. For their initial production Steinway contracted with the National Machine Company in Hartford, Connecticut.

The first catalog for Steinway's Daimler Motor Company, dated 1891, offered one, two and four-horsepower models. Complete marine units with reverse gear, shaft, propeller, tank and fittings were priced at $690, $910 and $1,225, respectively. In 1893 a seven-horsepower two-cylinder engine and a twelve-horsepower four-cylinder engine were added to the product line.

The 4-cycle Otto engine had been available since 1876 but, the new Daimler engines offered important advantages for use in boats and carriages. The four-horsepower Daimler weighed 678 pounds and developed 580 rpm while the comparable Otto weighed 1,200 pounds and operated at 225 rpm.

A showroom for Steinway boats and Daimler motors opened in Manhattan, prominently located next door to Steinway Hall. At first the engines seemed to sell well. By 1893 both Daimler engines and Steinway boats were being built at the Steinway plant on the East River at Long Island. At the 1893 Columbian Exposition in Chicago Daimler engines were exhibited. There was no Daimler automobile present, but, a Daimler launch received much welcomed publicity when its exhibit launch rushed to rescue the crew and passengers of a capsized boat in Lake Michigan. Steinway aggressively promoted the Daimler Motor Company but, profitable results were elusive.

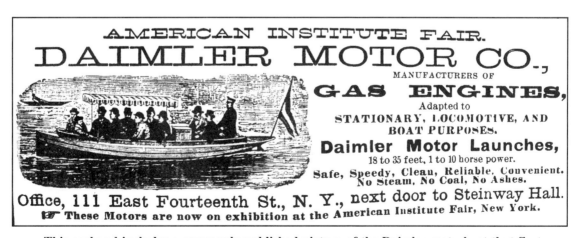

This early ad includes a commonly published picture of the Daimler motorboat that first appeared in the summer of 1886. This may have been the same boat that was exhibited at the 1889 Universal Exhibition in Paris. (See illustration on page 83)

WILLIAM STEINWAY,
PRESIDENT.

LOUIS VON BERNUTH,
TREASURER.

ADOLPH H. BURKARD,
SECRETARY.

ILLUSTRATED

CATALOGUE AND PRICE-LIST

OF THE

DAIMLER MOTOR COMPANY'S

Gas and Petroleum Motors

FOR

STREET RAILROAD CARS, PLEASURE BOATS, CARRIAGES,

QUADRICYCLES, FIRE ENGINES,

AS WELL AS ALL STATIONARY, MANUFACTURING OR OTHER PURPOSES.

Manufacturing Works and Principal Office:

Nos. 937, 939 and 941 STEINWAY AVENUE,

"STEINWAY," LONG ISLAND CITY, N. Y.

Branch Office: III East Fourteenth Street,

NEW YORK CITY.

1891.

On the inside pages the 1891 Daimler catalog offered complete marine units with reverse gear, shaft, propeller, tank and fittings.

An economic "Panic of 1893" hurt demand and prices had to be cut dramatically, reportedly by over 40% for the one-horsepower engine. When the economy improved, business improved. The optimistic Steinway funded an expansion of the plant that also included a dredged harbor to maintain customer's boats. However, in March, 1896, Steinway wrote, *I have serious apprehensions as to the monetary outlook and curse the Daimler Motor Company for its draining me of money and resolve to stop it.* Reportedly he had lost $500,000 in the engine business. That was big money in 1896.

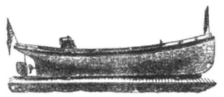

DAIMLER MOTOR COMPANY,

BUILDERS OF

HIGHEST GRADE SINGLE AND TWIN SCREW LAUNCHES,

The Pleasure Boat of the Day.

Safest, cleanest and speediest power boat built. No smoke or smokestack, no heat, dirt or smell, no coal, no gauge, no ashes, no licensed engineer or pilot required.

Run on one pint of gasoline per horse power per hour. No boiler, no steam or naptha under pressure. Under way in less than one minute. An unquestionable success.

Stationary motors from 1 to 10 horse power for pumping, electric lighting, hoisting and driving all sorts of machinery. Hundreds of these motors are in successful operation in all parts of the world.

Send for Illustrated Catalogue and Price List.

Works: 937 to 947 Steinway Ave.,
"Steinway," Long Island City, N. Y.

New York Office: 111 East 14th St.,
Next door to Steinway Hall.

With all their advantages, William Steinway must have been troubled to understand why his motorboats were not more popular. Steinway-Daimler powerboats had a slight price advantage over the Gas Engine & Power Company's "Naphtha" launches; Daimler engines were capable of higher speeds and quick starts than the Naphtha engines; and they burned only a pint of fuel per horsepower per hour, compared to the Naphtha's fuel consumption of about three quarts per horsepower per hour.

William Steinway did not live to see the internal combustion engine overcome the competition of the electric and Naphtha engines. One factor suggested by author Don Fostle may have been that the Gas Engine and Power Company built stock boats for immediate delivery while Steinway apparently only built on a slower, custom basis. Another factor was that, at a time when the average American wage was about $400 a year, even the smallest Daimler powerboats was affordable only to the wealthy. Those wealthy enough to purchase such a vehicle were undoubtedly reluctant to use a smelly, oily, exploding, gasoline engine. In 1896 the upper class still preferred the quiet and predictable, though somewhat more expensive, operation of the "Naphtha" and electric launches.

After Steinway died, on November 30, 1896, an appraiser declared his investment in the Daimler Motor Company to be worthless. His estate sold the assets of the company to a syndicate of investors that reorganized as the Daimler Manufacturing Company with Frederick Kuebler as General Manager.

In 1898 *The Rudder* reported that 200 boats and yachts of all sizes had been built and sold in the last three years. That year the Daimler Manufacturing Company built the yacht *Coyote* for Eugene Peterson of Washington, D. C. Reportedly the 86-foot yacht was the largest gas powered yacht in the world at that time. The new company continued to produce and promote their powerboats into the 20th century. However, when Daimler Manufacturing Company ceased production in America in 1908 they were building and importing only cars.

While it may not have been a financial success for Mr. Steinway, the company's promotion was undoubtedly a marketing success for the acceptance of the new technology. William Steinway must be given credit for the important role he played in promoting and popularizing power boating in America and with that, advancing the acceptance of the high-speed internal combustion engine.

References:

Catalog, "The American Mercedes," Daimler Manufacturing Company, 1906, reproduced with introduction, 1961

Fostle, D. W., "Speedboat," Published jointly by the United States Historical Society and Mystic Seaport Museum Stores, CN, 1988

"Gottlicb Daimler Zum Gedachtnis, Eine Dokimenten-Sammlung (Gottlieb Daimler In Memorium, a Document Collection)," Daimler-Benz AG, Stuttgart-Unterturkheim, Germany, 1950

Grayson, Stan, "Engines Afloat, Vol. I, The Gasoline Era," Devereux Books, Marblehead, MA, 1999

Human, Alfred, "Forgotten Pages in the Romance of Motor Boating," Motor Boating, February, 1934

"Our Builders, The Daimler Motor Company," The Rudder, 1898.

www.steinway.com, the official web site for the 150th anniversary (1853-2003) of Steinway & Sons.

Clark Sintz

Famous but Forgotten

Gottleib Daimler's high-speed 4-cycle engines were not the only internal combustion engines with promise in 1891. While the acceptance of the "exploding" engines was moving west from Cannstatt, Germany, pioneer motormen in the Great Lakes area of the American mid-west were independently making important advances with internal combustion engines of their own.

Of America's pioneer motormen, arguably no one had more influence on advancing the design and application of internal combustion engines than Clark Sintz. Sintz marine engines were the first commercially successful gas engines on the Great Lakes and they powered some of America's first experimental gas automobiles. Three of the most well known successors to Clark Sintz's engine companies, Foos Gas Engine Company, Wolverine Motor Company and Gray Marine Motor Company, continued into the second half of the 20th century. Clark Sintz's most notable contributions to modern engine design included:

1. First American builder to eliminate the separate compression cylinder, using the crankcase as the mixing-compression chamber. That feature reduced the size, weight and cost of building 2-cycle engines.

2. First to patent a totally valve-less, 3-port, 2-cycle engine, the basic design of all modern 2-cycle engines (2 port engines use a one-way valve on the intake port).

3. First to use spark advance, the basic design used by all modern electro-gasoline engines

According to author Stan Grayson, A. E. Potter, a mechanical engineer, reportedly said in *MotorBoat*, 1912, that the early developments of the 2-cycle engine were made around Grand Rapids, Michigan, and gradually extended to the East Coast. Potter was quoted as giving an "eye witness" account that the Palmer engine (1895) was copied from the Sintz and the Lathrop was later copied from Palmer. They in turn inspired other machinists who adapted Sintz designs and become engine builders.

When added to a tradition of boat building in Grand Rapids, Sintz's relocation to that city in 1892ignited a boom in power boat building of national importance. In the mid-1890s Grand Rapids may have been the small gas engine capital of America. By 1895 the Sintz Motor Company was no longer that city's only marine gas engine manufacture. Other contemporary manufacturers shipping boats and engines from Grand Rapids included the Wolverine Motor Works, another Sintz family enterprise, the Grand Rapids Gas Engine & Yacht Company, manufacturers of the *Monarch* engines, and the Monitor Vapor Engine and Power Company, the manufacturer of the first gasoline engine to be reviewed by *The Rudder*, December 1895. The manufacturing of Monitor and Sintz engines relocated to Detroit in 1900, adding to the concentration of gasoline engine manufacturers in that city *before* the days of the automobile industry.

Clark Sintz was a first generation German-American, born in 1850 on a farm in Springfield, Ohio. His father, Peter Sintz, Jr., was a prosperous farmer. He also owned a sawmill and a gristmill.

Clark's mechanical aptitude blossomed at an early age, most likely influenced by exposure to his father's machinery. When he was 12 he built a miniature steam engine and by the time he was 18 he built a full-size, slide valve steam engine.

During the 1870s, Clark established himself as a manufacturer of steam engines, together with boilers and a variety of steam powered farm equipment. In 1874 he married and had two sons, Guy born 1875 and Claude born 1878.

In 1876 Clark attended the Philadelphia Centennial Exposition where he certainly must have been impressed with the Otto gasoline engines on display. By 1882 Clark built his own internal combustion engine. Author Stan Grayson writes that Sintz stated in a brief article for *Power Boating* in 1914 that his first marine engine was made in Springfield in 1884 and that it was tested on the Detroit River. However, other reports suggest the year was 1885 or 1887. The 1901 catalog of the *Michigan Yacht and Power and the Sintz Gas Engine Company* states that the Sintz marine engine was first placed on the market in 1886. Why he traveled all the way to Detroit is not known. Perhaps he was looking for investors.

In 1886 Clark received his first patent for a "new and useful", 2-cycle engine. That engine had two cylinders side by side, one cylinder was to mix and compress the air/fuel mixture and the other was to receive the compressed mixture and the ignition. The ignition came from an external flame injected through a small port in the cylinder head.

In January 1887 Clark filed a second patent that was issued in 1888 for a horizontal stationary engine with a belted governor and an electric ignition system that included a built-in dynamo. Most outstanding was that it also introduced a feature that has become a fundamental feature on all engines: ignition advance (sparking before the piston reaches top dead-center). This was at a time when many engine builders, including Daimler, were still using external flame type ignition systems.

In 1888 Sintz associated with John Foos, one of Springfield's most prominent citizens, to organize the Gas Engine Company of Springfield. Foos owned a number of ventures, including the St. John Sewing Machine Company. By that time the sewing machine market in America had become saturated so, like many owners of excess/idle capacity, Foos welcomed the opportunity to manufacture a new product.

A few years later Sintz left the company. It is not known why, but it may have had something to do with Sintz's interest in marine engines and Foos' focus on stationary engines. Away from navigable water, in the farming community of Springfield, Foos's focus may have been less visionary but, it was well grounded and proved successful for Foos. The Foos

Gas Engine Company survived as an independent engine manufacturer until about 1925 when it was acquired by the Fulton Iron Works, St. Louis, Missouri.

Sintz continued manufacturing engines under his own name. By 1890 he was issued additional patents that included one for a 4-cycle design. According to author Stan Grayson, an 1890 Sintz brochure offered single cylinder, make-and-break ignition engines of one to six-horsepower for both stationary and marine applications. The stationary engines were popular with printers, among others, and sold for $200 to $485. The marine engines cost an additional $25 to $35.

In October 1892 Clark made application for the patent (received November 1893) on what became the basic design for millions of outboards, lawn mowers, motorcycles and chain saws: the 3-port, 2-cycle engine. With that design, he became the first American inventor[1] to use a closed base, making the backside of the piston the charging pump, and completely eliminated all valves.

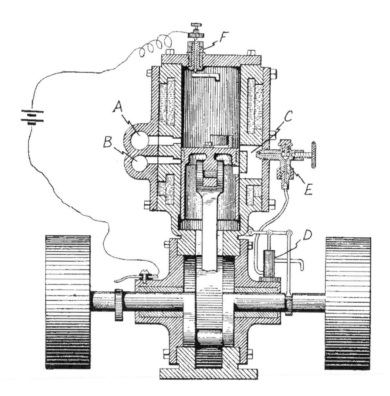

Sintz patent No. 509,255, issued November 21, 1893, shows his three port design for a two-cycle engine. A. exhaust port: B, intake port: C, by-pass port: D, fuel pump: E, fuel injector: F, make-and-break ignition.

Ignition advance and the use of the crankcase and backside of the piston as the charging pump were features that were eventually adopted by all 2-cycle engine manufacturers. However, Sintz's patent for the completely valve-less feature of the 3-port system was protected as late as 1906. In the April 1906 issue of *Cycle and Automobile Trade Journal*, Hugh Dulnar, one of the best known automobile journalists of that era, noted that the

---

1. Joseph Day received a British patent for a similar design in 1891.

Sintz 3-port patent was not expiring until November 21, 1910. At the time of the article, the patent rights were being enforced by James Whittemore, said to represent the Olds Motor Works, who was demanding payment from manufacturers of 3-port 2-cycle engines.

One of the early Sintz marine engines was sold to a wealthy boating enthusiast from Grand Rapids, Michigan named Addison A. Berber. Berber was so impressed that he persuaded Sintz to move to Grand Rapids where they formed the Sintz Gas Engine Company in the Fall of 1892.

At the same time, the Truscott Boat Manufacturing Company in St. Joseph, Michigan, formerly of Grand Rapids, had reserved a large exhibition space for the 1893 Colombian Exhibition in Chicago. A sales arrangement was made to include the Sintz engine in their exhibit. A small engine in the yacht tender *Dainty* was exhibited in the booth and a larger one was demonstrated in a launch in the exhibition lagoon.

Sintz powered, Truscott built, *Dainty* exhibited at the Columbian World Exhibition, Chicago 1893.

Among the visitors to the Colombian Exhibition were many automotive pioneers including, Elwood Haynes, Charles Brady King, Ransom Olds and Henry Ford. While the Daimler four-cycle engines were also exhibited, both Haynes and King ordered one-hp 2-cycle Sintz engines with the idea of using them to power carriages. King, however, made a few experiments and determined that a 4-cylinder, 4-cycle engine would be more suitable for a road vehicle. He decided to build one of his own design and converted the Sintz engine into an air compressor for use with his pneumatic hammers.

When Elwood Haynes got his Sintz engine back home in Kokomo, Indiana, he contracted with the Apperson brothers who, with the assistance of Jonathan Maxwell, completed one of the first gas powered American "automobiles" in July 1894. That Sintz-powered Haynes-Apperson car is now in the collection of the Smithsonian Institution and is the oldest surviving gas powered American automobile.[2]

_____

2. The original 1-hp engine was replaced with a 6-hp Sintz engine in 1896. It is the later engine that is in the vehicle in the collection of the Smithsonian Institute in Washington, D. C.

"Wolverine" Self-Starting Marine Engines

The **LEVER** Starts It Reverses It

The only SELF-STARTING and RE-VERSING marine gas engine on the market. The *lightest* engine for its power. The only engine suitable for large launches. Absolutely safe. Kept cool by water jackets. No noise. No smoke. No **"Cranking."** No vibration. Automatic generator. Removable igniters. Only engine using solid propeller, and *no* reversing gear. We make engines from 2 to 60 h. p.
Send for engine and launch catalogue to

WOLVERINE MOTOR WORKS
Grand Rapids, Mich.

For unknown reasons, about 1894 Clark left the Sintz Gas Engine Company. In what was most likely a maneuver to circumvent a poorly written non-compete agreement, Clark helped his sixteen year old son Claude establish the Wolverine Motor Company in December 1894. The patent for the four-cycle Wolverine engine was in Claude's name but, Clark was appointed guardian to handle the legal affairs of the minor.

It is easy to get ahead of our story, as by this time there were three corporate heirs to Clark Sintz's mechanical creativity: Foos, Sintz and Wolverine.

By the mid-1890s, advances in internal combustion engine design were making them reasonably reliable choices for launches and automobile experiments. Among the automobile experiments using Sintz engines that began in 1893, the following automobile pioneers strapped Sintz's engines on a chassis:

1. Elwood Haynes, described above.

2. Gottfried Schloemer and Frank Toepfer of Milwaukee, Wisconsin completed a Sintz powered horseless carriage by 1895. The restored vehicle is in the collection of the Milwaukee Public Museum but, it no longer has the original engine.

3. Reportedly, Claude Sintz built two engines he hoped to use in the famous race sponsored by the *Chicago Times-Herald* in 1895. They were not completed in time and instead were used as marine engines. Those engines may have been the four-cycle engines that became the foundation of the Wolverine Motor Works.

4. In 1897 the Reeves Variable Speed Pulley Co., of Columbus, Indiana, organized the Reeves Motor Carriage Company to manufacture a motor vehicle with a 2-cycle, six-hp Sintz engine. The June, 1897, issue of *Motorcycle Magazine* described the engine as a vertical type, with two parallel cylinders. The Reeves Company also built the 4-passenger "Sintz Motor Carriage" for the Sintz Gas Engine Company that was pictured in the September, 1897, issue of *Horseless Age*.

5. In 1898 Frank Edson & Louis Greenough, of Pierre, South Dakota, placed a Wolverine engine under the seat of a carriage with an enclosed body for six passengers. Commercial plans for the bus were unsuccessful until it was hired by the post office to ferry mail between the cities of Pierre and Fort Sully, South Dakota.

6. Between 1902 and 1904, Claude Sintz, Inc. built six automobiles. The automobile venture was unsuccessful, so the next year Claude reorganized as the Claude Sintz Company, Inc., to manufacture 4-cycle, double opposed marine engines.

A favorable review of the Sintz engine appeared in *Beeson's Marine Directory*, 1896. Their correspondent began the review as follows:

> *"Having given a great amount of attention for some time past to improvements in gas, kerosene and gasoline power motors, in my opinion the Sintz Marine Engines have many advantages over all others...*

He ended the review with the following testimonial:

> *"The writer has seen, he believes, nearly every method of vessel propulsion, but nothing previously seen interested him more than the performance of this machinery. It is the nearest to automatic action that has ever come before his notice."*

In 1897, Frank E. Kirby wrote the Sintz Gas Engine Company asking for circulars to distribute when others asked him to suggest the best gasoline marine engine available. Kirby's opinion would certainly have had some influence at the time. He was both the President of Detroit Boat Works, and the General Manager of the Detroit Shipbuilding Company. He was arguably one of the country's most important naval architect of the era.

By 1898 the Sintz Gas Engine Co. had four branch offices: Detroit, Philadelphia, Boston and New York City. The Detroit agent was O.J. Mulford. That year Mulford organized the Michigan Yacht and Power Company (MY&P), and it soon became the Sintz Gas Engine Company's best customer. In 1900 MY&P bought the company and moved the engine plant to Detroit, because, as Mulford explained, MY&P was building boats faster than the Sintz Company could build engines. The next year MY&P also acquired the King Marine Engine division from the Olds Motor Works and could then offer both two and four cycle engine options.

SINTZ Gasoline Engines and Launches...

THE. 1900 MODEL SINTZ GASOLINE ENGINE

Is the result of fifteen years of experience and an expenditure of hundreds of thousands of dollars. Having built more **Marine Gasoline Engines** than any other builders, we offer you a broader experience and the most perfect Marine Engine built. Let us send you our catalogue with testimonials, so you may see what our customers think of the "SINTZ ENGINE."

SAFEST, MOST RELIABLE, MOST COMPACT, BEST IN DESIGN, SUREST, SIMPLEST, OLDEST

Electric Gasoline Marine Engine

ON THE MARKET

ABSOLUTELY GUARANTEED

When passing through Detroit or Grand Rapids, stop over and see one of our engines in operation and take a ride on one of our FAST LAUNCHES.

SINTZ GAS ENGINE CO. Grand Rapids, Mich.

One of the last advertisements for the Sintz Gas Engine Company of Grand Rapids appeared in *Beesons's Marine Directory.* Later that year the company was acquired by the Michigan Yacht and Power Company and relocated to Detroit.

In 1904 the Michigan Yacht and Power and the Sintz Gas Engine Company consolidated, reorganized and introduced the Pungs-Sintz marine engine and the Pungs-Finch automobile. Mulford left the company at that time and the next year organized the Gray Motor Company.

The Pungs-Finch automobile received favorable reviews and was successfully manufactured until fire destroyed the factory in 1910. According to automotive historian and author Robert Szudarek, in 1906 Henry Ford reportedly told Pungs that it was the finest car he had ever seen.

Back in Grand Rapids, the Sintz family was successfully manufacturing the Wolverine engine. Between 1894 and 1900 Clark and Claude were granted six more patents. Some of the patents dealt with carburetion and ignition advancements.

One of Wolverine's most satisfied customers was a wealthy Connecticut businessman named Charles L. Snyder. Snyder and his brothers owned a banana growing and exporting business in Panama. Initially they purchased a few Sintz engines to install in banana hauling rowboats. The results impressed Snyder who in 1895 spent several months in Grand Rapids collaborating with Clark Sintz on a gas-powered narrow gauged locomotive to operate on his plantation in Panama.

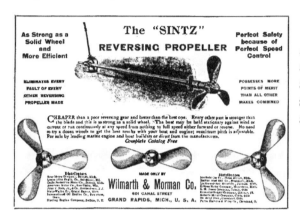

Another important Sintz patent was a reversible boat propeller. The adjustable blades permitted various speeds and a change in direction at a time before reliable transmissions.

In 1899 the Snyders sold their Panamanian interests to the United Fruit Company and, flush with cash, looked for new investments. In 1901 Charles Snyder bought the Wolverine Motor Company. Manufacturing remained in Grand Rapids until 1907 when it was relocated to Bridgeport, Connecticut. Snyder reported that the move was to better compete for the export engine market. Wolverine prospered for many years and produced marine engines, including diesels, until 1954. Service and parts continued to be offered until 1972[3].

Returning to the Sintz family, the sale of Wolverine in 1901 permitted Clark and his two sons to organize Claude Sintz, Inc., to manufacture a Sintz automobile. Reportedly Clark Sintz was the Manager, Claude was the Superintendent and Guy was a "traveling agent." The company was located in Detroit but, at the same time, Clark opened a new shop in Grand Rapids to manufacture the "improved" Clark Sintz marine, stationary and automobile engines. It seems likely that the automobiles of Claude Sintz, Inc. were to be supplied engines from Clark Sintz. However, they were only able to build some six automobiles before lack of capital forced the company to close in 1904.

Shortly after Claude Sintz Inc. closed, Clark left Grand Rapids and spent time in Panama as the mechanical Superintendent for the United Fruit Company, a position most likely obtained through continuing good relations with Charles Snyder. Later, according to author Stan Grayson, Clark designed a hydraulic transmission and a floatless carburetor for the Ford Motor Company. About 1915 he retired to a farm in Waveland, Mississippi. By 1921 he was again working in a machine shop. Sadly, in 1922 Clark was struck and killed by an automobile in Bay St. Louis, Mississippi.

3. In 1982 the remaining assets of the company, including some 16 tons of parts, were purchased by Wolverine enthusiast Larry Mahan who installed a beautifully restored 100-hp 4-cycle diesel, built in 1928, as auxiliary power for his sailing yacht "Larinda".

In 1905 Claude was back in Grand Rapids manufacturing a dual-opposed, horizontal, 4-cycle marine engines under his own name. This may have been a continuation of the manufacturing shop Clark left behind when he went to Panama. About 1907 the Sintz-Wallin Company of Grand Rapids was manufacturing the Sintz horizontal opposed, 4-cycle "Leader, non-vibrating marine engines," and Claude was the Treasurer and General Manager. Claude left the business and it was reorganized as the Leader Gas Engine Company. About 1914 the company disappeared from the public record.

In 1912 Claude formed the Claude Sintz Company, Inc., to manufacturer specialty parts for automobiles. The company still exists today as a tier one automobile components supplier. It is a member of the Deshler Group, a cooperative of companies primarily serving the auto industry.

In 1905 Guy was in Marshall, Michigan, doing business as the Guy L. Sintz Company, manufacturing a 4-cycle "Sintz two-cylinder opposed marine motor." Later he worked with several auto companies in Detroit, Pittsburg and York, Pennsylvania. In 1923 he joined Claude as factory superintendent. Sadly, he was incapacitated by a severe stroke in 1929. Claude remained active until his death in 1955, at age 78. In 1947 Claude was honored at Detroit's "Golden Jubilee" as one of the important pioneers of the automobile industry.

References:

DeAngelis, George and Murray Fahnestock, "Sintz's Important Contribution to the Birth of the Automobile," Antique Automobile, March-April, 1972

Barthel, Com. Otto F., "The Growth of Power Boating on Fresh Water in the Past Ten Years," Detroit Free Press, July 9, 1905.

Catalogs: Michigan Yacht & Power Company, 1901
              The Guy L. Sintz Co., 1906

Fostle, D. W., "Speedboat," United States Historical Society and Mystic Seaport Museum Stores, Mystic, Conn, 1988.

Grayson, Stan, "Engines Afloat, Vol. I," Devereux Books, Marbelhead, MA, 1999

Grayson, Stan, "Beautiful Engines," Devereux Books, Marbelhead, MA, 2001

Interview with Captain Larry Mahan, owner of Wolverine Motor Works, in Mystic, Connecticut, August 18, 2002

Szudarek, Robert, "How Detroit Became the Automotive Capital," Warren, MI 1996

Truscott, James M., "The Boat Building Truscott Family," Rudder, January 1945

Charles Brady King

Dean of American Automobile Pioneers

Charles Brady King, 1868-1957, may be one of the most fascinating and underrated figures among the automobile pioneers. From 1897-1902 he was a leading manufacturer of marine engines. However, in 1896 he was one of the first Americans to build an operable gas (IC) powered automobile and was associated with practically every person of importance in the early days of the automobile industry. It may have been that he was so absorbed in the creative side that he made no serious effort to establish himself as an automobile manufacturer. Consequently he has been understated and scarcely remembered for the important role he played in advancing design and development of the American automobile.

Oliver Barthel, left, and Charles Brady King in the first gas powered automobile exhibited on the streets of Detroit, March 6, 1896.

At the dawn of the American automobile era, King drove two pioneer automobiles that made history, and rode in two others. In the first one, he rode as an "umpire" in the first important automobile race in America. The race was held in Chicago on Thanksgiving Day, 1895, and he drove the second place finisher across the line when the driver fainted from exhaustion. The other was the one of his design and manufacturer that on March 6, 1896 became the first gas powered horseless carriage publicly demonstrated on the streets of Detroit. Six weeks later at the Detroit Horse Show, King exhibited the Duryea car that won the Chicago race. A few months later he rode with Henry Ford, who built his first automobile with help from King.

The visionary King was the first to propose the formation of a national organization to support what he recognized as the "coming revolution" in transportation. The idea received support and the "American Motor League" was organized in Chicago on November 1, 1895. It was the first association in the world relating to the introduction of the automobile. King was the founding Secretary. Following is the text of King's letter to the Editor of the *Chicago Times Herald*:

Dear Sir:

Realizing the fact that we have already a large number of people in this country interested in the coming revolution, the motor vehicle, and in order to pave the way for early success of this vehicle of the future, it is proposed to form a National

Organization which will have as its object the furtherance of all details connected with the broad subject, and to hold stated meetings, where papers can be read and discussions follow as to the respective merits of all points in question. Such an organization is needed now, and upon its formation would meet with hearty cooperation of the newspapers, the friends of good roads and the public at large. It is therefore proposed that such an organization be now formed and have as its name the AMERICAN MOTOR LEAGUE. This title is broad and is well suited to survive any change that the future may bring.

Yours truly,

(signed) CHARLES B. KING

In the Beginning

King's interest in transportation began at an early age. As the son of a military officer, his childhood was spent moving from one army post after another. As a result of that nomadic existence, King said, *"I kept trying to figure out some way of beating our schedule of 10 miles a day"*

C.B. King sketched the Detroit-Windsor ferry *Sappho* **on June 12, 1895, in the log book of Henry Joy's sailboat, the schooner yacht** *Pilot.*

In 1882 the family returned to Detroit where Charles' grandfather, Captain Lewis Davenport had been a transportation pioneer. In 1825 Davenport leased a little steamboat named Argo, and operated the first mechanically powered ferry service between Detroit and Windsor.

In the fall of 1887 King entered Cornell University to major in mechanical engineering. We know that he was active in college affairs and produced imaginative pen and ink drawings for the college yearbook. Another Detroiter and future business partner, John S. Newberry, Jr., also attended Cornell at that time.

King's education at Cornell was cut short when his father died in 1888. He returned to Detroit and worked as a draftsman with the Michigan Car Company. The Michigan Car Company was organized in 1864 by James McMillan and John S. Newberry Sr. to build (railroad) cars. By 1878, when Henry Ford worked there briefly, the railroad car company was Detroit's largest employer.

Car Capital of the West
(Before the Automobile)

King's relatives made Detroit the car capital of the west long before the days of the horseless carriage. The first train cars built west of Albany, NY, were built in Detroit in 1853 by a firm started by his uncle, Dr. George B. Russel (Russel married King's maternal aunt, Anna Davenport). In 1868 Russel merged with Detroit Car & Manufacturing Company and in 1871 they sold the business to the Pullman Co. In

---

1856 Dr. Russell organized the Hamtramck Iron Works and built the first iron blast furnace west of Pittsburgh. It was located at the foot of Concord, in Detroit, near the future site of the Olds Motor Works. In 1877 two of King's cousins, George and Walter Russel organized the Russel Wheel & Foundry Company to build railroad wheels. Their older brother, Henry, was the attorney for the Michigan Central Railroad Co. and in 1902 became the president of the Olds Motor Works.

In 1893 King designed a motorized tricycle and a horseless carriage with the intention of powering them with a Sintz marine engine that he purchased at the Chicago Colombian World Exhibition. Unsatisfied with the Sintz engine he instead designed and built his own two-cylinder, two-cycle engine in 1894, but after further experiments he determined that a four-cycle engine should be used. In 1895 he designed and built his first 4-cylinder, 4-cycle gasoline engine that was based on measurements from a high-speed Herreshoff marine steam engine. Valves from that engine were given to Henry Ford and used in his famous Quadricycle.[1]

King's next engine design addressed a problem of overheating exhaust valves that he experienced with earlier engines. The result became the basic engine design manufactured by the Charles B. King Company for the next five years. In his own words, from his personal papers in file at the National Automotive History Collection, King had the following to say about events of the early years:

"A real opportunity came my way in 1893 when the Russel Wheel & Foundry Company selected me to take charge of its exhibit in the Transportation building at the Chicago Worlds' Fair, or the Columbian Exposition. This assignment gave me a chance to study a multitude of engineering displays and to exhibit a patented invention of my own. This was a pneumatic hammer based upon a design which I originated in 1890 and thereafter used successfully for riveting and caulking. It was the only tool of its kind at the Fair, and received the highest award – a bronze medal and diploma . . . another invention of mine was on display . . .the King brake beam for railroad cars . . .

"At the Fair I saw, studied and later ordered a Sintz gasoline engine . .. started me planning and working on gasoline engines adapted to the propulsion of road vehicles. The Sintz people passed along to me an invitation which had come to them from their French agent, to participate in the worlds' first automobile road race then being promoted by the Petit Journal of Paris . . . held in July 1894...

"In 1894 I organized the Charles B. King Co. at 110-112 St. Antoine Street, Detroit, to manufacture pneumatic hammers and marine engines. The sale of my brake beam patent to The American Brake Beam Company of Chicago helped finance this undertaking . . ."

---

1. From the King Papers in the collection of the National Automotive History Collection of the Detroit Public Library. This was an important contribution to Ford as the valves were the most difficult component to machine at that time.

In another paper King stated:

"The initial start was made with the King Pneumatic Hammer, having actually been in operation before 1893 and through the years was the wage earner for my experimental car, engine, and construction work. In 1893, however, I made my first car drawing relating to the Sintz engine... found it unreliable and finally converted it into an air compressor for testing the King Pneumatic Hammer...

"In 1894 I designed and built a two cylinder, two cycle engine . . . But after tests and due consideration, I abandoned the two-cycle . . . "Being influenced by marine steam engine practice, I now designed and built a four cylinder, four cycle gasoline block engine for the bevel drive car, which I hoped later to enter in the Chicago Times-Herald Race of 1895 . . .

CHARLES B. KING,

112 AND 114

ST. ANTOINE STREET.

DETROIT, MICH

✳

MANUFACTURER OF

KING'S ✦ ✦

PATENT ✦

GAS ✦ ✦ ✦

ENGINES

FOR
VEHICLES.
LAUNCHES.
ETC

Left, an advertisement for King's Patent Gas Engines that appeared in the first issue of America's first automotive journal, *The Horseless Age*, November, 1895. Noteably King was offering gas engines of his design for others to put in vehicles, launches, etc. before he completed his first automobile.

"My original cylinder block had separate outside valves. . . This block was redesigned so that all valves, inlet and exhaust, with their manifolds were an intimate part of the block, and this all was water cooled; this also later becoming an accepted practice. A set of the valves removed from the first block, I gave to Henry Ford and were used by him in his ...Quadricycle...

". . .this block was redesigned. . . and this was the engine I used in driving the first car on the streets of Detroit ... The car in which the engine was mounted ... was a delivery wagon type with iron tires, as obtained from the Emerson and Fisher Company of Cincinnati. This I converted into a dependable car, putting in Hyatt roller bearings, efficient steering gear, two-speed foot controlled belt drive, foot throttle, carburetor adjustment, and gasoline tank under the driver's seat; the water tank being placed directly over the engine, at the rear of the car. To test this outfit and also my four cylinder engine, (as well as the other engines that were to follow) I made numerous tests on the streets of Detroit. Some of these tests . . . took place prior to the one recorded in the newspaper . . .

"I further adapted this four cylinder block design with steel rod frame to marine engine use later with little change . . . This block engine was copied on Henry Ford's "999" racer, except the stroke was shortened two inches and its valves operated differently . . ."[2]

The Duryea car received significant publicity as the winner of the Chicago Times-Herald race on Thanksgiving Day, 1895. King believed there would be an opportunity for the sale of Duryea engines to experimental automobile builders and he entered into an agreement to build engines under license. To create additional publicity for the engine, King arranged for the Duryea automobile to be exhibited at the Detroit Horse Show, April 23 – 26, 1896. The exhibition was held six weeks after King took the historic ride in his own horseless carriage on March 6, 1896.[3]

Charles G. Annesley

The four cylinder engine from King's first horseless carriage was later sold to Charles G. Annesley who is most often remembered as the man who bought Henry Ford's Quadricycle in 1896. Annesley was himself a notable automobile pioneer who built four electric carriages and three gasoline engines of his own before he left Detroit in 1900 and joined the Buffalo Gas Engine Company. The Buffalo Gas Engine company subsequently employed many of King's design features.

King did build one sample Duryea engine that was sold to the Emerson and Fisher Company for use in a horseless carriage they built for a circus show. King also corresponded with the Daimler Motor Company regarding a licensing agreement. However, he came to the conclusion that there would not be enough profit building motors under a 10% royalty arrangement. Instead he designed a simplified two-cylinder version of his historic four-cylinder engine. King's papers record that only three of them were sold for use in land vehicles. One of them was installed in his historic carriage and sold to Byron J. Carter in 1899. That vehicle became the foundation of the Carter-Friction Drive Car Company in Jackson, Michigan.

King Marine Engines

 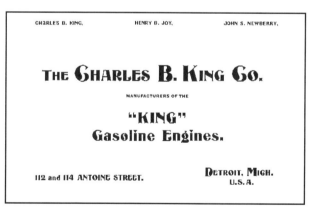

**Cover and Title Page of the
1898 catalog of *The Charles B. King Company***

---

2. King's long-time assistant, Oliver Barthel, designed the famous 999 racer with Ford.
3. Ford's historic ride was in June 1896, making his the third gas powered automobile to be demonstrated in Detroit.

King's notes state that he started marine engineering work in 1893 and that the Charles B. King Company was organized in 1894 for the manufacture of pneumatic hammers and marine engines. In the summer of 1897 the Charles B. King Company was reorganized with John S. Newberry and Henry B. Joy, as partners. This enterprise appears to have been entirely devoted to two-cylinder marine engines. The 1898 catalog offers one four-cylinder option, but it was actually two of the two-cylinder engines mounted in-line. The blocks were cast by the Leland & Faulconer Company.[4]

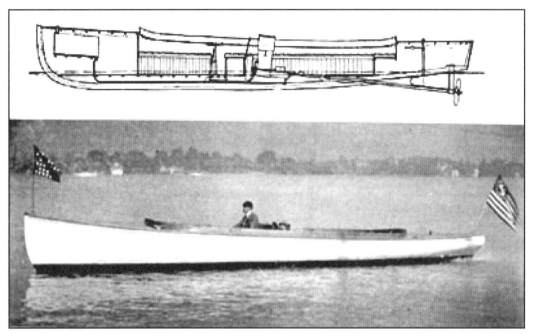

**The company's demonstration launch *Star*,
as it appeared in the 1898 catalog**

In February the company printed 5,000 second-edition copies of its 1898 catalog. Whether demand was actually growing that fast could not be confirmed because on April 24, 1898, Spain was forced to declare war on the United States. King and his partner, Henry B. Joy were two of the 14 officers and 267 enlisted volunteers from Michigan to serve on the U.S.S. Yosemite under the command of four regular officers. The Yosemite's first mission was to escort Marines landing at Guantanamo, Cuba. Her last mission was to blockade the harbor of San Juan, Puerto Rico

---

U.S.S. Yosemite

No other ship in the U.S. Navy has ever had so many well-educated and prominent sailors. In addition to Joy & King, the crew of Detroiter's included J. Walter Drake, the future president of Hupp Motor Company, two future secretaries of the Navy, Truman H. Newberry and Edwin Denby and the Dean of the University of Michigan School of Engineering and Architecture, Mortimer Cooley.

---

4. Leland & Faulconer had long been renowned for gear manufacturing and the company had recently established a reputation as an engine manufacturer. In 1896 they were contracted to make internal combustion gas engines for a boat shop owned by Frank J. Dimmer and later for the Chas. A. Strelinger Company and the Olds Motor Works.

Shortly before the Spanish-American War, King designed the hull and machinery for *Lady Frances*, a 70-foot twin-screw cabin yacht, commissioned by Boston owner J. A. VanderPoel. While King was away, Oliver Barthel managed the engine business and supervised the completion of the hull and cabin.[5] After the hull was launched it went to the Detroit Dry Dock Company, where it was outfitted with two self-starting, 30-hp, four-cylinder King engines. It was also equipped with a 2-hp gasoline engine powering an electric generator and a 1-hp gasoline engine powering a 14-foot launch that was carried aboard.

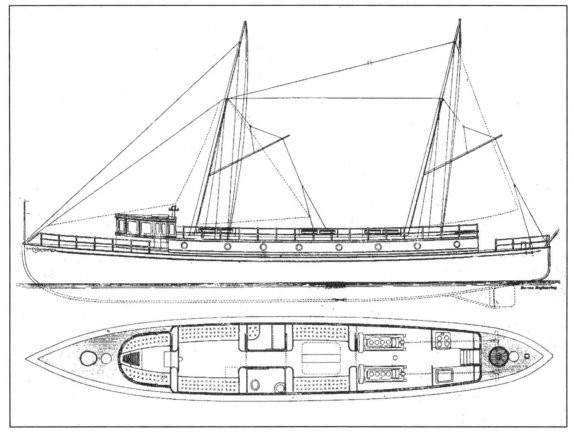

King designed yacht *Lady Frances*

1899 Self-starting King Engine

The 30-hp engines King designed for the *Lady Frances* were too large to be cranked by hand, so King designed a self-starting mechanism. The crankshaft was slowly rotated to bring one piston into a firing position. The cylinder was primed through the petcocks and a 10-gauge shell blank was screwed into the cylinder heads. When the shell's firing pin was struck by a hammer the engine would spin into action.

5. The hull and cabin were built by the Vinton Company, in Detroit, located a few blocks from King's office above John Lauer's shop at the foot of St. Antoine. The Detroit Dry Dock Company was located a short distance up river from the Vinton ship building yard. By 1907 it had been renamed *Amalie* and was owned by Joseph Cassidy when it caught fire and was destroyed at her mooring in Long Island, New York. At the time the yacht was valued at $6,000.

3.30 P.M.

An exerpt frim the log of Henry R. Joy's schooner yacht pilot. C. B. King sketched and in May 1899 Henry Joy recorded the following: "... *finally converted into an auxiliary... 6-hp engine put in place .. .Engine worked well and did not stop except on changing from dynamo to battery ..."*

In 1899 King began working on a more advanced automobile. Years he said that he regretted never completing it. The engine included several significant new design features. The four-cylinder "en bloc" engine included overhead valves operated by rocker arms, activated by rods from a camshaft enclosed in an aluminum crankcase. It is believed that was the first aluminum crankcase cast in Detroit and that it is was the largest aluminum casting made in the city up to that time. Without completing the automobile, in 1902 King converted it into a marine engine and installed it in the *Wal-Rus*, a cabin boat built by the Michigan Yacht & Power Company for his cousin Walter S. Russel.

In 1900 the King engine business was sold to the Olds Motor Works. King's records indicate that by that time he had built and sold 125 engines. King joined the Olds Motor Works as Superintendent of the Marine Engine Division. A disastrous fire in the spring of 1901 changed that company's plans. The King marine engine business was sold to Michigan Yacht and Power Company and Charles King joined that company as the Mechanical Superintendent. He also designed custom yachts during his stay with the company.

Upon acquiring King's engine business Michigan Yacht and Power Co. (MY&P) published a revised catalog that included the King engine along with their boats and the 2-cycle Sintz engines. At that time the King engine was offered in standard two and four cylinder engines up to 30-hp. King stayed with the company as the Mechanical Superintendent

---

The First Packard in Detroit

According to Oliver Barthel, Miss Grace Fletcher of Detroit, who in 1901 became Mrs. Charles B. King, was the first to buy one of Mr. Packard's cars in Detroit. Henry B. Joy, after seeing this car and driving it, bought one also. Barthel said that this was, "the introductory step in bringing the Packard Company to Detroit."

A page from the 1901 Michigan Yacht & Power Company catalog

until August 1903. At that time he left to design automobiles for the Northern Manufacturing Company with Jonathan D. Maxwell.

In 1902, King's friends and former partners in the marine engine business, Henry B. Joy and John S. Newberry, decided to get into the automobile business. It is not known why they did not back a King automobile company[6] but, they decided to buy a going concern. They led a group of Detroit investors to purchase the three year old Packard Motor Car Company.[7] In the fall of 1903 the company was relocated from Warren, Ohio, to Detroit, a significant enhancement to the Motor City's growth in the manufacturing of gasoline automobiles. About that time, King too moved into the automobile business full time.

Automobile Innovation: The *Silent Northern*

In 1894 Jonathan Dixon Maxwell assisted Elwood Haynes and the Apperson brothers to install a Sintz marine engine in a carriage. Several notable automobile brands ultimately emerged from that collaboration: the Haynes-Apperson; Haynes; Apperson; Northern; and the Maxwell. After Maxwell left the Haynes and Apperson enterprises he continued to work in the pioneer automobile business elsewhere. On King's recommendation, Ransom Olds recruited Maxwell to work on his experimental automobiles. That is believed

---

6. Indications are that King was interested in designing many things and automobile manufacturing could not hold his attention.
7. Originally name the Ohio Automobile Company, it was reorganized as the Packard Motor Car Company when it relocated to Detroit in 1903.

to have been the first significant instance at the start of a long trend of automotive talent migrating to Detroit.

The success of the 1901 Oldsmobile demonstrated to Detroit investors that the automobile business could be profitable. Maxwell seized the opportunity to interest William T. Barbour, president of the Detroit Stove Works, in organizing a new automobile company. Having been well received, he resigned from Olds and they organized the Northern Manufacturing Company. The first "Northern" looked unremarkably similar to the Olds runabout and was on the market in the spring of 1902. In August 1903 King left MY&PC to join Maxwell in the engineering department.

Shortly after King arrived, Maxwell left to organize the Maxwell-Briscoe Motor Company with Benjamin Briscoe. King became the Chief Engineer and designed a larger touring car powered by a horizontal opposed two cylinder engine of his design. The engine ran so quietly, they named the car the "Silent Northern." One of the most important features of the engine, and a first for automobile design, was that the transmission and crankcase were enclosed.[8]

NORTHERN

"*Dustless and Noiseless*"

18 h. p. side entrance $1700

The 24-inch Fly Wheel with Fan Blades

Sends a powerful *blast of air* under the car toward rear axle, destroying the vacuum caused by the swiftly moving car, and driving away all dust. Riders in the Silent Northern enjoy complete freedom from the "dust nuisance," regardless of speed. ¶ Northern mechanism—all under the hood—is the simplest, most accessible and most compact in the world. Notice that the engine is *tipped* downward, throwing the crank shaft on a *direct* line with rear axle. The Northern is the only *noiseless* car and only car at the price equipped with *four-inch* tires. It has more distinctive and *original* improvements than any other car at any price, and is more luxuriously upholstered and handsomely equipped than many cars sold at twice the price. Write for Catalog No. 11. Shows four styles of touring cars—and the Sturdy Northern Runabout, 7 h. p., **$650.**

Northern Manufacturing Company, Detroit, U.S.A.

Member Association Licensed Automobile Manufacturers.

---

8. Up to that time automobile engines did not enclose the crankcase and other parts. Most early automobile engine designs used the drip and spin-off type of lubrication, believing that only clean new oil should lubricate the engine. Marine engines had to be enclosed so King knew that it was a reasonable system.

The *Silent Northern* introduced many other innovative features attributed to King, including three-point engine suspension, integral motor and transmission assembly, and running board side steps. King is slao credited with introducing left handed steering, air-operated brakes, air-controlled clutch, and incorporating all operating controls on the steering column. Reminiscent of the experimantal engine installed in Walter Russel's yacht, King designed an overhead valve engine that was built by the Northern Manufacturing Company:

The plaque on the overhead valve engine reads:
Manufactured Under the
Chas. B. King Patent
Controlled by the
Northern Manufacturing Co.
Detroit, Mich. USA

In June 1908, super salesman William Metzger had a controlling interest in the Northern Manufacturing Company and merged it with the Wayne Automobile Company to form the Everitt, Metzger and Flanders Company (EMF). A few years later "E-M-F." became the automobile division of the Studebaker Corporation.

King did not stay after the merger and reportedly left to study automobile design and developments in Europe. But King was a natural artist as well as an inventor and engineer so, while in Paris he studied art. In Detroit he was a member of the Scarab Club, an association of artists, and his work was exhibited in Paris, Detroit and elsewhere.

The King Motor Car Co.

King reappeared to the Detroit scene on October 26, 1909, entering into an agreement with O.J. Mulford to organize the King Motor Car Co. While working on the design, they became involved in a precedent setting case in "automobile law" that established

ownership of engineering drawings. Julius Haltenberger, a draftsman employed by King & Mulford, took some of the drawings to Toronto and sold them to a rival concern. The first defense was that all Haltenberger could be accused of carrying away was the value of the paper. However, Judge Donovan, ruled that the real value was in the ideas on the paper. The Detroit News, September 11, 1910, reported that the decision was, *"one of far reaching importance in a city like this, which is the world headquarters of one of the world's greatest industries."* Along with the Seldon patent case[9], this was one of the most important early cases in automobile law. Earlier in the year King & Mulford had already reached an equitable agreement with the innocent Canadian participant who then became the Canadian licensee of the proposed King Motor Car.

The following article, Detroit News, September 21, 1910, explains the issues and the important legal precedent established by the Haltenberger lawsuit:

"BLUE PRINT CASE FINALLY SETTLED"
"EMPLOYER IS GIVEN OWNERSHIP OF AUTO DRAWINGS EMPLOYEE TRIED TO SELL."

Julius Haltenberger, a young Hungarian automobile inventor, was assessed $2,000 this morning by Judge Donovan for carrying into Canada and trying to sell to the Jules Motor Co., of Toronto, certain automobile tracings of the model King car. The blue prints were declared to be the exclusive property of Charles B. King and O. J. Mulford, who are contemplating the organization of the King Motor Car Co., to place their auto on the market, Judge Donovan placing the value of the model in dispute at between $20,000 and $30,000.

The decision is unique, in that there is very little automobile law on the books, and all of the auto people of the city have been watching the contest *which, as Judge Donovan states in his decision, has been full of bitterness, tediously long and full of intricate and expert matters. If not reversed by the supreme court, a precedent will be created regarding the ownership of blue prints upon which different persons work.*

One of the features of the case was the legal novelty of suing an attorney, John Atkinson, for the advice he gave Haltenberger, and charging him with being a conspirator to gain possession of the blue prints. Judge Donovan exonerated Atkinson completely, laying the entire responsibility upon Haltenberger.

'I find the attorney was grossly misled by Haltenberger,' runs the decision, 'who unfairly stated his case and so gained the very bad advice upon which he acted. This also applied to Charles M. Preston and Arthur J. Greenway, who were joined as co-

---

9. George Seldon received a patent that broadly covered all gas powered automobiles. Most of the gas engine automobile manufacturers paid a royalty and organized the Automobile Manufacturers Association of America to use a portion of the royalty to promote the industry. Ford 's court battle got the 4-cycle gas engine automobile excepted. The entire patent expired the following year.

> *defendants. No independent, actionable conspiracy has been clearly proven as to the defendants, aside from Haltenberger. And fraud cannot be made of suspicions; it requires convincing proof.'*
>
> *Judge Donovan states that it is his desire to protect the automobile industry of Detroit.*
>
> *'The King car is unique, with original features,' says he. 'They were mainly copied from King's original sketches, tracings and blue prints by Haltenberger, while under pay by the week, and he carried the copies to Canada and offered them for sale.*
>
> *'Such conduct would seriously undermine and seriously injure the greatest industry of Detroit, which support over 100,000 people, and such conduct must be held illegal and dangerously near to larceny. Advice of counsel cannot shield Haltenberger, who told counsel that he owned the prints, which was untrue, and that he owned an interest therein, when conditions precedent had not been fulfilled.'*

By the end of 1912 both King & Mulford had left the King Motor Car Company. King regained full possession of his patents and later sold them to various companies. Mulford merged Gray Motor Company with the Maxwell-Briscoe Company and other manufacturers when the United States Motor Company was organized in 1910. In 1912 he was busy rescuing the Gray Motor Company from the United States Motor Company bankruptcy. The only other brand name that survived was the Maxwell.

The Later Years

For the next several years King devoted himself again to experiment and invention, with a particular interest in aviation. In 1916 he was appointed to head the Division of Engine Design in the United States Army's Bureau of Aircraft Production. With forty engineers and draftsmen he directed the design of several aviation engines for experimental purpose. His office supplied all the reference data on which the design of the Liberty engine was based.

After WWI King and his wife retired to Larchmont, New York. Both Charles, and his wife, Grace Fletcher King, maintained close ties to Detroit and visited often. Charles continued on the Board of Directors of the Fletcher Paper Company and as a Co-Trustee of the Davenport Estate with Sidney T. Miller, a founding partner of a prominent Detroit law firm and president of one of the city's prominent banks. For many years he continued to maintain a Detroit residence in Indian Village Manor a prominent riverfront apartment building and on later visits stayed with his sister in Grosse Pointe.

Aside from engineering, King had interests in art and architecture and was a member of the Architectural League and the Scarab Club, a Detroit artists' association. His paintings and etchings were displayed in the Detroit Institute of Arts, the National Art Gallery in Washington, the New York Public Library and the Paris Salon. As a musician he was an accomplished performer on the drums, the flute, the bells that hung in a carillon tower on his estate, and several other instruments. In 1952 he made his last trip to Detroit to give his collection of books to the Detroit Public Library. Henry Ford Museum received his model collection of engines, cars and ships.

In 1946 King was honored at Detroit's "Golden Jubilee" commemorating his first public demonstration of a gasoline powered automobile on the streets of Detroit, a milestone in the history of the transportation revolution in that city.

Detroit Mayor Jeffries, above right, shows Charles B. King the bronze plaque commemorating King's historic 1896 horseless carriage. The plaque reads: *In Lauer's Machine Shop. Located on this site, Charles Brady King Designed and Built A Gasoline Powered Automobile. He Drove This Automobile Which was the First To Operate and Travel on the Streets of Detroit . . .* **(March 6, 1896)**

After a few fender-crumpling mishaps his driver's license was revoked when his insurance company canceled his auto coverage on his 85th birthday. King called the accidents "trivial" and the license ban "ridiculous," but he observed it. The man who drove the first car on the streets of Detroit was banned from driving on public streets. Four years later, in 1959, at the age of 89 Charles Brady King died at his home in Rye, New York.

For his final resting place King returned to Detroit. His eulogy was read at the Grosse Pointe Newberry Memorial Church and he is buried in Detroit's historic Elmwood Cemetery. When King died in 1957 the revolution he envisioned in 1995 was one of the greatest industries the world has ever known and the corporate successor of its "Silent Northern," Studebaker, was still one of the surviving automobile grand names.

The Umpire-Driver in America's First Automobile Race returned to Chicago in 1945 planning to participate in the Golden Jubilee Re-run of that race over the same course in Evanston and return on Thanksgiving Day. His picture was taken in a one-cylinder Cadillac in front of the Chicago Museum of Science and Industry in Jackson Park near the starting-point of the Race.

References

Horseless Age, an advertisement, November 1895

King, Charles, "The Golden Anniversary of America's First Automobile Race," Privately published, Larchmont, New York, 1945

Powell, Sinclair, "In the Beginning," Michigan History, November/December 1985

"The Reminiscences of Mr. Oliver E. Barthel," From the Collections of The Henry Ford, Ford Motor Company Archives Oral History Project, July, 1952

"Woodward Avenue Property which has been in the Same Family for a Hundred Years," The Detroit News Tribune, Sunday, June 18, 1911

The author's collection and the papers of the National Automotive History Collection and the Burton Historical Department, Detroit Public Library

Ransom E. Olds

Founding Father of Michigan's Automobile Industry

A carriage is a very poor place to experiment with a motor, said Ransom Olds in a speech he gave before a meeting of the Michigan Engineering Society, December, 1897.

Olds had good reason to know.

Along with Charles B. King and Henry Ford, he also demonstrated a gasoline powered automobile in 1896. However, unlike the other Michigan automobile pioneers, Olds had previously produced two other newsworthy self-powered carriages. The first Olds horseless carriage was a steam car built in 1886, shortly after he joined his father in the business of building steam engines. His second automobile, also a steamer, was built and sold in 1892. Before the end of the decade he had built a good number of experimental gasoline vehicles, and a couple of electric ones too. However, while he experimented with automobiles, his business for fifteen years was building industrial and marine engines.

Ransom E. Olds was closely associated with Lansing, Michigan, most of his adult life,

From Our Friends as We See "Em

but the events of his few years in Detroit, 1899-1902, laid the foundation for that city to become the center of the automobile industry. By 1904 Ransom's resume included leading the growth of a successful engine business founded by his father in 1880 and founding two successful automobile companies. Both of the brands he created, Oldsmobile and REO, were still in production in Lansing when he died in 1950, at the age of 86. The outstanding legacy of Ransom E. Olds is the success of the 1901 Oldsmobile and his leadership that inspired a generation of young mechanics, designers and investors to create a new industry. And it happened when he was in Detroit.

It is hard to overestimate the contributions of Ransom Olds to the automobile industry in Detroit and Lansing. Ford may have perfected the assembly line but, Olds introduced mass production. In 1901 the Olds Motor Works shattered the world's production and sales records for a gas engine automobile. By doing so, Olds changed the destiny of both cities. It has been said that over 150[1] of the topmost executives at the dawn of the automobile industry had been employed by, or otherwise had close association with, Olds and the Olds Motor Works (See *Olds Alumnae, Suppliers and Investors*, at the end of this chapter). His actions, more than anyone else's, showed that

---

1. Curcio, Vincent, "Chrysler, The Life and Times of an Automotive Genius," page 153.

the purely experimental stage was over, a market existed and there was money to be made in building automobiles powered by internal combustion engines.

Olds was the man who orchestrated the change from the shop to the assembly line, making the automobile affordable to anyone who previously could afford a horse and carriage. Biographer George S. May said that R. E. Olds was *"the man who for a ten-year period in the middle of a long life, sketched the outline of America's greatest industry and thereby influenced the future development of his city, his state, his country, and his world to an extent that was equaled or surpassed by few of his contemporaries."*

Between 1886 and 1901 Ransom Olds led a successful engine business with a national reputation. During that time he experimented with steam, gas and electric vehicles. That gave him the experience, capacity and talent to plan, produce and market an automobile that few others could duplicate. The decision to put that talent and all the company's resources into the service of assembling a single, simple, moderately priced automobile was a risk. The decisions he made in 1901 established a pattern of production and marketing that became the standard of a great industry.

From the Beginning: Boats & Engines

The Olds story began on the banks of the Grand River in Lansing, Michigan, with a family engine business. In 1880, when Ransom was about 14 years of age, his father, Pliney, organized P.F.Olds & Son with his older brother Wallace. Whether young Ransom first had an interest in the boats he saw on the river or the engines in the shop is uncertain but, it is apparent that he had a lifetime interest in putting them together.

While still in High School he began experimenting with the use of Olds engines in various boats. It was about 1882 when the enterprising young man built a 25-foot steamboat, *Mary Ann*, which he operated on the Grand River on Sunday afternoons, carrying passengers for a fee. This marked the beginning of Ransom's enthusiasm for power boating and for the rest of his life it would be his principal leisure activity.

By the time Ransom became fully employed at P.F. Olds & Son in 1883, they were advertising themselves as "Manufacturers of Steam Yachts and Vertical Steam Engines of 3, 5 and 10 horsepower." The Olds business became especially well known in the 1890's in the marine engine field.

That same year Ransom and his father acquired *Jumbo*, a launch powered by an Olds steam engine and a carrying capacity of 100 people. Ransom ran *Jumbo* on his Sunday cruises and that is where he first met his wife when she rode as a passenger.

In 1885 Ransom bought out his brother Wallace and became the "Son" in the business. The next year Ransom built his first experimental road vehicle, a 3-wheeled steamer reported in the Lansing newspaper, *State Republican*, August 5, 1886. During this period Ransom and other family members reportedly had a couple of motorized boats.

By 1891 the business was advertising the "Olds Gasoline Engine" in sizes of one and two horsepower. They were not internal combustion engines but were actually small stationary steam engines that used a gasoline burner to heat the boiler. One impressive feature was that it only took about 10 minutes to get up to steam. According to the testimonial letters they became particularly popular with newspaper publishers, and others who needed an engine for short periods of time, between long periods of idleness.

His second steam powered automobile was reviewed in the May 21, 1892 issue of *Scientific American*. That vehicle attracted the attention of the Frances Times Co. of London, England, who bought the car and shipped it to India. Tragically, Michigan's first automobile export was lost at sea.
Courtesy NAHC

Ransom Olds may have decided to build internal combustions engines after visiting the Chicago *Columbian Exhibition* in 1893. In August 1895 he and Madison Bates, a member of his staff, applied for a patent on a "gas or vapor engine." The first announcement regarding the new "Olds Safety Gas and Vapor Engines" appeared the following year in the March 14 issue of *Scientific American*. The first reported use of the new gas engine was to power launches on the Grand River. As a matter of fact, its use as a marine engine was the only use specifically mentioned in the *Scientific American* article and another article that appeared in the March 1896 issue of *Horseless Age*.

The Olds gas engine business grew steadily and by 1897 the company was operating with two shifts. To provide additional capital for expansion, the company was reorganized.

It increased its capital from $30,000 to $50,000 and, Pliney having retired, the name was changed to Olds Gasoline Engine Works.

1896 "Oldsmobile" driven by Ransom
Courtesy NAHC

The first Olds gas engine powered automobile was reportedly completed in June, 1896 but, not until August 11th was it was demonstrated for the benefit of a local newspaper reporter. It created sufficient interest to attract investors so that in 1897 the Olds Motor Vehicle Company was formed in Lansing for the stated purpose of manufacturing and selling motor vehicles.

According to automotive historian and Olds' biographer George S. May, there is no record that the Olds Motor Vehicle Company manufactured more than two to four vehicles.[2] and it is indicated that most of the investors regarded the venture as a relatively minor investment on their part, mostly undertaken to keep the Olds engine company in Lansing. George S. May quoted one of the investors, Eugene Cooley, when he recalled later,

> *"Here was a contrivance that would run on the roads by a means of power developed within itself. I did not see any great possibilities for it, but nevertheless any contrivance that would do that I felt was worthy of some encouragement. **I am sure I did not see any great future for the invention**, and I do not think others did, but we felt that if developed the power vehicle would have some sale and that a business possibly could be developed which would show a profit. I am free to say that I had not the faintest vision of what has eventuated in the automobile business."[3]*

The steady growth of the engine business created a constant need for additional capital and facilities. To secure growth capital Ransom made a decision that caused him to lose control of the company. He accepted the reorganization plan proposed by investors led by Samuel Latta Smith. Samuel Smith had made his fortune in the lumber, railroads and lake shipping businesses and thought the engine business would be good for his sons Angus and Frederic.

In May 1899 the Olds Motor Works (OMW) was incorporated to absorb the Olds Motor Vehicle Company and the Olds Gas Engine Company. The new company relocated to Detroit. The articles of incorporation stated that the purpose of the company was for the manufacturing and selling of "all kinds of Machinery, Engines, Motors, Motor Carriages and all appliances and equipment connected therewith or appurtenant thereto."

The new company did not emphasis automobiles and according to Fred Smith, the Detroit factory was built and equipped to make not automobiles but gas and gasoline engines.[4]

2. May, George S., "R. E. Olds, Auto Industry Pioneer," page 86
3. Ibid, page 87

Some space allocated to automobile experiments and future expansion. Soon after organizing OWM, Olds built his first electric powered automobile, making him the only Michigan auto pioneer to have experimented with all three engine options.

Ransom & Metta Olds seen riding in an electric "Oldsmobile." Picture is believed to have been taken in 1900 when they were touring around Detroit's Belle Isle Park Courtesy NAHC.

When the company was organized automobiles were merely an interesting speculation but, the gasoline engine was one of the most desirable investment opportunities of the day. Gas engine manufacturers were established along all the major waterways and ports in the country but, few were led by men with the experience and capacity, both technical and financial, as the Smith-Olds team.

About the time Olds moved to Detroit, Madison Bates, co-designer of the first Olds internal combustion engine, and James P. Edmunds became the first Olds alumni to strike out on their own. They organized the Bates and Edmunds Gas Engine Company in 1899. When Olds became interested in Diesel development in the 1920s he worked with Harry Hill who then had owned controlling interest in the company. Some time later Olds acquired the remaining interest and used the engines in his yachts *Reomay IV,* built in 1924, and *Mettemar,* built in 1930. The company reorganized in 1926 as the Hill Diesel Engine Company.

Industrial and marine engines continued to be the staple product of the Olds Motor Works after setting up operations in Detroit. Notably, in February, 1900, the company expanded the marine engine division by acquiring the Charles B. King Engine Company's marine engine business. King was hired to direct the production of marine engines. The King engine immediately began receiving special attention in the company advertising and plans were made to build a separate plant near the river specifically for the purpose of producing marine engines. Automobile activity continued to be limited to experimental design and development.

---

4. Smith, F. L., Motoring Down a Quarter of a Century," page 16.

The engine business continued to grow profitably and mitigated the expense of the automobile experiments. The accounts of both Ransom Olds and Frederic Smith agree that the first two years' losses in the automobile division were in excess of $80,000. Olds biographer George May said that the company probably would not have survived without the profits from the steady sales of engines, exceeding $180,000 in 1900.

Marine Motors

A Compact Reliable Gasoline Engine for Launches and Yachts, which starts easily, runs smoothly and noislessly :: :: :: ::

YOU ARE LOOKING FOR THIS KIND OF A MOTOR

ADDRESS:

Olds Motor Works

1305 Jefferson Ave., Detroit, Mich.

In February 1901 *The Rudder* magazine reviewed the Olds marine engines. They described them as powerful engines and said that the designers of the engines were *"thoroughly conversant with marine engineering practice."* They noted that the company's success was evident by the fact that the corporate launch had secured seven first prizes in launch races the prior year.

Detroit and automotive history were abruptly changed when fire destroyed the main building of the Olds Motor Works on March 9, 1901. Ransom read the news the next morning in the train station as he arrived from his usual winter vacation. He had the vision and capacity to reorganize immediately. Ransom had practical design and manufacturing experience behind his vision when he bet the future on an automobile powered by an internal combustion engine. Many others were still unsure.

They went to work immediately to convert the company foundry building into an assembly plant.[5] Suppliers were solicited and contracts were made for all the necessary components. Three days later they were back in business and established practices that became the industry standards: a testimony to Ransom's leadership skills and the financial backing of Samuel Smith.

---

5. Many historians continue to say that the 1899 factory was the first built exclusively for the manufacture of automobiles. It was not. The 1899 factory was built to manufacture gas and gasoline engines. It can rightfully be said that the foundry building became the first factory in Detroit to be organized for volume manufacturing of an automobile.

120

The 1901 "Curved Dash Olds"
Courtesy NAHC

Nine months later, by the end of the year, the OMW had built 425 curved dash Oldsmobiles, making the company the first mass-producer of gasoline powered automobiles in the world.[6] The Detroit suppliers that made this venture possible became hooked on the automotive business: Leland, engines; Dodge brothers, transmissions; Briscoe brothers, radiators; Everitt, frames and bodies; and many others in a long list of participants that became major players and leaders of the new industry.

Lansing business leaders seized the opportunity to entice Olds back to their city and offered incentives to relocate. A factory site was chosen and the Olds family returned to Lansing, leaving Fred Smith in charge of the Detroit facility. It is believed that this was the first case of an automobile company establishing production facilities in two cities. However, one outcome of this move was that it led to parallel management decisions and contributed to the growing differences between R. E. Olds and Fred Smith. Together they built and sold 2,500 automobiles in 1902 and 4,000 in 1903, making the company, and the City of Detroit, the largest manufacturer of automobiles in the world.

Due to irreconcilable differences, on January 5, 1904, R. E. Olds resigned from the company and took his family on an extended vacation. Upon returning he was informed that a group of Lansing friends and businessmen had organized the R. E. Olds Company and assigned the controlling interest to him. The Olds Motor Works opposed the name so it was changed to the REO Car Company and construction of a factory began in September 1904. In 1908 REO made and sold some 4,000 cars compared to only 1,000 Oldsmobiles that his former partners built without him.

By 1906 Ransom's role was no longer that of a pioneer seeking to innovate, prove that his ideas were successful, and survive in a new industry. He had already done that several times. Neither power nor greater wealth seemed to hold any great attraction for Ransom. Like so many of the pioneers, Ransom's interests were in the mechanical and organizational aspects of the business and he may have become bored with the tedious administrative tasks that were required to run a large automobile business once it had been firmly established. By 1907 Ransom was giving little attention to the day-to-day activities of his company. The one area in which he continued to maintain an interest and exert his authority appears to have been the design and mechanical features of the cars. However, his personal diaries indicate that he was spending more time working out the details of yachts in various stages of design, commissioning or outfitting.

---

6. It is often mistakenly reported that the Oldsmobile was the first mass produced automobile in the world. That is not true. In America that distinction rightfully goes to Albert Pope whose company produced some 500 electrics and 40 gas powered automobiles in 1898 and some 1,500 electrics in 1899.

Olds Yachts & Cruises

During the few years the Olds family lived in Detroit, from 1899-1902, Ransom owned a 35-foot cruiser named the *East Wind*. Later, he chartered a boat on which to spend a winter vacation in Florida. This led him to commission the 47-foot *Reo Pastime*. It was built in Muskegon and shipped to Florida to use during the family's 1906-1909 winter vacations. For 1909 he commissioned the 90-foot auxiliary schooner *Reomar* (I). *Reomar II* was a 98-foot auxiliary schooner built in 1911. After receiving *Reomar II*, the *Reomar*

I was traded for the first in a series of boats named *Reola*. *Reola II* was an 80-foot gas-engine powered Cox & Stevens design built in 1915. For the summer of 1912 Olds shipped the Florida based *Reomar II* to the Great Lakes and the family spent nearly the entire summer aboard.

Olds, rear, looking over the cabin deck of an unidentified yacht

About 1913 Ransom began developing *Elbamar*, a 600 acre summer/fall estate on the Detroit River at Grosse Ile, Michigan. In addition to the three story palatial main house, the grounds included a carriage house, ground-keeper/gate house, a home for Ransom's secretary, a three story stable, ice-house, greenhouse, windmill and a large boathouse. He had a herd of cattle, sheep and riding horses. The grounds also served as experimental gardens for his agricultural interests and perhaps one of his most important inventions, an improved gas engine powered lawnmower that he patented in 1915. The three homes survive today, sharing the waterfront with new neighbors.

About the same time, Ransom's agricultural interests led him to purchase 37,000 acres of land in Florida, at the northernmost tip of Tampa Bay. He personally invested more than $4.5 million to develop Oldsmar, a model rural city, with dairy farms and plantations along with a downtown center complete with a hotel, grocery, drug and hardware stores, a library, school, restaurant and a waterfront community center. In 1921 a powerful hurricane hit the city, devastating Oldsmar and the dreams of its founder. For the next 60 years, Oldsmar remained a sparsely populated rural community until the Tampa Bay area grew up around it.

Back in Grosse Ile, the *Elbamar* boathouse was built to accommodate *Reomar III*, a 100-foot steel Cox & Stevens designed motor yacht. The yacht was built in 1924 and required a crew of six. The 93-foot *Mettamar* was built for Olds in 1930. She was designed and built by the New York Yacht, Launch and Engine Co. and powered by a pair of 6-cylinder Hill diesels. Olds designed the engine with Harry Hill. Together they had come to own the gas engine company founded in 1899 by his former employees Bates and Edmunds.

***Reomar III*, a 100-foot yacht built in 1924 and powered by diesel engines designed by Ransom Olds and Harry Hill.**

The largest yacht owned by R. E. Olds was the 125-foot *Reomar IV* that had been launched as the *Sylvia* in 1926. Home base for that yacht was *Oldswoode*, a 150 acre estate that he bought in 1928/29 at Charlevoix, on Michigan's west coast.

The government conscripted *Reomar IV* for patrol duty in World War II. While it was used as his private yacht it required a crew of 14 under the command of a full time captain. After the war he returned to somewhat smaller boats including *Mettamar II*, a 57-foot Burger motor yacht built in 1948.

In addition to yachts he also owned numerous runabouts such as the *Oldswoode*, *Mettamora* and *Chieftain*.

The Olds family boating pleasures included extended cruises around the world. Beginning with a cruise to Europe in 1907. The following cruises were noted by author Patricia E. Heyden, in *Meta and R. E. Olds, Loves Lives Labor:*

    1908 Cruise down the St. Lawrence Seaway.
    1910 Cruised to Europe in July and returned in September.
    1913 Cruised to the Caribbean with a three week stay in Bermuda.
    1922 Cruised the Mediterranean with visits to Egypt and Palestine
    1924 Six month cruise with friends around the world.
    1926 Cruised to South Africa and Australia.
    1927 Cruised the British Islands
    1929 Cruised the North Cape of Norway, Ireland and Sweden.
    1937 Cruised to South America through the Panama Canal.

Over a long, creative and productive life Ransom Olds had many interests and accomplishments. It was his lifelong interest in power boating that led to innovations in steam, gasoline and diesel engine design and the founding of a great industry. The Olds family created a profitable business building stationary and marine steam engines before the gas engine era. With gas engines Olds became a wealthy man and mad a fortune using them to create two great automobile companies. Later his interests led him to do developmental work with marine Diesel engines. At the time of his 86th and last birthday he was eagerly awaiting delivery of the 58-foot *Reola IV*.

In the end the *Detroit Free Press* had the following to say about Ransom E. Olds in his obituary dated August 27, 1950:

> ". . .A pioneer in a select group of inventive geniuses whose mechanical skills, resourcefulness and promotions, ushered in the motor age. This grand old man had given his name and initials to two American automobiles, the Oldsmobile and the Reo. He was the industry's school master and had trained many who became prominent in the industry."

Epilog

Oldsmobile was the oldest American automobile brand when it was discontinued by General Motors Corporation in 2004

This ad for "The Oldsmobile" appeared in *The Carriage Monthly* in May 1901, two months after the fire that nearly destroyed the Olds Motor Works. It is interesting to note that the marine engine business had not yet been sold to Michigan Yacht & Power Company as a separate catalogue for marine engines was still being offered. It is also interesting to note that the company's business office relocated after the fire from 1305 Jefferson Avenue, a short distance to 61 Concord Avenue. The automobile assembly plant continued in what had been the foundry, at the Jefferson location, until all operations relocated to Lansing a few years later. When Ransom Olds returned to Lansing he left behind a distinguished cadre of alumnae that played leading roles in making Detroit the "Automobile Capital of the World." The following role call lists some of the most important graduates from Ransom Old's tuteledge:

OLDS MOTOR WORKS ALUMNAE

The following investors, suppliers and staff that worked with Ransome E. Olds and the Old Motor Works (OMW) in the first few years of the automobile industry. The lists include many of the founders and leaders of Michigan's automobile industry.

I. Olds Motor Works Alumnae - SUPPLIERS

Before OMW	Name	OMW & Later Business Interests
Briscoe Mfg Co. - specialized in sheet metal fabrication and has been credited with inventing the metal trash can	**Frank & Benjamin Briscoe**	1901-03 supplied radiators & body panels 1903 backed David Buick, 1903 co-founded Maxwell-Briscoe Co. 1908 co-founded Brush Motor Co. 1910 organized United States Motor Car Co.
After High School worked with Olds in Lansing, left to serve in the Spanish-American War	**Alanson P Brush**	1899-1901 Engineer with Leland & Falcouner Co. 1902-1905 Chief Engineer for Cadillac Motor Car Co. 1907 designed the first Pontiac 1908 co-founded Brush Motor Corp.
Built & serviced bicycles & marine steam engines	**Horace & John Dodge**	1901-1903 supplied transmissions and engines, 1903 chief suppliers and investors in Ford Motor Co. 1914 founded Dodge Brothers Motor Car Co.
Manager of the triming & finishing department of the C R Wilson Carriage Co. 1900 formed his own carriage triming business	**Bryon F. Everitt**	1901car bodies 1903 supplied the first 10,000 Ford car bodies. responsible for recruiting Fred & Charles Fisher to relocate from Norwalk, OH to Detroit. 1908 co-founded Everitt-Metzger-Flanders (E-M-F) Motor Car Co. Thereafter involved in numerous automobile companies
1897 created their first motorcycle 1899 created Holley Motor Co. 1903 produced a car called the Holley Motorette	**George & Earl Holley**	1904 Holley Brothers Company designed their first original carbureator for Olds. Thereafter it became standard on Ford 1907 moved company from Bradford, PA to Detroit
Master Machinist, co-founded Leland-Faulconer	**Henry Leland**	1901 supplied engines, 1902 organized Cadillac Motor Car 1917 organized Lincoln Motor Car Co.
Bicycle, gas launch and engine dealer Promoter of boat & automobile races and exhibitions 1900 opened Detroit's first auto dealership Represented electric, steam and gasoline powered automobiles.	**William E. Metzger**	1901 Olds distributor 1903 Sales Manager for Cadillac 1908 co-founded E-M-F Motor Car Co. Thereafter involved in numerous automobile companies.
1899 w/brother built gas powered vehicle for their dry cleaning business 1900 co-founded Owen Motor Carriage Co.	**Raymond M. Owen**	1901 organized R. M. Owen & Co. as the NY distributor for OMW 1904 switched to REO, 1910 co-founded Owen Motor Car Co. 1915 co-founded Owen Magnetic Co.,
Attorney	**Harris E. Thomas**	Olds legal advisor, 1902 co-founded the Clarkmobile Co. with Frank G. Clark (OMW investor)

II. Olds Motor Works Alumnae - STAFF

Before OMW	Role with OMW	After OMW
Assisted King & Ford with first automobiles	**Oliver Barthel** engineer	Consulted for numerous automobile projects
Brother of Oliver & Theodore Barthel	**Otto Barthel** pattent attorney	Attorney for numerous auto patents
Brother of Oliver & Otto Barthel	**Theodore Barthel** Test driver	1916 VP & GM of King Motor Car Co. 1926 trustee Liberty Motor Car Co.
	Guido G. Behn 1902-1906	1906 E. R. Thomas-Detroit (Chalmers) 1909 Hudson Motor Car, last as Director and Chief Engineer, (1927)
U of M and Nat'l Cash Register (with Hugh Chalmers and Alvin Macauley)	**J C Bayerline** purchasing agent **Frederic O. Bezner** 1903-1906 Purchasing Agent	1909 General Manager of Warren Motor Car Co. 1918 Executive of King Motor Company 1906 co-founded E R Thomas-Detroit/Chalmers
	James F. Bourquin	Superintendant Chalmers Motor Co., 1910 Factory GM, Paige Motor Car Co., Co-founder Liberty Motor Car Co.
University of Michigan (U of M)	**James J. Brady** 1901-1906	1906 co-founder E.R. Thomas - Detroit/Chalmers 1909 co-founded Hudson Motor Car Co.
U of M	**Roy D. Chapin** 1901-1906	1906 co-founded E R Thomas-Detroit/Chalmers 1909 co-founded Hudson Motorcar Co.
U of M	**Howard E. Coffin** 1902-1906, last as Chief Engineer	1906 V P & Chief Engineer ER Thomas -Detroit/Chalmers 1909 co-founded Hudson Motor Car Co.
	W. L. Daly	1910 Executive of King Motor Car Co., later, sales mgr, Columbia Motor Works
1901-1904 Chief Eng. American Motor Carriage Co., Cleveland, Ohio	**Geo. W. Duham** 1904-1909 last as Chief Engineer	1910 Chief Engineer, Hudson Motor Car Co. 1913 VP & Director Saxon Motor Car Co.
Railroad Accountant 1890-94 Wholesale dealer 1895-1902	**Charles D. Hastings** joined 1902,-1906 last as Sales Mgr for Detroit, Lansing & Export	1907 office mgr & sales exec for Thomas-Detroit Co./Chalmers, 1908 joined Hupp Motor Car Co., last as VP
1897 joined Olds in Lansing	**Robert C. Hupp** 1899-1904 last as mgr of repair dept.	1905 Ford Asst. Prod. 1908 President Hupp Motor Car Co.
U of M	**Roscoe B. Jackson** 1902-1906	1907 married J. L. Hudson's niece 1907 Factory Mgr of E. R. Thomas Motor Car, Buffalo, NY, 1909 co-founded Hudson Motor Car Co.
built and demonstrated first automobile in Detroit (1896) 1893-1900 manufactured pneumatic hammers and marine engines	**Charles B. King** 1900-1901 Chf Engineer and Mgr Marine Eng. Div.	1901-02 Michigan Yacht & Power Co., 1903-1908 Chief Engineer, Northern Mfg Co. 1910 King Motor Car Co.
Begn work with gas engines in 1888 Responsible for 1st Buick automobile, 1901	**Walter L. Marr** 1901	1902 Chief Designer and Superintendent of American Carriage Co. 1903 Marr Auto Car 1904 Buick Motor Car
1894 assisted Haynes & Appersons, to build Sintz powered automobile	**Jonathan Maxwell** 1900 -1902 last as Chief Engineer	Oct 1902 co-founded Northern Mfr Co 1903 Maxwell-Briscoe Motor Co.
	Wm G Murray 1900-1901 Mgr of Automobile Div	1902-03 Murray Motor Car, 1904- VP, American Motor League,

	Emil A. Nelson engineer	1906 Engineer Packard Motor Car Co. 1908-10 Chief Engineer, Hupp Motor Car Co. 1917 manufactured the Nelson automobile
1899 w/brother built a gas powered vehicle for their dry-cleaning business 1900 org. Owen Motor Carriage Co.	**Ralph Owen** 1901 factory mgr in Lansing	Jan 1910 co-founded Owen Mtr Car Co. (Subsequently merged with REO), 1915 co-founded Owen Magnetic Car Co.
Designed marine & stationary gas engines for others	**Eugene C. Richard** engineer	Buick engineer credited with patent for overhead valve design
1898 joined Olds in Lansing	**Richard H. Scott** 1899-1904	1923 president of REO 1904+ REO Motor Co., last as President (1923)
	Horace T. Thomas Engineer and test driver	Chief Engineer at REO
1898 joined Olds in Lansing	**Charles B. Wilson** 1898-1906, last as shop superintendant	1914 co-founded Wilson Foundry and Machine Co. 1917 Mgr of all Curtis Airplane plants 1920 GM of production facilities Willys-Overland & Willys Corp

III. Olds Motor Works Alumnae – INVESTORS

Before OMW	Name & OMW Role 1897-1904	Post OMW Business Interests
P. F. Olds & Son	**Ransom E. Olds** 1897 Treas & GM 1898 VP & GM	1904 resigned and organized the REO Motor Co.
Made fortune in lumber & mining Under his direction OMW relocated to Detroit in 1899	**Samuel Latta Smith** 1898 President 1904 retired	
Lansing Civic leader owner of Lansing Wheelbarrow Co.	**Edward W. Sparrow** 1897 President	
Secretary, Lansing Wheelbarrow Company	**Arthur C. Stebbins** 1897 Secretary	1904 organized Bates Automobile Co. with Madison F. Bates and Bliss Stebbins, (Bates is credited as the co-developer of the first Olds internal combustion engine. The Bates factory is now the R.E. Olds Museum)
Asst. Secretary of Lansing Wheelbarrow Co.	**Fred M. Seibly** Director	
Lansing carriage manufacturer, 1896 built body for the experimental Olds	**Frank G. Clark** Director	1902 organized Clarkmobile Co., 1910 Furgason Motor Co. 1911 Clark Power Wagon Vehicle Co. 1913 Columbia Motor Truck & Trailer Co.
Lansing industrialist	**Eugene F. Cooley** 1897 VP	
Son of Samuel L. Smith	**Frederic L. Smith** 1898 Sec/Treas 1904 VP & GM	
Son of Samuel L. Smith	**Angus Smith** 1904 Sec/Treas	1910, Owen Motor Car Co.
Lawyer, director of numerous co's, cousin to Charles B King, and son of Dr. George B. Russel, founder of Russel Wheel and Foundry Co.	**Henry Russel** 1904 President	

References

Curcio, Vincent, "Chrysler, The Life and Times of an Automotive Genius," Oxford University Press, Inc., New York, NY, 2000 Detroit Free Press, August 27, 1950.

Grosse Ile Historical Society files

Heyden, Patricia E., "Metta and R. E. Olds, Loves Lives Labors," Stuart Publishing, Lansing, MI 1997

May, George S., "R. E. Olds: Auto Industry Pioneer," William B. Eerdmans Publishing Company, Grand Rapids, MI, 1977

MacTaggart, Ross, "The Golden Century – Classic Motor Yachts 1830-1930," W. W. Norton & Company, Inc., NY, NY, 2001

Smith, Frederic, with an introduction by Roy Chapin, "Motoring Down a Quarter of a Century," Detroit Saturday Night Company, 1928

"Smith, S. L., Founder, Former Business Leader Dies," Detroit New, May 8,1917

David D. Buick

Father of the Brand that Built General Motors

David Buick c. 1899, left; c. 1920, right
Courtesy Lawrence R. Gustin

While making a small fortune inventing and manufacturing plumbing supplies with the Buick & Sherwood Manufacturing Company, David Dunbar Buick became an avid yachtsman and his passion turned to building small gas engines. By 1899 he organized Buick Auto-Vim and Powers Company and was building and selling marine engines. Indications are that the famous Buick overhead valve design was first employed to facilitate the manufacturing and service of marine engines[1].

Little is known about his early years. With his parents he emigrated from Scotland in 1856 and three years later his father died. His mother remarried and reportedly operated a candy store in Detroit. At a young age he jioned the work force.

From the little that is known, it can be understood that David Buick was always industrious and hardworking. He had a newspaper route before he left school at age 11. He then went to work on a farm for three years, and in 1869 returned to Detroit to work as an apprentice brass finisher for a manufacturer of plumbing fixtures, the Alexander Manufacturing Company. Later he worked at the James Flower and Brothers Manufacturing Company, first as an apprentice machinist and later as the foreman. It may have been there that Buick met his future partner, William Sherwood. Sherwood was working as a brass molder in 1873. Some reports indicate that Buick may have been the foreman in 1880 when Henry Ford was an apprentice at that company.[2]

About 1884 David Buick and William Sherwood bought the Alexander Manufacturing Company and reorganized it as the Buick & Sherwood Manufacturing Company. Buick was president, Sherwood was vice president and A.D. Babcock was the Secretary and Treasurer. The business prospered as a manufacturer and dealer in what they advertised as "sanitary specialties".

Between 1881 and 1889 Buick is credited with 13 inventions, including a lawn sprinkler, improvements to valves, flushing devices, and bathtubs. His most important achievement up

---

1. Rather than removing the entire engine, an overhead valve design allowed the engine head with the valve seats to be removed and separately taken to a machine shop for servicing.
2. December 1879 through August 1880

to that time was inventing a process to bond porcelain to cast iron. That invention modernized American kitchens and bathrooms and alone would have made him a wealthy man.

In their book *The Buick, A Complete History*, Terry B. Dunham and Lawrence R. Gustin summed up strengths that David Buick demonstrated in the days before the horseless carriage, "[he] *could run a business, keep an eye on the dollar, invent and then produce useful items, and attract talented employees. He worked hard and he demonstrated the strength of character to see his ideas through to completion.*"

However, Buick became more interested in making things than making money and like many Detroit machinists of the 1890s he became fascinated with developments of the internal combustion engine. Buick reportedly said that his enthusiasm for gas engines began in 1895. That same year another Detroiter, Charles B. King, began advertising his engines nationally.

Boats & Motors

In the 1890s Buick was an active yachtsman. His name often appeared in the newspaper as a race committee member or judge for important regattas. In 1899 he was Vice-Commodore of the Detroit Yacht Club. News clippings of the era report that Buick was winning sailboat races with his 27-foot sloop *Carrie B* (perhaps a nickname for his wife Caroline). According to Buick historian Terry B. Dunham, a brass cannon said to have been made by David Buick to start boat races in Detroit is still in the possession of his family.

By the late 1890s Buick was experimenting with internal combustion engines. Reportedly, it was Buick's growing obsession with engine experiments that annoyed William Sherwood and forced the sale of the Buick & Sherwood Manufacturing Company. In 1899 the company was sold to the Standard Sanitary Manufacturing Company of Pittsburgh for $100,000. Some time after the sale, Sherwood established the Sherwood Brass Company.[3]

Perhaps Buick had decided that at age 45 he was ready for a career change. In any case, with his share of the money David organized the Buick Auto-Vim and Power Company to manufacture stationary and marine engines. The Detroit phone book indicate that the business was located in the Boydel Building, along with the Dodge Brothers, a few blocks from the Detroit River.

Buick's reputation allowed him to sell everything they made with little advertising or marketing. However, it is believed that there was much more experimenting and testing going on. There is no information to indicate that sales were very significant.

We learn from the personal journal of C. B. Calder, the general superintendent of the Detroit Dry Dock Co., that W. S. Murray, an engineer working for Buick, visited him on February 28, 1900. Calder reports that Murray asked for their recommendation in regard to the best mill for boring out engine cylinders. Calder was told that Buick was going in the business to make 20 engines a day, a very optimistic rate by the current standards.

About that time Walter L. Marr first came to work with Buick. While in the employ of the Detroit Shipbuilding Company, Walter Marr was working with some friends on a gasoline marine engine when Buick strolled by the dock, stopped and watched him at work. It is accepted history that Buick recognized his ability at once and hired him on the spot. He immediately made him foreman at the Buick Auto-Vim and Power Company, and three months later he was the manager.

---

3. In 1970 Sherwood Brass became a division of Lear-Sigler.

Walter Marr was another mechanical genius. Reportedly he helped to build a gas engine as early as 1888. That engine was designed by the plant superintendent of Wickes Brothers; a Saginaw Michigan saw mill and steamboat engineering company that employed Marr from 1887 to 1896. The experiments with engines at Wicks Brothers gave Marr valuable experience with the early designs of internal combustion engines.

Regarding the early period with Buick, Marr later said that Buick's engineer, Murray, never built a satisfactory engine. Marr is quoted as saying, *"But he (Murray) was my boss and during the day I had to take his orders. But at night I would take the engine down and build it again according to my notions. I always had it back up the way he built it by the next morning."* A few months after Marr's arrival, Murray left and Marr had the opportunity to work on the engines using some of his ideas.

Marr said that when he was allowed to build the engine the way he wanted, he built an engine that beat any boat on the river in the 20-foot class. Marr later said he built an engine for Buick that beat everything in the 24-foot class on the Detroit River. He may have been referring to the same boat that was the subject of the following testimonial letter from Albert Stegmeyer seen in the 1902 and 1904 Buick catalogs: *(Editor's highlights)*

Detroit, Mich., Nov. 30, 1901

The Buick Manufacturing Co., Detroit, Mich.:
Gentlemen:

*I have been thinking seriously of selling the **20' launch that I purchased from you two years ago**, and getting a larger one for next season, and if you can guarantee to give me as good a 30' boat, with a 6 H. P. engine, as you did the 20' boat, I think we can make a deal.*

I wish to say right here that I consider your gasoline engine the best there is on the Detroit River.

You no doubt are aware that I discontinued the bath house, remodeling it into a Gasoline Launch Livery, which will hold 20 launches. Among these 20 launches there are all kinds of engines, some built by the parties that own the boats, and others built by the best gasoline engine builders and there is no one of them but what have more or less trouble. Whenever you go down to the livery you will see several owners of the different boats fixing up their engines, and it seems that there is always something the matter with them. For your benefit I would say that I have had absolutely no trouble at all with my engine, except putting on a larger wheel, as the engine was too powerful for the wheel that originally came with the boat. As for speed, I can beat every one of them, with the exception of a 30' launch which has a 12 H. P. engine against my 3 H. P. engine, but even so, this 30' boat does not beat me very much, and if you can do as well for me on a 30 launch for next season I will be more than pleased. Let me hear from you.

Trusting your engine will have the success it merits, I remain,

Yours very truly,

Albert Stegmeyer,
1470 Jefferson Ave.

From the Collection of Terry B. Dunham

Stegmeyer's testimonial letter indicates he was very pleased with a marine engine purchased from Buick in 1899, before Marr joined the business. A newspaper story about a boat race on the Detroit River appeared in the *Detroit Free Press*, August 8, 1902 that mentioned a Stegmeyer entry named the *German Village*.That boat may have been powered by an engine built by Marr and Buick.

Buick apparently supported Marr's automobile experiments without himself being very interested. In another account, Marr said that the only time he managed to get Buick into the automotive shop they went for a ride in the test car but, the ignition vibrator stuck and the car stalled. Buick was annoyed and boarded a passing streetcar. Marr said he quit Buick for the first time over the incident.

Both Buick and Marr were known for their quick tempers and history suggests that it was hard to work for either man. The split that grew out of the incident described above is documented in an interesting letter on Buick & Sherwood stationary from David Buick to Walter Marr, dated March 25, 1901: *"After considering the conversation we had the other day, and wherein you offered your resignation, I have concluded that it is best for both parties to accept the same, and to take effect at once. You will please turn over the keys and such other articles that you may have to Mr. Sherwood."*

In another letter dated April 5, 1901, Buick offered to sell Marr "the automobile known as the Buick Automobile, for the sum of $300." Perhaps Buick was strapped for cash or it is simply another indication that the automobile bug had not yet bitten. He also offered Marr a collection of vehicle bodies and engines for an additional $1,500. A subsequent letter dated August 16th confirmed the sale of the Buick Automobile for $225, documenting the first Buick sale, and at below sticker price.

The two letters are interesting because they document how little interest Buick had in automobiles up to that time. The second one suggests that after the sale of their company Buick and Sherwood continued to have some kind of working relationship. Buick did not complete another automobile for nearly two years after the sale of the first ufinished Buick automobile in August 1901.

About the time of Marr's first departure Buick hired another talented machinist named Eugene C. Richard. Richard was a French immigrant who had worked on engines in Philadelphia and most recently had worked for the Olds Motor Works at its Lansing location. He was also doing engine work part time for two other Lansing companies, Kneeland Crystal Creamery and The Peerless Motor Company. For the Peerless Motor Company he designed a 2-cycle marine engine that became the basis for the Peerless Marine Engine Company in Detroit.

Marr was eager to get in the Automobile business. When he left Buick he took a job at the Olds Motor Works in Detroit and helped build some of the first Oldsmobiles. Later that year he went to Cleveland where he became the chief designer and superintendent of the American Carriage Company. Sometime in 1902 he left that company and returned to Detroit, again spending some time with Buick. By 1903 he had developed his own automobile, the Marr Auto Car. It is estimated that some 24 cars were completed before a fire destroyed the plant along with 14 of the completed cars awaiting shipping.

After Marr left in 1901, Buick reorganized the Auto-Vim and Power Company as the Buick Manufacturing Company. On February 18, 1902, Eugene Richard filed for a patent on the valve-in-head engine and assigned the patent to the Buick Manufacturing Company. Marr often claimed the invention saying that he had begun building one before he left Buick and that he went in that direction because he thought it was the easiest way to build an engine. Richard said he remembered steam engines in Europe that had used the same principle and he simply applied it to the gasoline engines. At that time, perhaps unknown to either man, Charles Brady King had built a 4-cylinder overhead valve engine with an aluminum crankcase. He intended to put it in another experimental automobile of his design but, after that project sat incomplete, in 1902 he was persuaded to put the engine in *Wal-Rus*, a cabin launch built by the Michigan Yacht and Power Company for his cousin Walter Russel.

In any case it was an important event and somehow, among the ideas of Charles Brady King, David Buick, Walter Marr and Eugene Richard, the Buick Company was the first to market it as a new idea in gas engine design. The Buick engine earned a reputation for exceptional power and performance and the design eventually became an industry standard.

At first they did not appear to have understood the performance benefits: placing valves directly over the piston head creates a more compact combustion chamber, a faster fuel-burn rate, and consequently more horsepower than other engine designs of similar size. The overhead design also provided some distinct maintenance benefits. The first known catalog of the Buick Manufacturing Company, 1902, included stationary and marine engines and the only reference to the overhead valve design described the manufacturing and maintenance benefits. They noted that to re-grind or reset the valves it was not necessary to take out the whole engine, as it was possible to simply unbolt the head and carry it to the machine shop. A 4-hp engine weighed more than 100 pounds but, the head alone weighed less than 10 pounds. Performance benefits were not mentioned.

The portability feature was not considered to be important for automobile engines. In 1904 the Buick automobile engine had overhead valves set into a solid cylinder-housing that was bolted to the crankcase.

Automobiles

Sometime in 1902 David Buick appears to have been infected by the automobile fever. Eventually his experiments put him a couple of hundred dollars in debt to the Briscoe Manufacturing Company. One day in the spring of 1903 Buick asked Benjamin Briscoe[4] to visit the Buick facility where he explained that he had invested most of his money in a design for a new car. At that time Briscoe was interested in making his first horseless carriage purchase and by the time they had finished talking Briscoe agreed to buy the car and advanced Buick more money to complete it.

Briscoe was one of Detroit's original automotive suppliers. In 1901 he began building radiators and body panels for the Olds Motor Works. Within a couple of years the Briscoe Manufacturing Company had 1,200 employees and was making big profits.

When Buick needed additional cash, Briscoe agreed to it on the condition that the company reorganize. On May 19, 1903 the Buick Manufacturing Company was reorganized as the Buick Motor Company, with Briscoe holding 99.7% of the stock. In the process Briscoe's son-in-law and private secretary, Emil Moessner became the corporate treasurer. The stated purpose of the company in the incorporation papers was the *manufacture of power machinery, automobile equipment, automobiles, pumps, engines and other mechanical appliances.* It was not organized for the exclusive purpose of building automobiles.

---

4. Briscoe and Buick had been business associates and friends for a long time. When Briscoe started his sheet metal business, in 1888, Buick had given him work that helped him get established.

Buick remained as President and was given the option of repaying what he owed Briscoe by the end of September, about $3,500, to receive all the stock or relinquish control of the company. At that point Briscoe set in motion events that he later described as *"so fraught with romance that it made the Arabian Nights tales look commonplace."*

While Buick, Marr and Richard worked on finishing the car, Briscoe made up his mind to be more than a supplier and become an automobile manufacturer. Initially he thought of teaming up with Buick but, while Briscoe did not doubt Buick's integrity and ability as a craftsman, he had become wary of his business abilities. Buick's advanced designs were creating substantial cost overruns with meager results.

Briscoe asked auto pioneer Jonathan D. Maxwell to go take a look at the Buick automobile and give his opinion. Reportedly Maxwell returned and, without giving his opinion about the Buick automobile, suggested that Briscoe go into business with him. On July 4, 1903 Briscoe and Maxwell signed a contract and the Maxwell-Briscoe Motor Company was born. The Maxwell brand survived through dramatic and important chapters of the early automobile industry until Walter P. Chrysler acquired the company. In 1924, the Chrysler brandname was first introduced and the Maxwell name was dropped from the roles of the 1925 models.

Now that Briscoe was going to manufacture a car with Maxwell he wanted to close out his business with Buick. Sometime that summer Briscoe met with James Whiting, president of the Flint Wagon Works, and interested him in the Buick automobile. Negotiations with the Flint interests were begun by Briscoe but, the concluding negotiations took several months and were left to David Buick. In the meantime Briscoe went to France to study the manufacture of radiators.

Upon Briscoe's return in September, Buick called with the final details. Reportedly, he not only paid Briscoe what he owed him, plus interest, he also paid a bonus of an unreported amount. Briscoe and Buick had now set in motion the events that directly led to the foundation of General Motors.

The first Buick plant in Flint was operating by December, 1903, with 25 employees. In January 1904 the Detroit based Buick Motors Company was dissolved and the Flint based company was incorporated with Whiting as President and Buick as Secretary.

Only a few months prior to moving the company to Flint, David Buick's son Thomas wrote a sales letter to a boat builder in which he described the company's marine engine heritage. See page 135.

Notably, automobiles did not appear to be a priority for the reorganized company. Profits were still to be made, with less risk, manufacturing gas and gasoline engines. Strikingly, the earliest known Buick catalog printed with the Flint address in 1904 was devoted almost entirely to stationary and marine motors. Of the 30 pages only 3 referred to an automobile engine. No Buick automobiles were mentioned at all in the catalog but, automobile engines were offered so that others could use them.

The first Flint catalog in 1904 was much like the earlier catalog. However, in addition to the 5.5-hp, 4-cycle stationary and marine engines, two new models were added: a 4-cycle 12-hp Buick automobile engine of the double cylinder opposed type and a 1-hp Buick 2-cycle marine engine. The testimonial letter about the performance of Stegmeyer's boat was included again, along with several testimonials regarding the stationary engines.

THE BUICK MOTOR COMPANY

MANUFACTURERS OF

AUTOMOBILES, STATIONARY, MARINE and AUTOMOBILE GAS and GASOLINE ENGINES

TRANSMISSION GEARS, SPARK PLUGS, CARBURETERS, ETC.

GENERAL LINE OF BRASS GOODS   416-418 HOWARD STREET

Detroit, Mich.___Oct. 21, 1903___190__

Mr. J. G. Schmidt,
    360 Como Ave.,
Dear Sir:

      This is no doubt the first time that our name has been brought before you as manufacturers of marine engines. This is due to the fact that our output was limited, and that we were able to dispose of all the engines we could manufacture in certain localities, where our engines are known without doing any advertising or soliciting, but as we are now building a large and modern plant at Flint, Mich., it becomes necessary for us to extend our territory, and increase our sales to take care of the large output we will have. The fact that it has not been necessary for us to advertise or solicit orders would go far to prove that we have an engine of decided merit, and one which must be giving satisfaction.

      We have been manufacturing the 2 and 4 H.P. 4 cycle engine, but are now adding a number of sizes to the above. We are also making a 2 cycle marine engine, namely 1 1/2 H.P., which we will sell for a 3/4 H.P. This size we intend to make a special push on, as well as a special low price. We also intend making other sizes of the 2 cycle type, so that we will be able to take care of any wants our customers may have.

      It is a well known fact that the boat builder receives very few complaints, if any,--in regard to the boat itself--the complaints are usually made on account of the poor working of the engine. Now, we have had a great deal of satisfaction from the fact that the boat builders who are using our engines have had as few complaints in regard to them, as they have had from the hull they built. No matter what business a firm may be in, they usually have troubles of their own, without being saddled with trouble caused by goods which they purchase from outside manufacturers. We are absolutely certain that if you handle our engines your engine troubles will be a thing of the past.

      We wish to say that we do not build a boat so we cannot come in competition with the boat builders.

      If we have interested you, kindly let us know what your wants will be for the coming season. Ask us for prices or any other information you may desire, and it will be a pleasure to us to comply with your request.

      Thanking you for the favor of a reply, we beg to remain,

        Yours very truly.

From the Collection of Terry B. Dunham

There was not yet any mention of the engines actually being used in a Buick automobile. Nor is there any record of who may have used Buick's engine to build other automobiles.

Prior to 1904 there is no substantial evidence that Buick worked on more than two automobiles; the incomplete one sold to Marr in 1901 and the other delivered to Briscoe in 1903. Up to 1904 it was obvious that the emphasis of the Buick Motor Company was simply engines.

Getting production facilities set up in Flint exhausted the company's capital and ran up debts. Large orders for engines had been obtained but, production was not meeting expectation. Nevertheless, on May 27, 1904, *The Flint Journal* reported that a Buick automobile had been completed and tested on the city streets.

On Saturday July 9, 1904, Walter Marr and Thomas Buick started out to drive the first Flint-made Buick car[5] to Detroit. They spent the first night repairing a rear-bearing and arrived in Detroit on Sunday. On Monday they bought car license No. 1024 and on Tuesday headed back to Flint, driving 90 miles through a steady rain. Marr reportedly said that he did the driving and Thomas Buick kept busy wiping the mud off his goggles. On July 27th the car was delivered to the purchaser, Flint physician Herbert Hills. A total of 37 cars were built by the end of the year.

Hugh Dolner, one of the most prominent auto reporters of the time, wrote about the Buick company history and the details of the car. His report in the *Cycle and Automobile Trade Journal*, September 1904, stated that that a number of different car builders at the time were using Buick motors to complete vehicles. Unfortunately, history does not remember who may have been the other builders.

By the time the first car was built Whiting had become convinced that the company needed more money and a younger man to lead the business. At this point William Crapo Durant, semi-retired from the Durant-Dort Carriage Company, enters the stage. At the time, Durant did not have an interest in automobiles. He thought they were noisy, foul smiling and generally obnoxious to horses, humans and in particular to carriage makers.

William C. Durant,
creator of General Motors
Courtesy NAHC

Durant had been living in New York managing his investments when he was asked to come to Flint to listen to Mr. Whiting's proposal. On September 4th he was given his first ride in a Buick automobile. The bug bit and by November 1st he was in control of the company's future. The rest of the history of Durant, the Buick Motor Company and General Motors Corporation is well documented elsewhere, particularly in the previously cited book *The Buick, A Complete History*.

---

5. Believed to be the third automobile to be known at a Buick.

Epilog

David Buick's role in the company declined rapidly until he finally lost all managerial responsibility in early 1906, the year that Buick became the world's largest automobile producer. By the end of 1908 he had severed all ties with the company, except for some 300 shares of company stock. In 1921 Briscoe wrote that if Buick could have held onto to his stock his shares would have been worth $10,000,000.

David's son, Thomas Buick, left the company about 1906 to go into a brass foundry business supplying parts to the Buick Motor Company. By all accounts he did very well in that business and maintained an expensive estate on Grosse Ile, Michigan, until losing everything in a crisis in 1910. When he died in 1942, Thomas was a Fuller Brush salesman. His son David II worked for twenty-five years as a clerk at the Chrysler Corporation.

David Buick apparently did well for a while after leaving Buick Motor Company. First he was involved with the Buick Oil Company in Los Angeles, California where the family was prominent socially and built a handsome home in one of the fashionable residential areas. Unfortunately litigation later ensued over the ownership of some of the oil lands and the business failed.

David returned to Michigan to manufacture a revolutionary carburetor of his own invention, without success. In 1920 he had a controlling interest in the Lorraine Motor Corporation in Grand Rapids, Michigan, but that too failed.

The Buick name still had great public appeal and a group of investors thought that by getting David Buick to lend his name they would attract all the investment capital they wanted. In 1922 it was announced that David Dunbar Buick was returning to the automobile ranks. Initially the "Dunbar" venture appeared to hold promise and production was scheduled to begin in 1923. In the end the whole venture proved to be a financial sham and David Buick had been one of the deceived.

Later he was in a Florida real estate venture that ended up in bankruptcy. Broke, but not beaten, Buick returned to Detroit. In 1927 he worked as an instructor at the Detroit School of Trades. In April 1928, Bruce Catton, interviewed the slight framed 74 year old man. The man who first built the engine and cars that became the cornerstone of the world's largest manufacturing company could no longer afford to keep a telephone in his home, let alone buy one of the automobiles that carried his name. However, the old man told Catton,

"I'm not worrying, the failure is the man who stays down when he falls – the man who sits and worries about what happened yesterday, instead of jumping up and figuring what he's going to do today and tomorrow. That's what success is - looking ahead to tomorrow."

In the course of some five years, David Buick's fascination with gas marine engines became the foundation on which the world's largest manufacturing company was launched. David Dunbar Buick's vision and hard work may have made a hundred millionaires, but he died in poverty.

On the occasion of the 100th anniversary of the Buick Motor Company the Michigan Historical Commission placed a historical marker at the Renaissance Center in Detroit commemorating both the company and the man:

BUICK MOTOR COMPANY

David Dunbar Buick was one of many Detroiters who built gasoline-powered marine and farm engines during the late nineteenth century. Buick (1854-1929) opened his first motor shop, Buick Auto-Vim and Power Company, around 1900. Machinist Walter Marr built the first Buick automobile about the same time, and engineer Eugene Richard soon patented the powerful overhead valve engine synonymous with the Buick label. In 1903 the Flint Wagon Works purchased what was by then the Buick Motor Company and moved operations to Flint. Carriage maker William C. Durant took control of the company in 1904, propelling Buick to the top of the burgeoning market and using the capital to found General Motors in 1908. In 1998--nearly 35 million Buicks later--Buick's headquarters returned to Detroit.

MICHIGAN HISTORICAL COMMISSION • MICHIGAN HISTORICAL CENTER
REGISTERED STATE SITE NO. 475 1093
THIS MARKER IS THE PROPERTY OF THE STATE OF MICHIGAN

DAVID DUNBAR BUICK

David Dunbar Buick, for whom the Buick automobile is named, came to Detroit from Scotland with his parents in 1856 at age two. A plumbing inventor and businessman, Buick turned to building gasoline engines for boats on the Detroit River during the 1890s. By 1900 his first motor firm, Buick Auto-Vim and Power Company, was operating some six blocks north of this site near what is now the southwest corner of Beaubien and Lafayette Streets. The firm's overhead valve engines became famous for power. The first experimental Buick automobile was built in Detroit circa 1900. On May 19, 1903, David Buick incorporated the Buick Motor Company. That fall the firm was sold to the Flint Wagon Works in Flint where the first retail Buicks were built in 1904.

MICHIGAN HISTORICAL COMMISSION • MICHIGAN HISTORICAL CENTER
REGISTERED STATE SITE NO. 476 2003
THIS MARKER IS THE PROPERTY OF THE STATE OF MICHIGAN

Reference:

Detroit News Tribune, July 3 and 5, 1898

Dolnar, Hugh, "The Buick Motor Company's Side-Entrance Tonneau," Cycle and Automobile Trade Journal, September, 1904

Dunham, Terry B., "Searching for Mr. Marr, The Buick Engineer that Jump Started General Motors," The Buick Beagle, November, 2003

http://media.gm.com/division/buick/products/heritage/heritage.htm

http://www.1904buick.com

"Innovation in Power Racing," Detroit Free Press, August 10, 1902

Gustin, Lawrence R. and Terry B. Dunham, "The Buick, A Complete History", Automobile Quarterly Library Series Book, Revised Sixth Edition, 2002

King Papers, National Automotive History Collection, Detroit Public Library

Klug, Thomas A., "Dry Dock Engine Works," Historic American Engineering Record No. MI-330, August 2002, page 19 citing: Calder, C. B. Daily Journal of, Archival Collections of the Great Lakes, Jerome Library, Bowlong Green State University, Bowling Green, OH.

Scharchburg, Richard, "Walter L. Marr – Auto Pioneer 1865-1941," Wheels, Journal of the National Automotive History Collection, Summer/Fall 1999

Miscellaneous undated newspaper clippings

"Pretty Sight, Detroit's Yachtsmen Off for Marine City," Detroit Tribune, July 3, 1898

"Yachting," Detroit Tribune, July 5, 1898

Henry Ford

Reluctant Marine Engine Builder

From the Collections of
The Henry Ford

So much has been written about the Fords that it would seem little more could be added. However, largely unknown are details of any engine experiments between the time he completed the toy-like "Quadricycle" in 1896 and the first vehicle he produced for the Detroit Automobile Company in 1899. During that time yachtsmen/gas engine pioneers such as Steinway, King, Olds and Buick were personally interested in building marine engines. Ford, however, is not known to have had any personal interest in yachting or boats of any kind at that time. Nevertheless, there is evidence that some of his experimental gas engines were built and sold as marine engines. By deduction, Ford was not yet a wealthy man so, selling an experimental engine to reinvest in the next improved engine could be expected. At the time the best market for lightweight internal combustion engines as prime movers was on the waterfront.

Ford's work with marine engines began shortly after he moved from the family's farm to the City of Detroit. His first job was brief employment with the Michigan Car Company,[1] the city's largest employer. Later he worked at the James Flower and Brothers Manufacturing Company at a time when David Buick may have been the foreman[2]. Before joining the Edison Illuminating Company he worked with marine engines at the Detroit Dry Dock Company.

Regarding his experience at the Detroit Dry Dock Company, Ford told Charles B. King the following story:

> "You know I worked for the Detroit Dry Dock Co. . . I helped an apprentice put the engine in the car ferry Algonach. One day I was going down the engine room ladder with a Stillson wrench on my shoulder and Kirby[3] said, 'Don't go down that way - you are liable to break you neck. Take hold of the rail. Well, the next day, I was going down with a chain-falls on my shoulder and I slipped, and if it had not been for Kirby's advice, I would have gone straight to the bottom! You know, I have Kirby's name on the Engineering Building with the world's greatest men - wrote him and got his permission. He said he appreciated the honor."

During the early years, before the Detroit Automobile Company, Henry Ford was interested in any and all engine experiments. That curiosity led him to associate with many pioneer

---

1. In the 19th and early 20th century the term "car" most oftern referred to rail vehicles. The Michigan Car Company built railroad cars using a form of assembly line
2. December 1879 through August 1880.
3. Frank Kirby was Detroit's foremost naval architect. He is well known for having designed many of the Great Lakes excursion boats, such as the *Tashmoo* and the Bob-Lo boats, and also overnight passenger ships, such as the *Greater Detroit,* among others.

motormen. According to Ford biographer Sidney Olson, two of Ford's close friends were Charles Annesley and Barton Peck. Annesley and Peck had been college friends and both were sons of wealthy men that indulged their interests in motor vehicles[4]. They were known to have tinkered together in Peck's shop with plans for a gasoline engine to drive a motorboat[5].

Charles Annesley is best remembered to history as the man who bought both Ford's Quadricycle and the engine from King's first horseless carriage. He is also known to have himself built four electric and three gas powered automobiles by 1899, making him one of the prolific automobile pioneers in Michigan, up to that time. In 1900 he moved to Buffalo, New York to build marine engines with the Buffalo Gas Engine Company.

Barton Peck built his first automobile in 1897 and in 1898 received one of the first speeding tickets in America. It was in Peck's shop at 81 Park Place, in 1901, that Ford, Peck, C. Harold Wills and Oliver Barthel built the race car, "Sweepstakes," that launched the short lived Henry Ford Automobile Company. Reportedly Peck later became an enthusiastic aviation pioneer and is known to have bought the first Curtis flying-boat. He subsequently relocated to Florida where he made a fortune in real estate.

As an employee of the Edison Illuminating Company, Ford looked after the repairs of the company's steam engines. This led him to John Lauer's machine shop where Charles B. King and Oliver Barthel were experimenting with gasoline engines and plans for self-powered vehicles. It was during this period that they became friends and shared ideas.

The three men collaborated closely with each other in the early years. Riding on his bicycle, Ford escorted King and Barthel on the first public demonstration of a gas powered automobile on the streets of Detroit, indicating that he was one of the few to have had prior knowledge of the event. The valves in Ford's famous *Quadricycle* came from one of King's experimental engines. Later King escorted Ford on a nine mile test run from the city to the Ford family farm. In his book, *Psychic Reminiscences*, King retold the story as follows:

> "... Ford talked much with me about a test run to the old farm at Dearborn, his birthplace, a distance of nine miles, and the 'great hit' it would make with the 'old man' and the neighbors. He wanted me to go along, I consented, the day was set and we started. Ford drove the machine alone and I followed on a bicycle as his sole escort. Much tinkering was done on the way out. The ignition requiring the most attention. Considerable water was put in the tank. A number of frightened horses were passed until we finally reached the farm. I opened the big gate and Ford drove in and around to the kitchen.
>
> The door opened and there was the tall form of his father, William Ford, Justice of the Peace, Church Warden and Farmer. He stood there, said nothing. He was certainly lacking in enthusiasm. The neighbors were coming across the fields. I can see it as yesterday, because such things make deep impressions. About a dozen had arrived and their whole expression was one of sympathy for the Senior

4. Barton Peck's father was president of the Edison Illuminating Company of Detroit. It is not hard to imagine that the Peck-Ford friendship did not influence Ford's opportunities at the company.
5. *Young Henry Ford,* p. 62

Ford, rather than praise for Henry. In other words, it was a 'frost.' Ford sensed it, exactly as I did when the back door was opened. His picture had been shattered. He looked at me and said, let's get out of here.

I opened the big gate and we tinkered our way home, reaching the big city in the dark of that evening-realizing the frailties of human nature and the frailties of machine design."

Henry Ford, left, and Oliver Barthel, right, in Ford's famous racer 999.
Courtesy NAHC

Oliver Barthel

Oliver Barthel had been Charles Brady King's right hand man since the time before he rode by his side in the first public demonstration of a gasoline powered automobile on the streets of Detroit. While King and Henry Joy were serving aboard the *U.S.S. Yosemite* in the Spanish-American War, Barthel managed the sompany business. In 1900 King's marine engine business was sold to the Olds Motor Works and Oliver Barthel, went to work with Ford at the Detroit Automobile Company. On the side he worked with Ford to design and build the famous *Sweepstakes* racer in 1901. The next year he began the design for Ford's *999* racer. In the following years he was an Experimental Engineer for the Ford Motor Company and the Olds Motor Works. During the early years of the automobile industry Barthel also designed marine engines for the Strelinger Company and the Scripps Motor Company and he was responsible for the Olds Motor Works' race boat *Six Shooter*. For decades he was invited to officiate most corporate power boat regattas between Detroit and Buffalo.

They worked in boats

After demonstrating the *Quadricycle* in June 1896, more than two years passed before the first report in November 1898 that indicated he had completed his second automobile,[6] and seven years passed before he organized the Ford Motor Company in 1903. During those intervening years most gasoline engine built for transportation vehicles, worldwide, were marine engines. It is not known how many of Ford's engines went into boats during that time but, one Ford marine engine built in 1897 is well documented by Sidney Olsen[7]. That year Ford helped Fred Strauss to set up a machine shop at 151 Shelby Street in Detroit. Ford put up some of the money for equipment and paid rent for the first two months. The first engine they built was a stationary engine for a framer in Dearborn. The second engine was for William Hurlbut's yacht. The engine is well documented because it stalled on the river and Hurlbut refused to pay. Ford and Strauss went to see attorney Horace Rackham, who got the partners a settlement and later made a fortune on a $5,000 investment in the Ford Motor Company.

Ford historian Sidney Olsen indicates that Ford and Strauss built several marine engines together. Subsequently Ford was responsible for brining in Frank Dimmer as a full time partner for Strauss. Notably, Dimmer is remembered in the history of Henry Leland[8] as the man who in 1896 commissioned the machine shop of Leland and Faulconer to build small internal combustion engines for boats[9].

Based on the following letter from Ellery I. Garfield to William Maybury (courtesy NAHC), it is certain that more than a few marine engines were built by Ford in the years before the Detroit Automobile Company in August 1899. Garfield and Maybury would certainly have been well informed as close observers of Ford's work at that time. Maybury was a Ford family friend and along with Garfield was one of Ford's first financial backers. The letter reveals the use of Ford's experimental engines in launches and provides insight into issues of early engine development (highlights by the editor):

---

6. Ford biographer Sindy Olson says there are three pieces of evidence that he was still working on the vehicle in August 1898. The first press indication of a second Ford car was a three sentence mention in Horseless Age, November 1898. The report was clearly in error when it indicated that there were several of Ford's automobiles on the streets of Detroit and it may still have been only talk about a second. The first local news story was not until July 29, 1899 in the Detroit Journal. I t is clear that Ford had significant men ready to back an automobile venture as soon as he could demonstrate a workable model. The Detroit Automobile Company was organized based on the performance of the automobile reported in the July story.
7. *Young Henry Ford,* p 101-102
8. Founder of both the Cadillac and Lincoln automobile brands.
9. *Master of Precision,* p 60

FORT WAYNE ELECTRIC CORPORATION,

MANUFACTURERS OF THE

"WOOD"SYSTEMS

OF

ARC LIGHTING, ALTERNATING AND DIRECT CURRENT INCANDESCENT LIGHTING,

POWER GENERATORS, MOTORS, TRANSFORMERS, INSTRUMENTS AND APPLIANCES.

BRANCH OFFICES:

NEW YORK.	NEW ORLEANS, LA.	ST. PAUL, MINN.
CHICAGO, ILL.	SAN ANTONIO, TEX.	CINCINNATI, OHIO.
PHILADELPHIA PA.	ROCHESTER, N.Y.	ATLANTA, GA.
PITTSBURGH PA.	PORTLAND, ORE.	ST. LOUIS, MO.
BOSTON, MASS.	COLUMBUS, OHIO.	OMAHA, NEB.
SAN FRANCISCO, CAL.	KANSAS CITY, MO.	

CABLE ADDRESS "WOODARC." A.B.C. AND A.I. CODE USED.

IF FEDERAL ST. BOSTON, MASS. Sept. 21, 1897.

MAIN OFFICES AND WORKS
FORT WAYNE, INDIANA.

My Dear Maybury:---

I am in receipt of your letter of the 16th and note its contents with much interest. I was very sorry not to see you in New York; but it was impossible for me to go over and I see it was equally impossible for you to come to Boston.

I note what you say of the motor wagon and your conclusions with regard to it. <u>I do not wonder that you are somewhat discouraged, as I am, for Mr. Ford seems to have difficulties as well as all the others.</u> I think I said to you in one of my former letters that I believed one of the greatest drawbacks in motor wagons to be that they are all trying to see how light a wagon they can make. In this they have made a most grievous mistake.

I have been doing a great deal of thinking and the result is I have in my mind a very serious doubt as to whether gasoline engines are the proper thing for motor carriages; or for that matter any power that is produced by explosion. It may be I have written you on this subject before but possibly not. In any event I will give you my opinion. I wish you would think it over and see how it agrees with your notions.

Take for instance a carriage that is standing still, no matter whether it is a buggy or express wagon and suppose that a slight obstruction is directly in the way of the front wheel; or suppose the front wheels are in such a position that they have to go over a slight obstruction of some kind before the carriage can go ahead. In case of gasoline or any other explosive a certain kick is made by the explosion and there is no further explosion until the carriage has moved a certain distance, which of course, is very short.

The force of the kick is all you obtain. It is not a continued pressure, as in the case of steam or electricity. **With steam you open the throttle, and there is a slight push; the more you open it the greater the push, but it is steady and does not stop. It is continuous. While in the case of anything explosive, it comes with a rush for an instant only and then is all gone.10 This of course, must be a great strain on a light wagon or light machinery. This is where, I think we in this country have made a great mistake; in trying to build too light engines and wagons. It seems to me the idea of force must be a continuous one. Therefore I have been leaning for some little time towards steam.** Electric carriages I do not consider as amounting to anything, on account of cost of running them, the short distance they can be made to go and also their weight.

The Whitney Steam Carriage, about which I wrote you some time ago, and in which I took a ride at the Park, has been perfected, as they claim. I learned today- that the "Pratt & Whitney Co.," of Hartford, have entered into arrangements with the inventor to build all the carriages. Young Mr. Whitney, who has invented this carriage, is a nephew of Mr. Whitney of the "Pratt & Whitney Co." The wagon certainly looks very nicely. The man whom I saw today and who gave me the information told me he rode in it to Providence and back last Saturday. They started out with several bicycle men, who were going through to Providence. He said they kept with the bicycle people until they reached Dedham, about ten miles out, and then became tired of loafing, as he expressed it, went on and left them. They ran away from all cyclists and electric cars. They rode seventy miles without doing anything to their engine. They then put in a pail of water, and this was all that was done. They used gasoline for heating purposes. Their engine has two cylinders.

I know Prof. Thomson is in favor of steam or any power that will give as I express it, a continuous pressure. I saw Prof. Thomson last Thursday at a reception in Lynn and gathered from him enough to convince me that his ideas lay in the same direction that mine did. **The only objection I have heard thus far to the steam motor is the smell of gasoline**, which up to the present time they have failed to rid them-selves of.

<u>I can readily see how some of the engines Mr. Ford has made have been sold for small boats and work very well,</u> When they are on a boat and in the water and the explosion is made, the propeller of course will continue to turn as there is not a great amount of resistance. I have no doubt about the power they generate or the quickness with which they are operated when used on boats.

Your letter is dated the 16th and Mr. Ford's promise to you of thirty days would make it about the middle of October. I sincerely trust he will have something that will be a long way ahead of any other carriage at that time. If it is practical and he can over come the difficulties that have been in the way of all others, he will have something that is valuable, and of which we can take hold and make money. As you say he has been so long about it I shall be better satisfied when I see it.

I wrote you some little time ago in regard to my going to Detroit on the Boland case. I am informed by him that the case has been put off from the 14th to the 28th. Gen. Peach, who saw Mr. Boland in New York, thinks it will be put off again, but to what time he does not know. Mr. Boland and his Attorney, Mr. Putney, are very anxious to have me come at that time. They may possibly change their minds. In any event, if I do not come for them, I will come on when Ford says he has the carriage ready. . . .

Kindly remember me to all who may inquire and believe me to be,
Very sincerely yours,

[Ellery I. Garfield]

Mr. Garfield's letter is convincing circumstantial evidence. At a time when there appeared to be a ready buyer for every lightweight gas engine suitable for a boat, it seems very likely that Ford would experiment "perfecting" his engine and recover some of the developmental costs by selling them to eager buyers. Unfortunately, except for this and the marine engine sold to William Hurlbut, there is little documentary evidence for this practice.

Ford Yachts and Speed Boats

Ford did not demonstrate any particular personal interest in power boats in the early years. However, one of the few pictures on the walls of his Piquette Street office (1903-1910) features the Dodge Brothers' yacht *Hornet*.

Henry Ford in his office circa 1908.

A desire to travel to Cuba to investigate some iron ore property is generally credited as the reason Henry Ford acquired his first yacht. Reportedly he did not like to travel in public and wanted to go down on his own boat. He asked his Chief Engineer, William B. Mayo, to find an ocean-going yacht for the trip. After searching the East Coast for several weeks Mayo located the 202'7" yacht *Sialia*, named after the scientific name of the Eastern Bluebird. The yacht was purchased in January 1917. After returning from Havana later that year, the boat was conscripted by the U. S. government for war use.

Apparently hooked on yachting, Ford purchased a substitute yacht named *Widgeon* and renamed it *Sialia II*. In May, 1920, he was able to regain possession of the first *Sialia*. In 1925 he had the ship cut in two, added a 21-foot section and replaced the steam engine with a pair of diesel engines. *Sialia* was sold in 1929.

In 1935 Ford purchased the 138-foot Herreshoff built yacht *Truant*. The yacht had been built in 1892 for Truman H. Newberry, a Detroit industrialist, one time Secretary of the Navy and the man that beat Ford in his campaign for the U. S. Senate. In 1941 the boat was donated to the Sixth Naval Training Station in Chicago, where Henry Ford II was in training.

Located 20 miles from Detroit, on the northeast end of Lake St. Clair, the exclusive Old Club of Detroit could only be reached by boat until the 1930s. The club's 1927 special edition year book lists Henry Ford as a member along with many of Detroit's leading yachtsmen.

Edsel Ford, enjoying experimenting with war surplus Liberty aircraft engines and high-speed boats. Perhaps for that reason, Henry Ford was receptive to a proposal for an International Sweepstakes Race that would be a "laboratory of engine development." Ford provided the "seed" money for the prize. The 150-mile race was run in three 50-mile laps that severely tested the men, engines and hulls. For the first running of race, 1923, Edsel Ford's *Greyhound Jr.* competed with fourteen other boats.

In the 1924 International Sweepstakes Race, R. C. Dahlinger was driving Edsel's race boat *999*. Shortly after passing Horace Dodge Jr's *Baby Delphine III*, flames shot through the hatches of the Ford boat. Reportedly, the boat was going close to 60 mph when the driver and mechanic leaped from the burning craft. It is no wonder that Edsel was never allowed to be the driver of his boats in competition.

The 611-foot cargo ship *Henry Ford II* may have been the world's largest yacht. It was outfitted with luxury accomodations for Henry Ford and his guests and the ship was often rerouted to accomodate his personal schedule.

We have gotten ahead of our story. Ford boats, ships and marine conversion of Ford engines would fill another book. However, it is worth mentioning that the first vehicles produced at Ford's monumental River Rouge factory were Eagle Boats; submarine chasers designed by Frank Kirby and built under contract for the U. S. Navy.

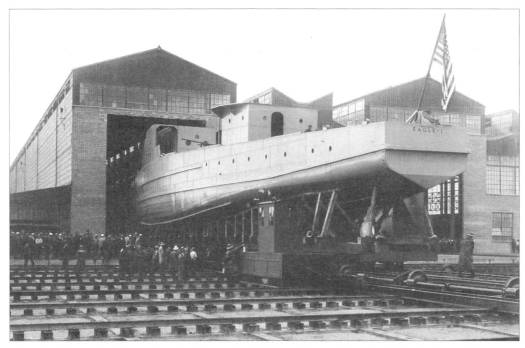

The first Eagle Boat being launched from Ford's River Rouge factory building that would become the Dearborn assembly plant for the Mustang.
Courtesy Dossin Great Lakes Museum

References:

Barthel, Oliver, and Mayo, William N., Oral histories in the Collection of the Benson Ford Research Center, The Henry Ford.

Barrett, J. Lee, Speed Boat Kings, Arnold-Powers Inc., Detroit, MI., 1939

Horseless Age, November 1898

Leland, Mrs. Wilfred C. and Minnie Dubbs Millbrook, *Master of Precision,* Wayne State University Press, Detroit, MI, 196, 1996

Maybury, William C., Papers in the Collection of the Burton Historical Collection,Detroit Public Library, with copies also found in the King Collection of the National Automotive History Collection.

Olson, Sidney, Young Henry Ford, Wayne State University Press, Detroit, MI, 1963, 1997.

King, Charles B., "Psychic Reminiscences," Self published, 1953

Off to the Races II:

Experimental Era for the Real Racers, 1904-1912

Numerous engine innovations commonly attributed to the automobile first appeared in boats competing during this formative era of powerboat racing. High speed engines were being developed for automobiles but, their endurance and reliability was tested and improved under the trying conditions of unlimited powerboat racing. The first American Power Boat Association (APBA) Gold Cup race was won by C. C. Riotte's *Standard*. Marine engine manufacturer C. C. Riotte is credited with powering *Standard* with the first six-cylinder gasoline engine in America. He is also credited with building the first 500-hp gas engine in the world. In the 1905 Gold Cup race high speed automobile engines broke crankshafts and smashed cylinders while a modest boat powered by a two-cycle marine engine rated at 450 rpm cruised to victory over boats powered by Mercedes, Lozier, Winton, Olds and Packard engines designed primarily for automobiles. In 1906 the Gold Cup was won by an innovative super-charged two-cycle marine engine. Among the contenders was an innovative four-cylinder engine block with eight pistons and two crankshafts powering two propellers. For 1908 the defender employed an innovative V-8 with 3 valves per cylinder and a hemispherical combustion chamber.

By 1907 the powerboat racing circuit included events designed to promote endurance and enhance the gas engine's reputation for reliability. The 120-mile *Rudder Cup* race was first run on Lake Erie that year. In 1911 marine engine manufacturer William Scripps sponsored a 6000-mile race across both Lake Erie and Lake Ontario. In 1912 he equipped a 35-foot Mathews built boat with only a 16-hp production Scripps marine engine and sent it on a 6,000-mile voyage from Detroit to St. Petersburg, Russia a few months after the invincible ocean liner *Titanic* tragically disappeared. All gas engine manufacturer manufacturers learned valuable lesions form the examples demonstrated by power boats. This is there story.

By 1904 power boat racing was a motor sport of national and international interest with the American Power Boat Association (APBA) Gold Cup and the International Harmsworth Trophy as esteemed prizes for showcase events. At first this appeared to be a natural opportunity for automobile manufacturers to get some well deserved publicity for their achievements with designs that were pushing engine speeds up to

Courtesy NAHC

The pure racing boat emerged as wet, uncomfortable and not overly safe vehicle. It required careful housing and handling and was capable of accommodating only the necessary crew and equipment. The new all-out racing craft were called "auto-boats."

1,000 rpm. During the period from roughly 1903-1912, racing hulls and high speed marine engines evolved to be distinctly different from the everyday designs for boats and engines. The first power boats to be seriously termed "high-speed" were ones designed for the 1904 championship races. The trend was to diverge from everyday forms and heavy sea-worthy construction to the lightest possible construction stuffed with the most powerful machinery available. It became obvious that to contend for records under the American Power Boat Association (APBA) rules, a real racer had to be built solely and exclusively for racing, making the boat of little use for anything else.

Baby Reliance III

Perhaps one of the best known and extreme examples of hull to power ratio was the Chris Smith designed *Baby Reliance III*, a 20-foot planning hull with a 12-cyclinder, 150-hp Van Blerck engine. The equipment occupied most of the hull leaving minimal space for the required crew. Absent mechanical difficulties and if the waters were calm, it was a champion. The *Baby Reliance* series of fast boats, designed and built by Chris Smith roared to prominence at the end of this era. Chris Smith race boats are well remembered for having dominated the championship races in the early years of the hydroplane era.

Although the marine engine is the parent of the automobile engine, by the early 20th century many dare-devils were becoming familiar with the *explosive* engine by way of the on-land sport of "automobiling." Many of the speed seeking automobilists discovered that by transferring the high speed engine of an automobile from a chassis to a hull, they developed new opportunities for high-speed thrills. They also found that on the water they were much less hampered by restrictive legislation.

In Eastern waters the 1904 APBA race circuit was dominated by "automoboatists" who often entered boat racing to promote the engines they built or represented. Many of the most notable boats reviewed in the national publications that year were named for the engines: Standard, Mercedes, Panhard, Napier, Speedway, Winton and Fiat. Others promoting their engines but using less commercial names were *Shooting Star*, designed and built by the Lozier Motor Company; Six Shooter, built for the Olds Motor Works; *Japansky*, designed and built by the Gas Engine and Power Company; and both *Vingt-et-Un II* and *Challenger*, designed by Clinton H. Crane and built for Smith & Mabley, a manufacturer (Simplex) and importer of luxury automobiles (in 1904 Smith & Mabley reportedly contracted for 25% of the Mercedes automobiles produced that year). They built, raced and promoted fast boats, believing that their wealthy automobile customers were also interested in speed on the water.

The race for the first APBA Gold Cup was in June, 1904. Eight entries were received, but only three appeared on race day and one of them broke down. *Standard*, owned and operated by gas engine pioneer C.C. Riotte, not only won the race but also set a new record for gasoline powered boats by averaging 22.57 statute miles per hour over the 32 mile Hudson River course. The 59-foot auto-boat was powered by a six-cylinder 100 hp "Standard" engine, reportedly the first six-cylinder gasoline engine built in America. On June 24, 1904, the New York Times reported that *Standard* made barely one-third of a mile per hour less than the fast steam yacht *Kanawha* in a championship race the previous week. Then, on July 6, 1904 *Challenger*, a Smith & Mabley racer built as the first American challenger for the International Harmsworth Trophy, made a 21-mile trial run on the East River at the rate of 26.5 statute mph.

C. C. Riotte

On May 10, 1908, *Motor Boat* magazine published an obituary of C. C. Riotte titled, "A Tribute to Genius." Riotte was credited with building the first six-cylinder gasoline engine in America, and he was also credited with the first gasoline engine to produce 500-hp. Riotte began making gasoline engines as early as 1891, and about 1893 was building marine engines under the trade name of Empire Motors, later the C. C. Riotte Co. and in 1900 the Standard Motor Construction Company. (Standard remained in the marine engineering business into the 1920s.)

Nathaniel Greene Herreshoff believed he could build a small steam boat that would outperform the gasoline powered speedboats and made a respectable showing with the 40-foot *Swift Sure*. However, in a match race at Newport in 1903 *Vint-et-un* won decisively.

Herreshoff steam racer *Swift Sure* **and the APBA Gold Cup winner** *Standard*

The Rudder magazine published a picture of *Standard* and *Swift Sure* on the cover of their February 1905 issue. However, by that time Herreshoff was already convinced that for small fast boats, the day of the steam engine was over. In 1904 he built a hull similar to *Swift Sure* and powered it with a Daimler-Mercedes gas engine. The new boat was named *XPDNC*. In another match race with *Vint-et-un* the Herreshoff boat won decisively.

The second APBA Gold Cup race has been held in September 1904, the only time the Gold Cup race was run twice in the same year. *Standard* had been sold and was not available to compete. Ten other competitors were able to start on the first day, including many boats closely identified with their engine manufacturers, such as *Shooting Star* (Lozier), *Challenger* (Smith & Mabley), *Macaroni* (Fiat), *Speedway* (a brand name of Gas Engine & Power Company), *Mercedes U.S.A.* and *Mercedes IV*.

Vingt-et-Un* and *Vingt-et-Un II
Courtesy NAHC

The winning boat, *Vingt-et-Un II*, provided great promotional value for her original owners, Smith & Mabley. However, by the time of the second race it was owned by Philadelphia publisher Willis S. Kilmer representing the Chippewa Yacht Club.

Consequently the races for 1905 were moved westward to the home of the Chippewa Yacht Club in the Thousand Islands area of western New York.

It was soon clear that the "auto-boats" would dramatically alter the future of high speed power boat racing. By the end of the first year the deed of gift for at least one prestigious trophy, the Larchmont Yacht Club's Gold Cup, was changed to ban dealers engaged in the manufacture or sale of automobiles or boats.

Noted yacht designer W. P. Stephens expressed some distain for the "auto boats" in a story published in *The Rudder*, December, 1904, in which he commented, *"Now that the first season of the "auto-boat" is over, and the "automoboatist" has been taught a few tough lessons as to the difference between dust and spray, and between the resistance due to air and a rolling wheel as compared to water and a material bulk of displacement...."*

Writing for Power Boat magazine the following December, 1905, Stephens commented, *"It is seldom that any sport, old or new, begins a season with the promise which attended the opening of the present year in power boating. . . For the summer a variety of events, national and international were scheduled. . . "*

Stephens described the fleet as one of the most wonderful ever launched – on paper. He further remarked:

> *"After this brilliant outlook the retrospect is at first disappointing in the extreme, showing nothing but wrecks and failures; labor and money wasted by builders, owners and clubs, and all to little permanent gain. . . many of the leaders are out first and foremost. . . for free advertising, and as a class they are utterly ignorant of practical boating and yachting as well as the elemental principals of naval architecture."*

On the bright side, Stephens agreed that the development of the automobile engine within the past few years had been too important to be ignored: *". . .where the designed speed had been moderate from an auto-boat standpoint, a fair amount of success has been obtained."* The example cited was *Shooting Star II* designed and built by the Lozier Motor Company. Both boats demonstrated a high degree of reliability and regularity of performance.

Contrary to the trend, Herbert J. Leighton was the one boat and engine builder in America whose custom boats and engines defied the "auto-boat" trend and were still able to dominate the APBA Gold Cup races in 1905, 1906 and 1907. Three consecutive Gold Cup victories were followed in 1908 with an impressive second place. Leighton had been building boats and custom marine engines in western New York since the mid-1890s. He achieved high power, high speed and reliability with seaworthy boats and 2-cycle engines, most notably the three boats named Chip.

CHIP (I), left, was the Gold Cup champion for 1905

CHIP II, below, was the controversial Gold Cup champion for 1906 and 1907. The Packard powered *Swallow* was the high speed champion in 1906, but *Chip II* won with a technical advantage under the handicapping rules that were in use at that time.

For the 1905 APBA Gold Cup the owner of *Vingt-et-Un II* declined to enter her in defense of the cup. Under the circumstances the most available boat to defend the cup for the Chippewa Yacht Club was Jonathan Wainwright's *Chip*, a 27-foot open launch designed by Leighton and powered by a 10-hp, 2-cycle Leighton engine rated at 450 rpm. The most sensational of the challengers was *Flying Dutchman* powered by two Mercedes auto engines. Unfortunately, under full load during a trial run, one of the Mercedes engines broke a crankshaft. Contenders *Radium* and *So-Long* were running on "doped" gasoline using seven ounces of ether to 18 gallons of gasoline, and both were disabled

***CHIP III*, above, was a serious Gold Cup contender in 1908. It was powered by two straight-six, two-cycle Leighton engines. However, they were not enough to defeat *Dixie II* powered by a revolutionary V-8 hemi-head, four-cycle engine.**

with smashed cylinders. The APBA Gold Cup winner on corrected time was the little speedster *Chip*. The risks of running high-speed automobile engines under full load for extended time was becoming obvious.

The remaining seven contenders included the Lozier's *Shooting Star* and E. J. Schroeder's *Skeeter*. Both boats were considered to be top contenders for the Bourne Trophy, awarded to the fastest boat overall. The high speed prize went to *Shooting Star*, and the owner, E. J. Schroeder, set his sights on a faster boat.

One example of the type of dare-devil automobilists that took to the water that year was the hard driven, wealthy speed enthusiast Edward Russell Thomas.[1] By 1904 Edward Thomas had already been in so many serious automobile accidents, often caused by his own recklessness, that he decided that he would no longer drive high speed automobiles on public roads.

In search of new speed thrills Thomas turned to Smith & Mabley and Clinton H. Crane to design and build *Dixie*. The contract was given under the condition that they could guarantee a racer that would go 30 mph. *Dixie* was a modification of *Challenger* designed earlier by Crane for Smith & Mabley to make a run at bringing the Harmsworth Trophy to America. *Dixie* was designed to conform to the Harmsworth measurement rules and was powered by one of Smith & Mabley's 150-

In 1907 the Clinton Crane designed *Dixie* was the first American speed boat to win the International Harmsworth trophy. Courtesy NAHC

---

1. Some historians have confused Edward with Edwin Thomas. There is no known relation to the power boat enthusiast and automobile manufacturer from Buffalo, Edwin Ross Thomas, owner of the E. R. Thomas Motor Car Company.

hp Simplex engines. In July and again in September 1905, Thomas swept the field of "auto-boats," including those powered by Lozier, Winton, Olds and Packard engines. Without having competed in the APBA Gold Cup or Harmsworth races but, apparently having satisfied his quest for speed on the water, he sold the boat at the end of the season. The buyer was E. J. Schroeder, the owner of *Skeeter*, one of the fastest boats at the APBA Gold Cup races earlier that year.

Although the Inter-Lakes Yachting Association's (ILYA) power boat races played an important role in the prototype era, it was not devoted to power boating and has never hosted any premier national power boat championships. However, a special feature at the annual ILYA Regatta in 1905 was a crowd pleasing speed exhibition over the long course by *Six-Shooter*. *Six-*

1905 Oldsmobile, *Six-Shooter*
Courtesy NAHC

Shooter was the Olds Motor Works' "auto-boat" that was campaigning on the national circuit that year. Participants in ILYA's main power boat race were many of the same cruising-racers seen in prior years, such as *Restless, Thelma, Bab, Zenda* and *Ruby*, finishing in that order. Presumably to demonstrate the range of engines from the Thelma Motor Works. *Little Thelma* placed third in a power dinghy class race.

For 1906 the APBA introduced new rules that appeared to unfairly handicap boats with 2-cycle engines. However, the new rules did not measure a piston's stroke, only the bore of the combustion chamber so, Leighton created an engine with a small bore and an unusually long stroke. *Chip II* was powered by an innovative Leighton 2-cycle engine that rated only 16.75-hp under the new rules. In addition to the two explosive cylinders it had a third cylinder equipped with a double-acting pump used as an air compressor to "super-charge" the deep cylinders. The third cylinder was not counted in the new rating rules. Confident of complying with the rules, the Leighton engine was nevertheless kept well under cover until race day.

Triton

Another challenger, *Triton*, was also powered by a notably innovative engine designed to take advantage of the measurement rules. The novel 4-cycle engine designed by its owner had <u>eight distinct pistons, but only four explosive chambers</u> to be measured. The pistons were set at such an angle that they met in common combustion chambers while operating two distinct crankshafts, in two separate crankcases, driving two propeller shafts.

The leading challenger for the 1906 Gold Cup was the Packard powered *Sparrow* owned by C. J. Swain of Philadelphia. The hull was designed and built by E. H.

Godshalk & Co. and powered by a 4-cylinder, 4-cycle Packard engine rating 31.8-hp. (Other race boats using the Packard marine engines were E. H. Godshalk's *Swallow*, a near duplicate of the *Sparrow*, Van Balcom's *Nemesis* and Henry B. Joy's *Geisha*.) About half an hour before the start helmsmen Clarence A. Godshalk handed the Regatta Committee a protest based on the observation that *Chip II* obviously had three cylinders, not the two that were officially measured. *Chip II* beat all the contestants on corrected time so the committee was obligated to investigate the protest.

Packard powered *Swallow* was the favored APBA Gold Cup contender in 1906
Courtesy NAHC

The race committee's official measurer re-measured *Chip II*, and he again refused to include the supercharger as a third cylinder. The race committee was informed that the rating would not change. The Regatta Committee disagreed and the Gold Cup was placed in the custody of the APBA until the Executive Committee could make a decision. In the end, the trophy was awarded to *Chip II*, and the rules were again revised.

Overall speed did not increase much between 1903 and 1906. In September 1906 *Standard* achieved a speed record of 29.3 statute mph at the National Motor Boat Carnival on the Hudson River. The gain over *Challenger's* 1904 record was only three statute mph, but that was a 10% increase.

In July 1906, *The Rudder* published an article by A. S. Atkinson titled "Problems of the High-speed Power Boats." Steam engines continued to be the dominate motive power in the world and large, sturdy, high-powered steam boats continued to hold the world speed records. Accordingly it was natural that naval architects found the accomplishments in high speed torpedo boat and torpedo-boat destroyer designs to be the most fruitful for study and comparison.

In an article in T*he Rudder*, Atkins reported that, in the quest for more speed, naval architects were debating whether the speed of boats could best be increased by modifying the sharp lines of hulls that cut through the water or by strengthening them so more powerful machinery could be installed. To be competitive a powerboat had to be built to maintain high speed around the course through rough as well as smooth water. Flat-bottomed Hydroplane hulls that slide over the water were already being built in France when the concept was beginning to be explored in America.

While still under the radar of national attention, Detroit designer and boat builder John L. Hacker built one of the America's first planning speedboats, *Au Revoir*, for W. Murray

Smith in 1905. Hacker followed with several winning racers named *Kitty Hawk* built for Lee Counselman (VP & General Manager of Chalmers Motor Car Co., successor to the Thomas-Detroit Motor Car Company). However, eastern respect was withheld until H. H. Timken (co-founder of the Timken Roller Bearing Axle Company) took the 26-foot *Kitty Hawk II* east in 1911. He soundly beat *Sand Burr II*, a highly regarded and widely campaigned boat designed by Adolph Apel, a leading designer of fast boats from Atlantic City, New Jersey.

John L. Hacker

Hacker is best remembered as a designer of finely sculptured runabouts but, over his many years of designing boats, c.1901-1961, he was responsible for a number of unlimited racing winners, including Gold Cup winners *El Lagarto* in 1933-34-35, *My Sweetie* in 1949, and the winner of the 1952 President's Cup, *Miss Pepsi*.

Back in the Great Lakes, power boating was generally taking a different direction by 1906. As in the East many of the leading participants represented engine companies and race committees adopted the APBA rules. However, motorboat regattas on the Great Lakes were more inclusive continued to feature a variety of classes that included pleasure boats, speed boats and "Long Distance" racing designed to promote reliability of hulls and equipment.

The first notable long distance race was July 7, 1906, hosted by the Toledo Yacht Club. The prize for the 120 mile race was a silver cup presented by Thomas Fleming Day the Publisher of *The Rudder*. Alexander Winton entered a boat named *Jim*. The scratch boat was *Bab*, remembered as the winner of Detroit's first powerboat race in July 1900. The winner on corrected time was *Independence*, a 32-footer built by Mathews Boat Company, powered by a 2-cyclinder, 2-cycle Ralaco engine rating 12-hp.

Pungs-Finch (Sintz) powered Wilanna
winner of the 1906 Mathews Cup

The 14th annual Inter Lakes Yachting Association (ILYA) Regatta was held the week of July 19, 1906 with a greater number of entrants than in any previous year. One hundred and seventeen sailboats started in the five classes. The power boats were reported to be so thick around the docks that there was not enough room to moor a rowboat. In the cabin cruiser class, the Pungs-Finch (Sintz) powered *Wilanna*, owned by Detroit Motor Boat Club Commodore C.W. Kotcher, easily won the trophy presented by the Mathews Boat Company. In the speed boat class the Smalley powered *Arrow* from Bay City narrowly won the free-for-all and decisively won the handicap races. Other speed boat contestants included the Gray Motor Company's *Little Grayling* and the Scripps Motor Company's *P.D.Q.*

By this time the auto manufacturers were convinced that building fast boats and engines was more difficult than they had at first imagined. Increasing auto sales also demanded their complete attention to meet production goals. Most of them withdrew from power boat racing rather than risk a loss of prestige that might reflected poorly on their automobiles.

Naval architect W. P. Stephens and others had warned that there were significant differences between dust and spray. Marine engines have to be built to run at full speed under load for long periods of time. Under those conditions many engines designed for automobiles tended to overheat, or, worse, break their crankshafts or cylinder walls and burn bearings. For the most part, automobile manufacturers decided to stick with what they knew best. They left the building of marine engines and boats to others. But they learned a great deal about improving engine reliability from the experience.

The controversy following the 1906 Gold Cup and the departure of the automobile manufacturers seems to have robbed the 1907 race of all interest. The only challengers were local boats. Under the new rules, written with the benefit of the previous year's experience and with no end to data at their disposal, the results were practically the same. Defending the cup against four other boats divided equally between 2 and 4 cycle engines, *Chip II* was again the winner. Commenting on the results, *Chip II's* owner and three times winner of the cup, Mr. Jonathan Wainwright, stated that in his opinion the present rules were very poor and that never again would he race any of his boats in a handicap race.

In August 1907, the Toledo Power Boat Carnival offered riverfront entertainment with a parade of boats, and a race of "Auto-Boats," won by *Gray No. 6*, a small Godshalk hull powered by a stock 3-cyclinder, 2-cycle 18-hp Gray engine. The featured event was the second annual Long Distance Race in Lake Erie for *The Rudder Cup*. *Clymene*, owned by L. F. Eaton of Detroit, won on corrected time. O. J. Mulford's *Grayling*, launched that very day with three stock 4-cylinder, 2-cycle, 40-hp Gray motors, won the prize for the fastest time over the 120 mile course.

In Detroit the Detroit Motor Boat Club and the Country Club of Detroit both ran motor boat races that received some national press coverage. The latter was run on September 2, 1907 and was notable for including both 2 and 4-cycle Detroit engines manufactured by among others, Scripps, Cross, Pungs-Finch, Dingfelder, Gray and Packard. As in most important races on the Detroit River and Lake Erie, automotive pioneer Oliver E. Barthell was the official measurer.

In 1907 E. J. Schroeder shipped *Dixie* to England. America's interest in high speed boat racing was restored when he defeated *Daimler* and *Daimler II* to bring the Harmsworth Trophy across the Atlantic to America for the first time.

To prepare for the 1908 Harmsworth defense, Schroeder began plans for *Dixie II*. The successor to the Smith & Mabley Company, Simplex, was no longer making the light, powerful engines that helped make the first *Dixie* a champion. Designer Clinton Crane turned to his brother, a custom automobile builder and a brilliant engineer (he later served as president of the Society of Automotive Engineers). Henry Crane proposed an innovative design, a V-8 with 3 valves per cylinder and a hemispherical combustion chamber head. Using exotic steel and aluminum alloys, the 220 hp engine's weight was reduced to about 10 pounds per hp.

THE STORY
of The
2OO MILE RACE
On Lake Erie 1907

For the 1908 Harmsworth Trophy the leading challenger was the Duke of Westminster's twin screw *Wolseley-Siddely*, right, powered by two straight-eight Wolsclcy cngines totaling 414-hp and weighing 10 lbs/hp. Over the course's 32 statue miles the more powerful British boat closely followed *Dixie's* lead and roared across the finish line, 33 seconds too late. The next year at the Monaco Regatta's long distance race in the Mediterranean Sea, *Dixie II* suffered its only loss of its 108 race history. The winning boat was *Woseley-Siddely II*, a larger, more powerful and more seaworthy racer that was better able to ride the open sea.

After the Harmsworth race, the season's next big race was for the APBA Gold Cup. For 1908 the APBA removed all restriction except, like the Harmsworth rules, the overall length of the boats were limited to 40-feet. Wainwright and Leighton prepared *Chip III*, a new 40-footer powered by two straight-six, 2-cycle engines with a maximum speed of 1,100 rpm. *Chip III* performed admirably well but the undisputed champion of the year was the Clinton Crane designed *Dixie II* with the Henry Crane designed V-8 "hemi-head" engine.

Nothing much had happened to the speed record made by *Standard* in 1906 until *Dixie II* covered the 30-mile course of the 1908 Harmsworth race at a speed of 32 mph. That same year *Dixie II* traveled a measured mile at a record 36.05 mph, a gain of 20% over *Standard's* record. *Dixie II's* owner Schroeder was undoubtedly pleased with the Crane brothers' product.

For 1908 Clinton Crane designed *Dixie II* and his brother Henry built the first known V-8 "hemi-head engine

The Duke of Westminster's *Woolseley-Siddely* narrowly lost the 1908 Harmsworht trophy

In 1908 Detroit power boaters were very active. Writing about the Detroit Motor Boat Club's (DMBC) second annual regatta for Power Boating magazine, W. M. Bayless, Jr. claimed that Detroit probably had the largest and liveliest strictly power boat organization in the country and that the city probably had more power boats than any other city on fresh water. He predicted that the DMBC regatta would become one of the power boat classics, of equal importance with the annual ILYA Regatta. That year the DMBC regatta attracted so many entries that they had to divide them into eight classes, five for pleasure boats and three for the all-out racers. The pleasure boats were divided into cabin and open launch classes based on overall length and handicapped by a "predicted log" type of rating in which the boats could not run the course faster than their rated speed.

In the Class S Speed Boat challenge O.J. Mulford and William Pungs, former partners in the Michigan Yacht & Power Company, faced off in what may have been a "grudge match," but neither finished. The class R unlimited speed boat class had five starters, four of which were owned by marine engine manufacturers: Wadsworth (Detroit), E. R. Walker (Smalley), Dingfelder and Scripps. Class A attracted the most attention because it contained the big fellas, including a perennial favorite, Commodore Kotcher's *Wilanna*.

Along with four others was Mulford's old *Little Lady* owned by Vice Commodore Scripps and re-powered with Scripps engines. The fastest pleasure boats were in a fleet of 10 starters. First place went to Mulford in *Coot*, a little boat measuring only 18-feet and powered by a 12-hp Gray engine.

Two weeks later the 1908 ILYA race week attracted 43 entries for the four classes of motor boat races. Notably, this was the last time the writer found a Naphtha launch, *Resolute*, among the starters in a sanctioned power boat race. The Class A Cruiser fleet included: Alexander Winton's 64-foot *Lola*; O. J. Mulford's 62-foot *Grayling*; 32-foot *Marie* powered by an Olds engine; the 68-foot *Wilanna* and 57-foot *Bab*, both powered by Sintz engines; along with eleven other starters. First place went to the Scripps powered *Grace A. V.* The 14 starters in the Speed Boat Class included boat and engine manufacturer R. E. Wadsworth and his partner H. Scherer with four entries, Alexander Winton with the *Winton*, Mulford with *Rainmaker*, Scripps with *Scripps* and R. J. Morgan with *Morgan* powered by a Pope-Toledo automobile engine. *Rainmaker*, *Scripps* and *Silver Fizz* (Wadsworth) finished "nose and nose" in that order.

Rainmaker, above, *Scripps*, right

The first Detroit Long Distance Race was run on August 22, 1908 in three groups. Boats over 40-feet raced across Lake St. Clair, up the St. Clair River to Marine City and back, a distance of 96 miles. The two classes of pleasure boats under 40-feet went only as far as Grande Pointe, at the north end of Harsens Island, and back, for a distance of 60 miles. The speed boats ran a distance of 99 miles, 11 times around Belle Isle. The pride of first place and the silver *O. J. Mulford Cup* went to Mr. Hanna's *Grace*, in the over 40-foot class. Bob Keller's *Old Sport* received a trophy given by the Dodge Brothers for pleasure boats under 32-feet. A. Groesbeck's *Corning* won the speed boat class and the cup donated by the Scripps Motor Company. Second place went to Henry B. Joy's Packard powered *Geisha*. The "scratch boat," the one that gives time to everyone in its class, was *Scripps*. *Scripps* also had the honor of establishing a new American long distance speed record – averaging 27.76 mph over the 99 mile course.

The 1908 Great Lakes season was coming to an end when the Motor Boat Club of Buffalo sponsored the "speed championship" of the Great Lakes. Five starters sped 5 times around the club's 5 mile course. The Smalley powered *Admiral*, co-owned by Mr. Craig and E. R. Walker, honorably represented Detroit. *Courier*, powered by a Sterling engine, won the silver trophy presented by Edwin Ross Thomas (Edwin Thomas may best be remembered for manufacturing the *Thomas Flyer* that won the first "around the world" automobile race in 1907).

For 1909 a "new" *Dixie II* was built with a stronger hull that was flatter in the aft section and had a rounded transom. The same "hemi-head" engine was used but, after some tweaking, including the addition of a second carburetor, its power was increased from 220 to 250-hp. Six boats entered the 1909 APBA Gold Cup, including the "new" *Dixie II* as the defender. It was a foregone conclusion that *Dixie II* would win. It is interesting to note, as a mark of progress, that none of the participants were handicapped by mechanical difficulties.

Also notable is that by this time high speed power boat racing had become a tradition in the Mississippi Valley recieved some national attention. The annual regatta of the Mississippi Valley Power Boat Association in 1909 drew boats from all over, particularly boats from Chicago, St. Louis, Davenport, and Cleveland, to name a few.

Cero II, the last of the racing speedboats

The last known high-speed steamboat to compete in a championship race was *Cero II*, owned by Rob Deming of Cleveland. In the 1910 Annual Regatta of the Mississippi Valley Power Boat Association, the 31-foot *Cero II* made a respectable showing, winning the race for 32-footers and the mile speed trials, with an average speed of 32.9 mph.

1910 promised to be the year of impressive showcase races but, instead it was a great disappointment. Only four of the eight entries for the APBA Gold Cup started, and only *Dixie II* completed the course three days in succession.[2] Later, based solely on good luck, *Dixie II* successfully defended the Harmsworth Trophy. *Pioneer*, the most modern and fastest of the challengers, was stopped when its carburetor caught fire. Owned by the

The Duke of Westminster's innovative *Pioneer* was the fastest contender for the 1910 Harmsworth trophy

Duke of Westminster, *Pioneer* was an innovative six-step Fauber designed hydroplane powered by a 12-cylinder, 400-hp Wolsely-Siddeley engine.

---

2. Schroeder had sold *Dixie II* by this time. The new owner, Frederick K. Burnham entered her as a challenger for the cup she had won the prior year.

The defending champion, *Dixie II*, was the last displacement (non-hydroplaning) hull to win the Harmsworth trophy. The era of the displacement hull had come to an end.

Following the poor, albeit successful, performance defending the 1910 Harmsworth race, Burnham formed a syndicate and commissioned Clinton Crane to build a fourth Dixie for the 1911 defense. There was one condition, to go a guaranteed 45 mph. Crane tested four models in the testing tanks of the US Government before settling on a single step hull design. Henry Crane was commissioned to build a second "hemi-head" V-8 engine identical to the first and both were installed.

Dixie IV's first race was the 1911 APBA Gold Cup. Challengers for the cup included a diverse array of power, and a mix of non-planing displacement hulls along with the new "skimming" hulls, such as *Viva*, a single step hydro powered by four 6-cylinder, two-cycle Emmerson engines; *Mit II*, a hydroplane with an 8-cylinder 100-hp Sterling engine; *Hornet*, a twin screw displacement boat with two 4-cylinder Leighton engines; and *Wasp*, a twin screw Fauber hydroplane with two 6-cylinder Leighton engines. All bets were on Dixie and Wasp[3]. *Dixie IV* won easily the first day, but a burnt bearing kept her out of the second race. While *Mitt II* was not the fastest boat, she won the APBA Gold Cup on points over the three days.

Later that year, *Pioneer* put up a spirited challenge for the Harmsworth Trophy and was closing in on the final heat, when her engines overheated. *Dixie IV* easily cruised to the finish line.

Nothing of importance had happened in the way of overall speed for several years, so it was a notable accomplishment when *Dixie IV* broke the world's speed record over water.

 This was the first time a gasoline powered boat claimed the world's unlimited speed record. At slightly over 45 mph *Dixie IV* narrowly exceeded the record held by the 132-foot steam yacht *Arrow* since 1902.[4]

Dixie IV was the first gasoline powered boat to claim the world speed record from the steam boats

Dixie IV was fast but, it was unmanageable in rough water. Later in the 1911 season, at a race at Buffalo, *Dixie IV* hit the wake of a tug boat, flew out of control, up a stone break-wall and seriously wounded several people. That ended *Dixie's* racing career and Clinton Crane never again designed hydroplanes. In his words, "*I saw no way of making them safe and useful.*" After that Crane left the profession of naval architecture. As a side interest, he continued to design sail yachts from time to time. His next career as a civil engineer led to him presiding over the St. Joseph Lead Company.

3. Viva, Hamilton Waspare believed to be the last two-cycle Gold Cup contender.
4. *Arrow's* quadruple expansion steam engines may have developed as much as 10,000-hp and under optimal conditions could have been expected to exceed 45 mph, but by the time *Dixie IV* broke the record, *Arrow* was down to one engine and quietly operating as a stately pleasure yacht.

In October, *Motor Boating* magazine reported on a unique race resulting from a $5,000 bet between Commodore A. F. Smith, owner of the 16-foot hydroplane *Hazel*, and Frank J. Gould, owner of the 185-foot steam yacht *Helenita*. Gould ran almost a straight line for the 77 miles from Huntington to New London, Connecticut. The little gas powered *Hazel* went a considerable distance longer by following the Long Island shore most of the way but, by doing so he stayed in smooth water and arrived way ahead of *Helenita*. The result was considered to be another triumph for the reliability of the marine gasoline engine.

1911 may be most notable as the year that definitively marked the transition from a fleet dominated by non-planning displacement hulled racers to a fleet dominated by hydroplanes. However, 1912 was the "year of the hydroplane," and the APBA rules were amended to put hydroplanes and displacement hulls in separate classes.

John Hacker dsigned Kitty Hawk II
won a sensational 40 mile race at Detroit in 1912

1912 was the year that Detroit area designers Chris Smith and John Hacker rose to prominence and became widely recognized as challengers to the Crane, Fauber and Apel designed racers. Most of the contenders were powered by engines designed as marine engines, either custom built or as limited production engines built for high speed race boats by Great Lakes area manufacturers such Sterling (Buffalo), Leighton (Syracuse) and Van Blerck (Detroit/Monroe). A new dynasty of boats designed by Chris Smith and John Hacker dominated power boat racing and runabout styles for the next 20 years.

In 1912 Detroit hosted a birthday party regatta for itself called the *Cadillaqua Championship*. For the first time in Detroit, classes were distinctly divided into groups of hydroplanes and displacement hulls. Great things had been expected of New York Yacht Club Commodore J. Stuart Blackton's *Baby Reliance III*, a 20-foot hydroplane built by Chris Smith and powered by a 12-cylinder,150-hp Van Blerck engine. She had made a phenomenal record earlier at the Mississippi Valley Regatta in Davenport, Iowa but, was unable to start the second heat in Detroit. The star of the event was *Kitty Hawk II*, a 26-foot hydroplane designed and built by John Hacker with a Van Blerck engine that won the 40-mile championship in a sensational race against Carl Fisher's (co-founder of the Indianapolis Speedway) *Eph*, designed and built by Chris Smith, and Lawrence Buhl's *Neptune*, another John Hacker design. *Neptune* was ahead until she caught a steamship's wake and sank. Another contender was *Thelma IV* owned by the Thelma Motor Works of Detroit.

At the three day regatta of the Motor Boat Club of Buffalo, September 12, 13 and 14, 1912, *Baby Reliance II* swept the field winning both the 30-mile free-for-all, the championship for boats under 32 feet, and the overall International Interlake Championship. With a course speed of 46.75 mph, the 20-foot *Baby Reliance II*, powered by an 8-cylinder 150-hp Sterling engine, claimed the title of the fastest boat in the country.

Maple Leaf IV took the Harmsworth back to England in 1912

By contrast, the 1912 Harmsworth Race was a dramatic reminder that relying on speed alone was risky. Neither *Ankle Deep*, *Baby Reliance II*, nor *Baby Reliance III* had the combination of speed and endurance to beat E. Mackay Edgar's *Maple Leaf IV*, the third of her name to represent England's challenge. Consequently, in 1912 Edgar took the Harmsworth Trophy across the Atlantic and back to England.

In December 1912, *Yachting* magazine published "The Strife for Speed and What It has Accomplished," by Dickson Wylie. Without getting into the material and design details, Wylie made the argument that real advancement in speed on the water, under sail or in power boats, was due to wealthy racing men, whose utter disregard of expenses paid for the experimental work. He noted that the first real power boat racers appeared in 1904, and pushed the speed record for gasoline engine powered boats to 26.5 mph. Over the next eight years the speed nearly doubled to 45.22 mph, narrowly edging out the water speed record previously held by large steam powered boats with engine horse power rated in the thousands. The costs were staggering but, the resulting innovations in aerodynamics and technical engineering provided great benefit to builders of all types of gasoline powered vehicles on land and sea.

The contrast in dimensions of defenders *Ankle Deep* and *Baby Reliance II* dramatically marked an end to the era of Clinton Crane type displacement hulls and heralded the emergence of the Smith and Hacker designs that dominated the next era.

Over time planning hulls became the norm for most all pleasure boats, and the super-charged, hemispherical-heads and other innovations used on experimental marine engines built for the real racers were adopted by automobile engineers as well. Marine and automobile engine manufacturers continued to learn from each other, both on and off the race courses, for years to come. However, it would be another decade before American automobile manufacturers would again hope to promote their engines by way of power boat racing.

While custom hydroplane hulls and limited production high speed marine engines were transforming speed boat racing, reliability was always on the mind of yachtsmen, fisherman and others who depended on their marine engines to get them out and back safely. Production marine engine manufacturers wanted publicity for their reliability off the race course. Long Distance Reliability Cruises helped to prove that small gasoline engines were a reliable alternative in a world that was still largely based on steam or sail power for long distance boating.

In 1908 Detroit marine engine manufacturer and publisher, William Scripps sponsored a "reliability cruise" across Lake Erie, beginning in Detroit and ending at Buffalo. He said the purpose was to place a penalty on defective design, material and workmanship, and to promote the building of reliable boats and motors. In 1911 he sponsored a 600-mile reliability cruise that crossed both Lake Erie and Lake Ontario, beginning in Detroit and ending at Hamilton, Ontario.

For 1912 Scripps planned a dramatic 6,000 mile race against the elements in a sturdy little boat powered only by a 16-hp heavy-duty internal combustion marine engine. Scripps believed that if successful, the voyage would prove an object lesson for the whole world and would help hurry along the adoption of that type of motor as the universal marine engine.

For the challenge he commissioned the Mathews Boat Company to build a boat strong

enough to cross the Atlantic but, small enough to be noteworthy. For additional news worthiness, the Skipper of the voyage was Thomas Fleming Day, a veteran of long distance cruises under power and sail and the Publisher of *The Rudder* magazine.

On June 25, 1912, the double ended 35-foot *Detroit* was launched. The engine selected was a stock 2-cylinder, 4-cycle, 16-hp Scripps marine engine. The little craft carried 1,200 gallons of gasoline, 75 gallons of oil, 150 gallons of water and a crew of four with gear and provisions. To add some additional stability there was a 24-foot mast carrying a modest 240 square

Courtesy Dossin Great Lakes Museum

feet of sail. The 6,000 mile voyage from Detroit to St. Petersburg, Russia, was made all the more dramatic as the supposedly invincible ocean liner *Titanic* sank only a few months earlier. The voyage successfully proved to the world that the small, American built, gasoline engine was entirely reliable.

1912 can be said to have marked the end of the prototype experimental era. The real racer no longer bore any practical resemblance to the earlier speed launches that carried friends and family for leisurely voyages when not participating in motor boat regattas. The gasoline marine engine had earned a reputation as a reliable source of power for both high speed and long distance performance.

The new era would be equally exciting and innovative, and Detroit motormen would remain very much at the center of the activity.

References:

"Au Revoir," Power Boat News, October 7, 1905

"The Country Club Regatta," Boating, September 1907

Crane, Clinton, "Clinton Crane's Yachting Memories," D. Van Nostrand Co., Ny 1952

"Detroit Motor Boat Club's Splendid Regatta," PowerBoating, August 1908

Fostle, D. W., Speedboat, Mystic Seaport Museum Stores, 1988

Gamble, Hugh S. "Growth and Trend of Power Boat Racing," Yachting, august 1909

"Gold Challenge Cup Races of the American Power Boat Association," PowerBoat News, September, 1906

"Gold Challenge Cup," The Rudder, September 1907

"More Auto Boat Races," Motor Boat, July 1904

"Power Boat Race on Lake Erie for Rudder Cup," The Rudder, August 1906

"Rainmaker – A Fast One," Motor Boat 1908

"Six Shooter," PowerBoat News, May 20,1905

"Sparrow: A Remarkable Little Craft," The Rudder, December, 1906

Speltz, Robert, The Real Runabouts, Graphic Publishing Co., Lake Milles, IA, 1977

Stephens, W. P., "American Power Boat Association Bold Challenge Cup," Power Boat News, September 1905

Stephens, W. P., "The Power Boat in 1904," The Rudder, December 1904

Stephens, W. P., "The Power Boat in 1905," The Rudder, December 1905

"The 1907 Regatta of the Inter-Lake Yachting Association," Boating, August 1907

"The 1908 Regatta of the Inter-Lake Yachting Association," PowerBoating, September 1908

"The 1909 Inter-Lake Yachting Association Regatta," Yachting, November 1909

"The Development of High-Speed Launch or Automobile Boat," Scientific American, March 1904

APPENDICES

Guide to reference abbreviations found in the Appendices:

AGE: Wendel, C. H. "American Gasoline Engines Since 1872," MBI Publishing Company, Osceola, WI, 1999

AMUM: May, George S., "A Most Unique Machine," Wm. B. Eermans Publishing Co., Grand Rapids, MI, 1975

Bay City Directory: "Bay City Directory," R. L. Polk & Co., Detroit, MI

BLIS: "Annual Report of the Bureau of Labor and Industrial Statistics," State of Michigan, Lansing, MI

Boating: "Boating," The Penton Publishing Co., Cleveland, OH

Book of Detroiter: Marquis, Albert N., Editor, The Book of Detroiters, A Biographical Directory of Leading Living Men of the Dity of Detroit, A. N. Marquis & Company, Chicago, 1908

Detroit Directory: "Detroit City Directory," R. L. Polk & Co., Detroit, MI

Gas Engine: "Gas Engine," a monthly magazine, The Gas Engine Publishing Co., Cincinnati, OH

Hiscox: Hiscox, Gardner D., "Gas, Gasoline, and Oil Engines, including Producer Gas Plants," 18th Edition, The Norman W. Henley Publishing Company, New York, NY, 1910

Homfeld: Homfeld, Max, F., "753 Manufacturers of Inboard Marine Engines, Privately Published, St. Michaels, MD 1991

Lansing Directory: "Lansing City Directory," Chilson, McKinley & Co., Lansing, MI

MDL: "Annual Report of the Michigan Department of Labor," State of Michigan, Lansing, MI

MotorBoat: "MotorBoat," The Motor Boat Publishing Company, NY, NY

MSA: "Abstracts of Reports of Corporations," Michigan State Archives, Lansing, MI

MSG: "Michigan State Gazateer and Business Directory," R. L. Polk & Co., Detroit, MI

OME: Grayson, Stan, "Old Marine Engines, The World of the One-Lunger," Devereuz Books, Marblehead, MA, 1998

Power Boating:

REO: May, George S. "R. E. Olds, Auto Industry Pioneer," Wm. B. Eerdmans Publishing Co., Grand Rapids, 1977.

SCAC: Kimes, Beverly Rae, and Clark, Henry Austin, "Standard Catalog of American Cars (1805-1942)," 3rd Edition, Krause Publications, Inc., Iola, WI, 1996

Saginaw Directory: "Saginaw Directory," R. L. Polk & Company, Detroit, MI

Szudarek: Szudarek, Robert G. "How Detroit Became the Automotive Capital,"(Warren, MI: 1996.)

The Rudder: "The Rudder", The Rudder Publishing Company, New York (formerly Watertown), NY

Yachting: Yachting, Outing Publishing Company, New York, NY

Algonac Machine & Boat Works
Algonac
This was a boat-building and engine manufacturing firm that began sometime prior to 1915 but did not incorporate until the first week of July 1921 The president, Jan Matthijs Smits, Jr., was an electrical and mechanical engineer who graduated from the University of Constance in Germany and was a member of the Royal Engineering Society of Holland. Smits married Cordelia Currie of Algonac in 1915, at which time he was listed as owner of the firm.

In early December 1921, Algonac Machine & Boat Works took over the equipment of the Hess Marine Motor Company, formerly of Detroit. The company filed its notice of dissolution in the week ended May 24, 1924.

Four-Cycle

Trade Name	R.P.M.	H.P	Weight	Year	Notes
				1915	
Hess Mono	900	5	225	1921	High tension magneto ignition

Sources: Algonac Courier, December 31, 1915, p. 1.
Motor Boating December 1920 or 1921, pp 45-46
MSG 1917; 1919-1920; 1921-1922; 1923-1924.

Alpha Motor & Foundry Company
Detroit, Michigan

Trade Name	R.P.M.	H.P.	Weight	Year	Notes
				1911	

Sources: Motor Boating, December 1911, p. 75.
Motor Boat, February 25, 1912, p. 216.

American Boat Company: See listing for Gray-Hawley
Detroit

American Engine Company
Detroit
410 Boston St
The company claimed to have been in business since 1892.

Two and Four-Cycle

Trade Name	H.P.	Weight	Year	Notes
			1910	
American-Detroit			1914	"Now Sold Direct"
American	2.5 - 30	140-600	1921	2 port, jump spark ignition

Sources: Motor Boat, December 1910, p. 205
               Motor Boating, December, 1914; December; December 1921
               OME, 188
               Yachting Ad, 1912

Arrow Machine Works
Detroit

Trade name	R.P.M.	H.P.	Weight	Year	Notes
				1911	

Sources: Motor Boating, December 1911, p. 73.

Auto Marine Appliance Company
Detroit
685 Atwater
The company was organized to manufacture engines and other equipment. Incorporation occurred on March 6, 1909, with a capital of $100,000. Officers of the firm in 1910 consisted of M. W. Marshall as president; T. J. McCarthy, vice-president; and Frederick McNaughton as secretary-treasurer.

Trade name	H.P.	Weight	Year	Notes
			1911	

Sources: Detroit City Directory, 1911

Baird & Henselwood Company
Baird Machine & Manufacturing Company
Detroit
51-53 Fort Street East and subsequently at 26 Goebel
The company was advertising by 1908. William J. Baird was president and treasurer of the firm, with Andrew Baird as vice-president and Crawford Baird as secretary. Baird also owned and operated W. J. Baird & Company, a firm specializing in machinery. In 1910 they were offering sets of castings, forgings and blueprints for the "Yale" marine engine. The idea appears to have met with poor success, perhaps because the machine work required was too complicated for the average shop.

Trade Name	R.P.M.	H.P.	Weight	Year	Notes
Yale		9		1908	

Sources: AGE, p 44
               Motor Boat, July 10, 1908, p. 120.
               Detroit City Directory, 1911; 1912

Belle Isle Launch & Power Co.
Detroit
This enterprise may have been a predecessor of the Belle Isle Motor Co. C.B. Merriam
was cited as the manager of the company in a newspaper article in 1902.
Source: "Handicap in Power Racing," Detroit Free Press, August 17, 1902.

Belle Isle Motor Company, - 1907
Concrete Form & Engine Company, 1911
New Belle Isle Motor Company, 1911
Belle Isle Boat and Engine Co.
Detroit
Foot of Parkview Ave (later known as Motor Boat Lane)
By 1907 the officers of the Belle Isle Motor Company
were E. R. Ryno, Pres & GM, Wm B. Gregory, V.P.,
and R. H. Franchot, Sec-Treasurer. The firm merged
with Collapsible Steel Form Company and
reincorporated on January 1, 1911, as the Concrete Form
& Engine Company. The 1911 Detroit City Directory listed
the "New Belle Isle Motor Company" at the same address.

The American Boat Company, incorporated in 1912, shared a common address with the
Gray-Hawley Manufacturing Company on Motor Boat Lane. By 1923 American Boat
Company appears to have been affiliated with the Belle Isle Boat and Engine Company.
William B. Gregory was then president of both companies and Edgar M. Gregory was
vice-president and treasurer of the American Boat Company; Cora M. Zimmer was
secretary. The American Boat Company forfeited its Michigan charter and filed for
dissolution on May 28, 1924.

Two-Cycle

Trade name	H.P.	Weight	Year	Notes
Skidoo	2	52	1907	Sold with knock-down "Skidoo" boat frames and plans
Little Hammer			1907	
Belle Isle	2.5-10	73 –210	1911	
Belle Isle			1914	
Belle Isle			1915	Manufactured by Concrete Form & Eng

Sources: Boating, 1907, p 55
Motor Boating, December 10, 1911, pp. 156, 371; December, 1914
Detroit City Directory, 1911
Pike, Howard A., "How to Build an 18-Ft. Launch" (a brochure from the Belle
Isle Motor Company, c. 1907) Library of Michigan, Rare Book Collection.

The Beilfuss Motor Company:
Organized by Richard A. Beilfuss in Detroit in 1902. The company relocated to Lansing
in 1904.
See listing in "Other Michigan Marine Engine Builders" for more details.

C. H. Blomstrom Company, 1901
C. H. Blomstrom Motor Company, 1904
Blomstrom Manufacturing Company, 1906
Detroit
64 Second   (1901)
1284-1294 Riverside St (1903)
75 Clark (1904)
Leib & Wight (1906)

From "Our Friends as We See 'Em"

Carl H. Blomstrom is an extraordinary example of the pioneer motormen in Detroit that built small gas engines for boats and automobiles. He built both. Reportedly he built his first marine engine in 1891. While he was employed by the Lake Shore Engine Works in Marquette, Michigan he received several patents for two cycle marine engines, one each in 1900 and 1901.

In 1901 he relocated to Detroit and it was reported that in September 1902 he build a new factory and installed machinery to manufacture forty engines and eight boat hulls daily. His idea was to manufacture small low-powered boats in such numbers that they could be sold cheaply. About the first of January 1903 the $100 power boat was put on the market and by the first of April *Sail and Sweep* magazine was reporting that 300 had been sold, some with contracted hulls but, presumably all with Blomstrom engines.

In 1903 the company offered the $100 power boat as a fifteen and one-half foot hull equiped with a three-quarter horsepower engine, it also offered the same boat with a one and one-half horsepower engine for $125. Company advertisements also offered additional hulls and engines alone in sizes ranging from the three-quarter to eighty horsepower. In 1904 the company reported employing 69 people and during a State of Michigan canvas of boat builders conducted sometime in 1905 the company claimed to have built 200 boats that year to date with a value of $12,000. About that time the company published a fifty-five page catalog as the *"C. H. Blomstrom Motor Company, Builders of Gasoline Launches, Marine Gasoline Engines, Solid and Reversing Propeller Wheels, Office and Works at River Street and Clark Avenue, Detroit, Michigan."* Details are sketchy but, by early 1905, the lure of the automobile business began to absorb most of his efforts.

In addition to mass producing marine engines and launches, Blomstrom was also responsible for no fewer than five different automobile brands. He built his first experimental car in 1897 and another in 1899. By the end of 1903 he had built 25 small single-cylinder automobiles that he named after himself. It is not known when he stopped building boats and marine engines but in 1905 he was clearly well known as a business leader and the manufacturer of both boats and cars, as indicated by the caricature shown above.

Blomstrom's boat & engine factory after expansion to manufacture the Queen

In October 1904 the Blomstrom Manufacturing Company was incorporated. The Corporate Secretary was identified as Samuel R. Kaufman of Marquette, Michigan, presumably a member of the Kaufman family that owned the Lake Shore Engine Works and the community bank in Marquette. (From 1896 to 1901 Blomstrom had been employed by the Lake Shore Engine Works. In 1908 he was reported to be the manager of that company.) By the end of 1906 that company is known to have produced 1,500 automobiles designed by Blomstrom and marketed as the Queen. At that time the company merged with Car DeLuxe, with the Kaufman family evidently in control. The new company dropped the Blomstrom name, even as it consolidated operations at that company's factory at 75 Clark Avenue and the Detroit River. The new company ceased operations by the end of 1909 and the assets were sold to the Everitt- Metzgar-Flanders Company (EMF) before it was absorbed by Studebaker.

In August 1906 Carl Blomstrom incorporated the Blomstrom Manufacturing Company and occupied and 3-story brick factory at Leib & Wight Streets in Detroit. The new company manufactured the Blomstrom 30 that was described in the press as "the last thing in motor car design throughout." The Bloomstrom 30 was discontinued after 1908 as Blomstrom's interest shifted to the Gyroscope automobile he was building in another area of the factory. Only a few Gyroscopes were manufactured in 1908-09 before he decided to abandon the automobile and instead concentrate on the unique Gyroscope engine that featured a vertical crankshaft and horizontal flywheel. It was reported that the running of the vertical engine created a gyroscope effect that resulted in less vibration and a smother operation.

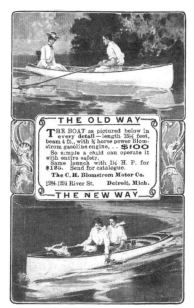

Never without ideas, in 1913 Blomstrom was the designer and one of the principal stockholders of the Rex Motor Company. Produced only in 1914, the Rex featured front-wheel drive and a competitive price of $395. At only 580 pounds, the fourteen horsepower engine reportedly attained speeds of over forty-five mph. In 1917 Blomstrom appeared in New Jersey with the Frontmobile, another front-wheel drive automobile. The Frontmobile was an elegant looking roadster but, reportedly it was hopelessly complicated and patents were pending on virtually every element. It did not survive beyond 1918. Bloomstrom tried to revive the vehicle with a new company, Camden Motors Corporation, but that venture was liquidated in 1922. He died in February 1923.

Trade Name	R.P.M.	H.P.	Weight	Year	Notes
Blomstrom				1901	
Blomstrom	600	¾ - 80		1903	$100 power launch
Queen				1905	Automobiles

Sources: AGE, pp 61, 270
            Book of Detroiters, 1908, page 65
            Catalog, The C. H. Blomstrom Motor Company, 190?. Library of Michigan,
               Rare Book Collect.
            Michigan Bureau of Labor and Industrial Statistics, 1906, pp. 373, 375
            "Our Friends as We See "Em", Newspaper Cartoonists' Association of
               Michigan, 1905
            Sail and Sweep, The Illustrated American Magazine of Aquatic Sports", Vol.
               II, No 4, Ap. 1903
            The American Boating Directory—1906 (Cleveland, OH: Penton Publishing
               Co., 1906.) p. 9
            SCAC, p 133, 253, 254, 619, 664, 665, 887, 1255
            Szudarek, p 93, 94, 131, 286

Bosserdet Yacht & Engine Company: See listing for Smith - Bosserdet
Detroit
Jefferson Avenue at the foot of Parkview Avenue (Motor Boat Lane)
This company, incorporated on October 13, 1910 with R. R. Mitchell as president and
Henry C. Bosserdet as the treasurer and manager. The company appears to have been
the successor to the Smith-Bosserdet Motor Company that was operated by Henry C.
Bosserdet in 1908.

By 1911, Richard B. Chase was president of the firm; Alfred E. Bosserdet, vice-president;
Harry S. Ayers, secretary and Henry Bosserdet, treasurer. In 1915 Randall H. Mitchell
was president again and Harry S. Ayers was secretary.

The company forfeited its Michigan charter and filed for dissolution on August 3, 1917.

Trade Name	R.P.M.	H.P.	Weight	Year	Notes
Bosserdet				1910	

Sources: Detroit City Directory, 1911
          MSG, 1911-1915

Brushmarine: See Wilpen Co. (1911)

Buick Auto-Vim and Power Company, 1899
Buick Manufacturing Company, 1901
Buick Motor Company, 1903
Detroit/Flint
416 Howard, Detroit
West Kearsley Street, Flint
Buick Motor Company was formed by David Dunbar Buick, who in the 1880s and 1890s
had been a successful inventor and manufacturer of plumbing and sanitary fixtures (Buick
& Sherwood Manufacturing Co.). Most importantly he was credited with inventing the
American process for bonding porcelain to cast iron. As early as 1896 Buick became
interested in the internal combustion engine and began experimenting soon thereafter. In

1899 he sold out his interest in Buick & Sherwood and organized the Buick Auto-Vim and Power Company to build gasoline engines for farm and marine use. However, the first known listing for the company in the 1900 Detroit phone book describes their expertise as "Gas & Gasoline Engines & Automobiles" but, there is no indication he had any serious interest in automobiles. In 1899 Buick was the vice-commodore of the Detroit Yacht Club when he met Walter L. Marr. Reportedly Marr was working with some friends on a motor for a speedboat when Buick first noticed his talents. Buick hired him on the spot and made him foreman at Buick Auto-Vim and Power Company. Marr once said he built the first marine motors for David Buick, including one that beat everything in the 24-foot class on the Detroit River. Buick Auto-Vim and Power Company reorganized as the Buick Manufacturing Company in 1901 and became the Buick Motor Company in 1903.

1903 Buick marine engines as they appear in the 1903 catalog, 2-cycle, left, 4-cycle, right

The earliest known catalog for the Buick Manufacturing Company of Detroit, 1902, and the first for Buick Motor Company of Flint, 1904, both described the companies as "Manufacturers of Stationary, Marine, Automobile, Gas and Gasoline Engines." Neither catalog mentioned any Buick automobiles. Buick automobiles would become well known only after W. C. Durant gained control of the company in 1904. The 1903 catalog offered both 2 and 4 cycle marine engines. The first known ad to feature a Buick automobile did not appeared until the October 1904 issue of Cycle and Automobile Trade Journal, which had previously published ads for the Buick engines.

Trade Name	Model	cylinders	RPM	HP	Year	Notes: Name Changes
					1899	Buick Auto-Vim and Power
					1901	Buick Manufacturing Co
Buick	2 cycle	1	600	1	1903	Buick Motor Company
	4 cycle	1		10	1903	

Sources: Catalog, Buick Manufacturing Company, Detroit, 1902
Catalog, Buick Motor Company, Flint, 1903
Cycle and Automobile Trade Journal ad, 1904
Detroit Phone Directory 1900
Detroit Directory 1899
Dunham, Terry B., and Gustin, Lawrence R., "The Buick, A Complete History," Automotive Heritage and Communications, LLC, 2002, p 13, 21

Caille Perfection Motor Company
Detroit
1336 Second Ave (1907)
The Caille Brothers are credited with developing the automatic gaming "slot" machines and in 1904 an early attempt at automobile manufacturing with the "Du Brie – Caille."

Inboard marine engine manufacturing began in 1906. Later they produced the "Neptune" brand of outboard motors. Officers of the company in 1912 consisted of A. Arthur Caille as president; Adolph Caille, vice-president; Edgar Elliott, secretary; and Theo. L. Smith, manager. In 1912 they offered a 1.5 hp horizontal 4-cycle stationary engine for $48. In 1914 their advertising claimed they were the "World's Largest Builders of Two-Cycle Marine Motors." At some time they also offered four-cycle engines under the brand name "Aistocrat."

Two-Cycle

Trade Name	R.P.M.	H.P.	Weight	Year	Notes
Perfection		21/2 -3		1906	
Perfection		2-12	300	1908	2 hp $45 complete; 5 hp $95; 6 hp 2-cyl $160
Caille	6-800	2-30	90-200	1911	
Neptune				1914	2.5 & 3 hp Outboard
Caille	500-1000	21/2-30	140-600	1921	2-port, jump spark ignition*
Motorbo				1922	Made for Sears Roebuck and Co.

Sources: Motor Boating, December, 1914; December 1915
Popular Mechanics ad, 1906
Rudder Ad, 1907,
Power Boating, 1908, p 158, 275
SCAP, p 494

Columbia Engine Company – See listing for Detroit Engine Co.
Detroit
26 Mt. Elliott Ave.
Columbia Engine Company was a marine engine manufacturing firm that was part of a group of engine and boat building firms owned by Hugo Scherer and Frederick E. Wadsworth, including Thrall Motor Company; Detroit Engine Works; Detroit Boat Company, Michigan Steel Boat Company and Detroit Motor Car Supply Company, all located at the same address.

Trade Name	cylinders	H.P.	Weight	Year	Notes
Columbia	1,2	2-50		1912	

Sources: AGE, p 103
             Yachting Ad, 1912

Concrete Form & Engine Company: See listing for Belle Isle Motor Company

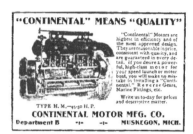

Continental Motor Manufacturing Company
Continental Motors Corporation
Muskegon/Detroit

The company was founded in 1905 in Muskegon by two brothers-in-law, Ross Judson and Arthur Tobi, to build a four-cycle, four-cylinder automotive engine featuring an in-line, L-head configuration. Subsequently they supplied engines for marine, aviation and stationary applications. At the 1908 Chicago Boat Show the company exhibited a 40 hp, 4-cylinder 4-cycle "auto-Marine" engine that weighted 725 pounds (18 lbs/hp). *Power Boating* magazine reviewed the engine and noted that it lived up to the company's high grade reputation in the automobile trade. In 1927 they produced their first aircraft engine, a converted Wright nine-cylinder radial. Two years later they introduced an original design, seven-cylinder radial, Model A70. After 1929 all Continental marine engines were conversions made by Gray Marine Motor Company. In 1944 Gray Marine Motor Co became a wholly owned subsidiary. In 1969 the company itself was acquired by Teldyne and Gray was promptly divested. The company slowly moved out of Michigan and by 1980 closed its last Michigan plant in Muskegon.

Four-Cycle

Trade Name	cylinders	R.P.M.	H.P.	Weight	Year	Notes
Continental			40-50		1908	Muskegon
	4	1,000	20-55		1911	
Reliance-Continental					1914	Detroit

Sources: Motor Boat, July 10, 1908, p. 11
             Motor Boating, December 1911, p. 76; December, 1914, February 1926, p. 287
             Power Boating 1908

Claus: See International Motor Company (1908)

Cragg: See listing for Gilmore-Cragg Motor Manufacturing Company (1912)
          and Park Motor Works, Inc. (1914)

M. O. Cross Engine Company
Detroit
830 Bellevue (1908)
This company may have begun making engines as early as 1895. A 1907 ad in *The Rudder* claimed that the company was established in 1895 and a 1908 ad claimed they had passed the test of 12 years hard running by all classes of people. A 1904 advertisement noted that the Cross engines were suitable for both marine and stationary use.

Four Cycle

Trade Name	H.P.	Year	Notes
Cross	2-150	1907	Company dates to 1895 A Cross engine powered "Let-Me-C" was entered in the 1907 Country Club of Detroit Regatta

Sources: AGE, p 113
Lloyds' Register of American Yachts, 1912.
Power Boating Ad, 1908
Rudder Ad, 1907

Delray Motor Works
Detroit
An 8 hp Delray engine was illustrated in the *Automobile Trade Journal*, March 1, 1908. The cylinder jackets and all the intake and water pipes were made of brass indicating that it was designed for marine use.

Trade name	cylinders	R.P.M.	H.P.	Weight	Year	Notes
	4		225		1908	Retailed for $225

Source: AGE, p 125

Detroit Aeroplane Company
Detroit
897 Canfield
The company was incorporated in 1910 with offices located at 607 Breitmeyer Building. Frederick Weinberg was president of the firm and Curt Weinberg the secretary-treasurer. Frederick also served as the construction engineer for the company.

Two-Cycle

Trade Name	Model	cylinders	R.P.M.	H.P.	Weight	Year	Notes
		2	1,2	1,000	1-3	44-64	1911

Sources: Detroit City Directory, 1911; 1912

Detroit Auto-Marine Company
Detroit
65 E. Congress St.
A 1906 advertisement noted that the company was formerly "Detroit Lackawana Company." It is likely that the company began as an affiliate of the Lackawana Motor Company from Lackawana, New York.

Two Cycle

Trade Name	cylinders	R.P.M.	H.P.	Weight	Year	Notes
			1-20		1906	

Source: Detroit Yacht Club's Annual Free-For-A;; "Sweepstakes," program, September, 1906

Detroit Auto Specialty Company, Inc.
Detroit
909-911 Greenwood (1911)
The company was incorporated September 30, 1905, with a capital of $75,000. Oscar C. Schimmel was president of the company, with Bernard Ginsburg as vice-president and Joseph L. Maniere as secretary and treasurer.

Two-Cycle

Trade name	cylinders	R.P.M.	H.P.	Weight	Year	Notes
Liberty	1,2	7-900	1.5-14	50-300	1911	
Liberty Dwarf					1911	

Sources: Detroit City Directory, 1911
OME, 197

Detroit Engine Works
Detroit
1250-1280 Jefferson Avenue (1909)
Indications are that the company may have been organized as early as 1896 to build 2-cycle engines for marine and stationary use. Hugo Scherer was president of the firm with Frederick E. Wads-

worth as secretary and treasurer. Scherer and Wadsworth also owned and managed the Detroit Motor Car Supply Company, Thrall Motor Company, Columbia Engine Company, Detroit Boat Company (Blue Bird line of boats) and the Michigan Steel Boat Co. In 1907 the

Michigan Steel Boat Company offered steel rowboats for $20 and a 16 foot launch with engine for $96 complete. That same year the Detroit Boat Company claimed to be the largest manufacturer of pleasure boats in the world.

In 1908 the Detroit Engine Works advertised a surplus 2-hp 1907 model for $29.50 and claimed 10,000 in use. Reportedly all "Detroit" boats were powered by "Detroit" engines.

Two-Cycle

Trade name	cylinders	H.P.	Weight	Year	Notes
		3,5,7,10		1907	
Detroit	1,2	2 - 20	85 - 425	1911	
Detroit	1,2	2-50		1914	Kerosene Marine Engines offered

Four-Cycle

Trade Name	cylinders	R.P.M.	H.P.	Weight	Year	Notes
Detroit	4	50/900	40	650	1911	

Sources: AGE, p. 130-132
Boating, 1907, pp 41, 79
Detroit City Directory, 1911
Field & Stream, April 1909
Motor Boat, January 10, 1915
Motor boating, December, 1914; December 1915
Power Boating ad, December, 1908

Detroit Gas Engine & Machinery Co: See Strelinger Engine Co
Detroit
81 E. Congress (1906)
The Rudder reported in March 1906 that the company claimed they were building 10,000 engines that year, "complete from foundry to user." The date of origin is unknown but the enterprise is believed to have originated by 1898. Oliver Barthel, one of the best known engine designers of the time, reportedly designed the early engines.

In 1907 they advertised that they built and sold 5,000 engines in 1906 and were said to be building 10,000 engines that year. By the end of the year they were in receivership and sold to the Strelinger Marine Engine Co.

Trade name	H.P.	Weight	Year	Notes
	1-20	1@37.5	1905	"Convert your rowboat to a launch" 1hp $37 (11/2 hp $32.15 engine only)
Major	1.5-25		1907	

Sources: AGE, p 131
            Boating, 1907, p 58
            Operating Manual, 1907, Dossin Great Lakes Museum
            OME, p 198
            Rudder, December 1905; March 1906

Detroit Motor Car Supply Company – See listing for Detroit Engine Works
Detroit
1270-1280 Jefferson Avenue
Detroit Motor Car Supply Company was one of the many engine and boat building companies owned and operated by Hugo Scherer and Frederick E. Wadsworth. In 1912 this company offered the "Shadow" marine engine that appears to have been a re-branded "Detroit" engine.

Trade Name	R.P.M.	H.P.	Weight	Year	Notes
Shadow				1912	

Sources: Motor Boating, December 1912, p. 30.
            OME, 198

MAX DINGFELDER

AUTOMOBILE and
YACHT.....

GasolineEngines

Manufacturer
Repairs and
Supplies.

958 JEFFERSON AVE.

Dingfelder Motor Company
Detroit
958 Jefferson
Foot of Crane Avenue
Max Dingfelder advertised as "Builders of Marine Motors, Complete Auto Pleasure and Work Boats." As early as 1903 he manufactured a number of small two-passenger automobiles that weighed 500 lbs and had a 3-1/2 horsepower one-cylinder engine. The automobile received a good review in *Cycle and Automobile Trade*, June, 1903. In 1906 he won a race sponsored by the Detroit Yacht Club with his boat named *999*.

In 1907 a four-cycle, four-cylinder, 34.5 horsepower Dingfelder motor was used in a 40-foot yacht named *Shabadagee* in the Detroit Country Club Regatta. That same year an article titled "Motor Boating in Detroit" noted that the Detroit Yacht Club's ferry was a 48-foot launch equipped with a 30 hp Dingfelder engine.

Little information is available after the first annual Detroit Motor Boat Show in 1908 where Dingfelder Motor Company exhibited a line of marine engines that included a six cylinder of 60 horsepower, a four cylinder of 30-40 hp. and a two cylinder of 15-20 hp.

Four-Cycle

Trade Name	cylinders	H.P.	Weight	Year	Notes
	1	3.5		1903	
Dingfelder	2,4,6	15 - 60		1908	

Sources: Motor Boat, September 25, 1907, pp 1-4
           Motor Boating, April 1908, pp 183-189
           Detroit City Directory, 1909
           Szudarek, p. 79.

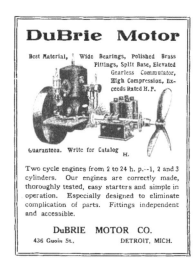

Du Brie Motor Company
Detroit
428-446 Guoin St. (1906)
Stanley Du Brie was one of the best known designers of two cycle marine engines at the turn of the century. He graduated as a mechanical engineer from the University of Ohio in 1896 and soon thereafter built an automobile and established the Du Brie Motor Works in Freemont, Ohio, for the manufacture of 2-cycle marine engines of his design. In 1900 he sold the business and built an experimental automobile for the Charles Beck Manufacturing Company in Penetog, Ontario. About the same time he also designed a 2-cycle marine engine for Peter Payette Company, also in Penetog, reportedly Canada's largest manufacture of gasoline marine engines at the time.

By 1904 he had relocated to Detroit and built a prototype Du Brie – Caille automobile that used his 2-cycle engine, but there is no indication that production followed. However, it did receive a rave review in *Cycle and Automobile Trade*, by Hugh Dolnar, one of the leading automobile journalist at that time.   (By 1906 Caille was manufacturing its own line of marine engines.)

Reportedly Du Brie marketed 10 engine sizes in 1906.   In 1905 he designed the first engine for the Gray Motor Company and most likely was the contract manufacture for all of their engines in 1906 and some in 1907. (In 1906 Du Brie and Gray used the same address.)

 Reporting on the new Peerless engine in 1907 *Boating* magazine noted that it was the latest DuBrie design, the result of 15 years of practical experience. They went on the say: "*Among the engines which Mr. Du Brie designed are the Sandusky, the Payette, one of the most popular engines in Canada today; De Loach, a 2 cycle, 2 cylinder automobile motor, the Du Brie - Caille, the first 2 cycle auto with direct drive; the Bense marine and stationary engine, the Waterloo, and in 1905 he designed the engine which bears his name and the following year, the Gray motor.*" At the time of the 1908 Detroit Motor Boat Show, S. A. Commons was the Secretary of the company. A 3-cylinder DuBrie engine powered the 26-foot boat *Zip* in the Detroit Yacht Club Long Distance Race of 1908.

In 1910 he built a prototype Templeton – Du Brie automobile with a 2 cycle engine and while there was some production it did not continue past 1910. Little is known of his activities over the next 10 years.

In the 1920's a new Du Brie Company was established in Detroit. In addition to building Du Brie designed engines, the company also marinized Ford Model T engines.

Two-Cycle

Trade name	R.P.M.	H.P.	Weight	Year	Notes
DuBrie	850	- 100	-850	1906	10 models (100 hp retail $1,000)
		2.5-27		1908	4-hp Gasoline $77.50 4-hp Kerosene $91.00

Sources: Boating, 1906, p 38; 1907, p 55
              Power Boating April, 1908, pp. 183-189
              SCAC, p 494, 1456
              The Motor Boat Ad, 1907

Ecorse Boat and Engine Works
Ecorse
An advertisement in the 1911 *Michigan State Gazetteer and Business Directory* listed the firm's services: "Ecorse Boat & Engine Works/Henry E. Suttkus, Prop./Motor Boat and Automobile Repairing/Engines Built, Bought, Sold and Exchanged/W. Jefferson Avenue/ Ecorse, Michigan."

Trade Name	R.P.M.	H.P.	Weight	Year	Notes
				1911	

Sources: MSG, 1911-1912; 1915

Edwards Motor Co.
Detroit
1181 W. Jefferson

Four-Cycle

Trade name	cylinders	R.P.M.	H.P.	Weight	Year	Notes
	2,4		2.5 - 10		1908	

Source: Power Boating Ad, 1908

Emmons Specialty Company
Detroit

Trade Name	R.P.M.	H.P.	Weight	Year	Notes
Oarsman				1913	

Sources: Motor Boating, December 1913, p. 163.

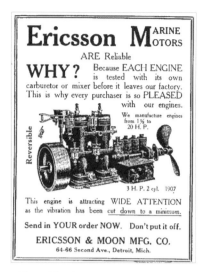

Ericsson & Moon Manufacturing Company
Detroit, Michigan
64-66 Second Ave (1907)

Two-Cycle

Trade Name	cylinders	H.P.	Weight	Year	Notes
Togo	1,2,4	1.5 - 8		1906	
Ericsson		1.5 - 20		1907	

Sources: Boating Ad, 1906; 1907

Fishback Motor Co: See listing for Thrall-Fishback
Detroit
By 1907 Fishback merged or was acquired by Thrall. The Fishback name was dropped by 1909.

Source: OME, 203

Gilmore-Cragg Motor Manu-facturing Company See listing for Park Motor Work, Inc. (1912)
Detroit
601 Wayne County Bank Building

Two-Cycle

Trade Name	R.P.M.	H.P.	Weight	Year	Notes
Cragg		1.5 - 36		1912	Three port

Source: Yachting Ad, 1912

Gray-Hawley Manufacturing Company and
Detroit
937-943 Jefferson Ave (Motor Boat Lane)
The company was incorporated in 1905 and began manufacturing engines about the same time. Officers of the firm in 1910 consisted of Emmet P. Gray as president and George E. Hawley as secretary-treasurer. In 1908 they acquired the St. Clair Motor Company of Detroit, another marine engine manufacturer.

The company was also affiliated with the American Boat Company, incorporated on October 4, 1912 and was then located at the same address. American Boat Company appears to have been affiliated with the Belle Isle Boat and Engine Company when it filed for dissolution on May 28, 1924.

According to a Gray-Hawley advertisement in the 1919 *Michigan State Gazetteer and Business Directory*, the company produced mufflers for 82 of the leading auto, truck and tractor manufacturers, with special models for Ford cars. The company listed that they also manufactured lock pedals, exhaust horns, motor boats, express cruisers, row boats and boat supplies and fittings.

Trade Name	R.P.M.	H.P.	Weight	Year	Notes
Little Skipper				1911	

Note: There was no connection between the Gray-Hawley Manufacturing Company and the Gray Motor Company.

Sources: Detroit City Directory, 1911
MSG, 1915 - 1924
OME, 205

Gray Motor Company (1905-1923)
Gray Marine Motor Company (1923-1968)
Detroit
436-442 Guoin St. (1906)
Leib & Congress (1907)
Oakland Ave, Highland Park (1910)
Mack & Belt Line (1917)
Canton & Lafayette (1923-1963)

Gray Motor Company was one of the largest and longest lasting of the early marine engine manufacturers. The company was organized by Ora J. Mulford, formerly the president of the Michigan Yacht and Power Company and the Secretary of the Sintz Gas Engine Company. When the company was incorporated in December 1905 the officers were Ora J. Mulford, president, Paul Gray, vice president and David Gray, secretary-treasurer. The first year all engines were manufactured under contract with the DuBrie Motor Co., located at the same address. The next year Gray was in its own factory but may still have contracted for some of the engine manufacturing as sales quickly exceeded the first factory's capability. A second, larger building was constructed for 1908.

The company became a subsidiary of the United States Motor Corporation (USMC) in 1910. At that time the officers were Ora J. Mulford, president; Frank Briscoe, vice-president; and E. C. Hough as secretary-treasurer. At that time the company relocated to the Oakland Avenue plant that became part of the headquarters for the Chrysler Corporation for over 50 years. USMC was forced into bankruptcy in 1912 and Mulford was able to buy back his engine company. For a few years they added stationary engines and an outboard to their product line-up.

In 1917 the company relocated to a plant on Mack at Belt Line Road, near Detroit's Eastern Market. In 1920 the company reorganized, increased its capital with new investors and manufactured of the Gray automobile from 1921 to 1926. In 1923 Mulford exchanged his investment for sole ownership of the marine engine division. The new company was reorganized as the Gray Marine Motor Company and operations relocated to the former factory of the Northern Manufacturing Company, on Canton and Lafayette, near the Belle Isle Bridge.

In the 1930s the company played a major role in moving to market the lightweight 2-cycle diesel engine that General Motors had been developing but, had not yet put into production. Gray Marine successfully demonstrated the benefits of the engines and began to market them before WWII. As a result, the Gray Marine Diesel was selected by the Navy to power the personnel Landing Craft that were so decisive in winning the war.

O. J. Mulford died in 1944 and to settle his estate, the company became a subsidiary of Continental Motors until 1969. Until 1963 Gray operated with its own factory and sales management, under the direction of John W. Mulford.. For the last five years Gray's were produced in the Continental factory in Muskegon. New engine production ceased in 1968. Subsequent companies have continued to provide repair services and parts.

Two-Cycle, Four-Cycle and Diesel

Trade Name	Years Produced	Notes
Gray	1906 - 1968	Built and marketed 2 and 4 cycle gas and diesel engines
	1910-1917	outboard and industrial engines
	1920-1926	automobiles

Sources: Author's file.
Grayson, Stan, "Engines Afloat: Volume I," Devereux Books, Marblehead, MA.

Henry Hammer
Hammer-Sommer Auto Carriage Co.
Hammer Motor Co.
Detroit
313 Riopelle
Henry Hammer was building marine engines for some time before organizing the Hammer-Sommer Auto Carriage Company in 1903 to manufacture an automobile using his 12-hp 2-cylinder engine. By December 1904 the Hammer Motor Company was organized by Henry Hammer, Leon J. Paszske, Foster F. Allen and Harry F. Nickoalds as a successor to the Hammer-Sommer Auto Carriage Co. They built marine engine and an automobile called the "Hammer" in 1905

Source: Szudarek, p 80
SCAC, p. 672

Herreshoff Motor Co.
Detroit
In 1909 Charles Frederick Herreshoff, of the famed boatbuilding family, introduced a line of automobiles powered by a 24-hp, 4-cyclinder engine that he had originally designed as a marine engine. The company slogan was *"As on blue water so on dry land pin your faith to Herreshoff."* The company closed in 1914 and Charles left Detroit to organize the Herreshoff Lite Car Company in Troy, NY. The model name was changed to "Howard" in 1915. Production ceased in 1921.

Source: SCAC, p 699

Hermann Engineering Co.
Detroit
Trade Name: Aristrocrat
Source: MotorBoating, December 1915

Hess Motor Company: See listing for Algonac Machine & Boat Works
Detroit

R. S. Hill
Detroit
78 E. Fort St (1907)
24 E. Woodbridge (1908)
In an advertisement in the 1907 Detroit City Directory, Hill described his engine as follows: *"The Engine you have been looking for; safe, sure and noiseless. A new and perfect model. Distinctly new and prominent features—such as water-cooled bearings making a large saving in grease. The grease always being stiff makes it easy to keep the engine clean. Grooved shafts prevent blowing from case. End bearings having half boxes to take up wear. Crank pins have center oilers, all bearings babbitted with the best Babbitt. Workmanship and materials the best. These new features make it a superior engine."*

Trade Name	cylinders	R.P.M.	H.P.	Weight	Year	Notes
Victor	1,2		15-20		1907	

Sources: Boating Ad, 1907
             Detroit City Directory, 1907-1908
             Power Boating Ad, 1908

Holmes-Howard Motor Co.
Detroit
Trade Name: Holmes-Howard

Source: MotorBoating, May 1915; December 1915

Frank J. Horton
Detroit

Trade Name	R.P.M.	H.P.	Weight	Year	Notes
				1913	Rotary engine

Source: Motor Boating, December 1913, p. 210.

Huron Motor Works
Detroit

Two-Cycle

Trade Name	R.P.M.	H.P.	Weight	Year	Notes
Huron		2.5		1908	$62.50 complete

Sources: Boating, 1907, p 62
           OME, 208

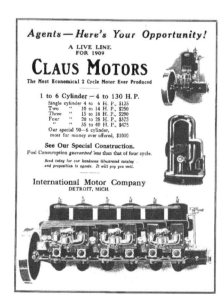

International Motor Company, Inc.
Detroit
868 Military Avenue
The company reportedly moved into a new facility by the time of the 1908 Detroit Motor Boat Show. Officers of the firm included X. B. Konkel as president and J. Lesinski as secretary. Engine designer, Claus was well known for having been the assistant superintendent of the Cadillac Automobile Company.

International Motor Company forfeited its Michigan charter and was listed as out of business in May 1910.

Two-Cycle

Trade Name	cylinders	H.P.	Year	Notes
Claus	1-6	4-130	1908	Claimed that fuel consumption was better than the best 4-cycle, "guaranteed."

Sources: MSG1909-1910
Power Boating April 1908, pp. 183-189

Kawalsky: See listing for Waterman Marine Motor Co.

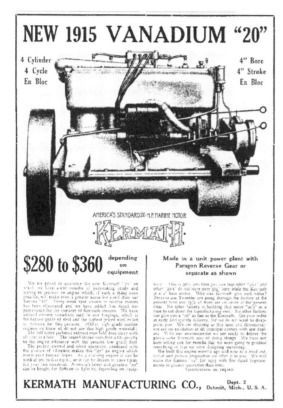

Kermath Manufacturing Company
Detroit
47 East Fort (1912)
James Kermath was the founder of the company that began manufacturing automobile parts and in 1907 built a complete car, the "Kermath Speed-Away." In 1910 they began to focus on marine engines. By 1912 Morton Engine Company was advertising the 12 hp "Kermath by Morton." Kermath may have achieved the pinnacle of progressive design improvements with the "Sea Wolf" Series introduced in 1926, an in-line 6-cylinder with overhead cams, and 4 valves per "hemi-head" cylinder.

Until the mid-30's all engine blocks and main castings were built in-house and they continued to maintain low compression ratios and non-counterbalanced crankshafts. In 1929 they combined two six cylinder Sea Wolfs on a common crankcase producing a V12 Sea Raider that reached 580 hp. In the mid 30's they began to marinize Ford and Lincoln-Mercury engines. But Kermath never used any of the high-performance V*'s that became popular and economically available after WWII. The company survived as a marine manufacturer until 1954.

Trade Name	H.P.	Year	Notes
Kermath		1912	Sole distributor was Morton Motor Co.
Kermath		1914	Vanadium 20 "America's standard 20 hp Marine Motor" $280 -360, depending on equipment

Sources: Aamodt, Jim, "Kermath – A True Classic, Part II & III", www.acb-bslol.com
Motor Boating, December, 1914; December, 1915
"Kermath, A Legend in Engines", www.mahagony bay.net
Yachting Ad, 1912

Charles B. King Company
Detroit
Charles B. King advertised engines for boats and automobiles in the first issue of "Horseless Carriage" in 1895. From about 1897 to 1900 the Charles B. King Engine Co., was a partnership with King, John S. Newberry and Henry B. Joy. Joy later led a group of investors to acquire the Packard Motor Car Co., in 1902 and relocated it to Detroit in 1903.

In February 1900 the King engine became part of the Marine Engine Department of the Olds Motor Works and King was retained as its superintendent. In 1901 the marine engine department was acquired by the Michigan Yacht & Power Company and King again was retained as the superintendent until leaving to join Jonathan Maxwell at the Northern Manufacturing Company (manufacturers of the "Silent Northern" automobile).

Four Cycle

Trade Name	R.P.M.	H.P.	Weight	Years	Notes
King				1895-1903	Used in first automobile on the streets of Detroit, 1896

Sources: Catalog, Charles B. King Engine Co., 1898
Catalog, Michigan Yacht & Power Company, 1901, second edition
King Files, National Automotive History Collection, Detroit Public Library

Krupp Marine Iron Works
Detroit

Two & Four-Cycle

Trade Name	R.P.M.	H.P.	Weight	Year	Notes
Krup		- 100		1912	

Sources: Motor Boating, July 1912.
OME, 210

Lauth Auto & Engine Company
Port Huron

Trade name	R.P.M.	H.P.	Weight	Year	Notes
				1911	

Sources: Motor Boating, December 1911, p. 83.

Leland & Faulconer Manufacturing Company
Detroit
Bates & Congress, 4th floor, 1890
Trombly & Dequinder, 1893
The company was founded in 1890 to make machine tools and gears. Soon however, they were manufacturing steam engines and about 1896 began making small marine engines for Frank J. Dimmer's boat shop at Wayne and Woodbridge Street. Later they made larger marine engines requested by Charles A. Strelinger for his retail trade (Strelinger had provided financing and space in his building to get Leland Faulconer started). In 1901 the company built transmissions and 3-hp engines for the Olds Motor Works. In 1902, the head of the company, Henry M. Leland, began managing Cadillac Motor Car Co. and built the first prototype "Cadillac" automobile in his shop. The two companies merged in 1905. In 1917 Leland organized the Lincoln Motor Co. to build Liberty aircraft engines. Following the war the surplus Liberty engines became very popular for use in "all out" race boats.. In 1922 the company was acquired by the Ford Motor Company.

Sources: 1904 Marine Buyers' Guide.
AGE, p 282
Leland, Mrs. Wilfred C. and Millbrook, "Master of Precision, Henry M. Leland," Wayne State
University Press, Detroit, MI, 1966, 1996, p 60, 61.

Liberty/Liberty Dwarf: See listing for Detroit Auto Specialty Co.

George A. Lisk
Detroit
338 Scotten (1907),
1193-1195 W. Jefferson Avenue.

By 1907 Lisk was known as a boat and marine engine builder. At the 1908 Detroit Motor Boat Show he exhibited one, two and four cylinder models of his 4-cycle engine.

Four-Cycle

Trade Name	cylinders	R.P.M.	H.P.	Weight	Year	Notes
Lisk	1,2,4		3.5-20		1907	
Lisk	1,2,3,4,6		3.5-30		1908	
Lisk	1,2,3,4,6	700	5-40	200-800	1911	
					1915	

Sources: Boating, 1907, p 54
Power Boating, April, 1908, pp. 183-189
Detroit City Directory, 1909
Motor Boat, December 1912
Motor Boating, December 1911; April, 1913; December, 1914, December, 1915

Little Giant: See listing for United Manufacturing Company (1906) and
Strelinger Marine Engine Company (1916)

Little Hammer: See Belle Isle Motor Company

Little Skipper: See St. Clair Motor Company (1907) and Gray-Hawley Manufacturing
Company (1911)

Major Marine Gas Engine Company (See Also Detroit Gas Engine and Machinery
Company)
Detroit
277 E. Jefferson

Two-Cycle

Trade name	H.P.	Weight	Year	Notes
Major Jones	1-1/2		1908	$48.50 complete

Sources: AGE, p 289

Maximotor Makers
Detroit
1524 E. Jefferson
The company occupied the former facilities of the Michigan Yacht & Power Company /
Sintz Gas Engine Company / Pungs-Finch Auto and Gas Engine Company.

Trade name	Model	R.P.M.	H.P.	Weight	Year	Notes
	A, B, C, D		40-100		1913	

Sources: Motor Boating, January 1913, p. 103; July 1913, p. 74.; December, 1914;
December, 1915
OME, 213

Modern Motor & Machine Company
Detroit
958 Jefferson Avenue
Little is known of this company except that they were building boats and engines by
1906. The company forfeited its Michigan charter and went out of business on June 20,
1911.

Trade name	R.P.M.	H.P.	Weight	Year	Notes
				1906	

Sources: The American Boating Directory—1906 (Cleveland, OH: Penton Publishing
Co.) p. 10.

Monitor Vapor Engine & Power Company
Grand Rapids / Detroit

The company began building boats and engines in Grand Rapids by 1894. The Monitor engine received a feature review in *The Rudder*, December, 1895. It appears that the company relocated to Detroit in 1900 as it was no longer listed in the Grand Rapids Directory and it was in Detroit that the company filed for dissolution on December 5, 1903. The company was re-established in Newark, NJ by George Gere, one of the original officers from 1894.
See listing in "Other Marine Engine Builders for more detail.

Morton Motor Company See listing for Kermath Manufacturing Company and

Peninsular Auto Parts Company
Detroit,
Morton began building 4-cycle marine engines in 1904. In 1912 they were marketing the new 12 hp "Kermath by Morton." and claiming to be the sole distributor. In 1918 Peninsular Auto Parts Company was marketing a "Morton" engine.

Trade Name	R.P.M.	H.P.	Weight	Year	Notes
Morton				1904	
Kermath by Morton		10-12		1912	
Morton				19148	

Sources: "Kermath, A Legend in Engines", www.mahoganybay.com
Motor Boating, December, 1914; December, 1915
OME, 219

Oakland: See Wilpen Company

PACKARD MARINE ENGINES SWEEPSTAKES MODEL

The Packard Sweepstakes Model has demonstrated its right to first place among all marine engines.

Packard Baby Gar, equipped with a Packard Sweepstakes Model Marine engine made a perfect score in the Wood-Fisher Trophy Races at Detroit, September 1922, finishing second. First place was taken by another Baby Gar of similar size but 400 lbs. lighter in weight, and powered by a motor of greater piston displacement.

Packard Baby Gar also made a perfect score in the Fisher-Allison Trophy Races at Hamilton, Ontario, August 1922, running second only to another Baby Gar with motors of approximately double the piston displacement.

PACKARD MOTOR CAR COMPANY, DETROIT

Packard Motor Car Company
Detroit

James Packard was one of America's most fascinating automobile pioneers and electrical geniuses. Before building his first internal engine he had been a champion bicycle racer, pioneer power boater (with a naphtha launch) and founder of the Packard Electrical Company. In 1899 he built his first automobile and organized the Ohio Automobile Company. By 1903 Detroit investors headed by Henry B. Joy persuaded Packard to move the company to Detroit where it was renamed the Packard Motor Car Co. (Joy had previously been a partner with C.B. King in his engine business from 1897 to 1900.)

The first known Packard marine engines were a limited production that appeared in race boats between 1904 and 1908. In 1904 they were known to power two race boats, the *Sparrow* and *Swallow*. *Sparrow* was the undisputed high performer in the 1906 APBA Gold Cup race, but lost on corrected time after much contesting over the unique 2-cycle design of the engine in *Chip II*. In 1908 H. B. Joy was reported racing his Packard Powered cruising class launch *Geisha*.

Packard built many of the WWI Liberty aircraft engines that were converted for high-performance marine use after the war. The first production marine engines that the company built appeared in 1921, the 275 hp 1M-1551 (1st Marine – 1551 cubic inches) based on one of their aircraft engines.

At Gar Wood's request Packard began converting some V-12 aero engines to defend the Harmsworth trophy in 1928. That engine work evolved into the 3M and 4M-2500 engines that powered the WWII PT boats. After the war they built the 5M-2500 V-12 and the 1M-3300 V-16, as well as smaller 6 and 8 cylinder engines for civilian use.

From 1951 to 1956 they also built diesel engines of 300-800 hp. The last of which reportedly did not leave Navy service until 1990.

Four-Cycle

Trade Name	Model	H.P.	Years Produced	Notes
Packard		34	1904	"Sparrow" Gold Cup contender
			1908	"Geisha" – H. B. Joy's race boat
	1M-1551		1921	
	1M-2500		1928	
	4M-2500		1941	Powered a PT boat 60 mph using 110
				gallons of high octane gas per hour.
	Diesel		1951	

Sources: Motor Boating, January 1925, pp. 154-155; February 1926, pp. 220-221.
       OME, p 217-218

Park Motor Works, Inc.
See listing for Gilmore-Cragg Motor Manufacturing Company (1912)
Detroit

Trade name	cylinders	R.P.M.	H.P.	Weight	Year	Notes
Gilmore					1914	

Sources: Motor Boating, December, 1914

Peerless Marine Engine Company (See Sibley-Haufley Machine Co)
Detroit (1907) / Buffalo, NY
325 Jefferson
The Motor Boat magazine reported in 1907 that "after several years of engineering" Peerless had perfected a method that prevented salt water rusting of the interior of the water jacket and had begun treating all of their engines. *Boating* magazine reported that the new engine for 1907 was designed by Stanley R. Du Brie, one of the best known two-cycle marine engine designers of the time. For reasons unknown, a short time later the company relocated to Buffalo, N.Y.

Two-Cycle

Trade Name	cylinders	R.P.M.	H.P.	Year	Notes
Peerless	1,2	550	9, 15	1907	Detroit
Peerless	2		50	1914	Buffalo

Note: the relationship with the Peerless Motor Company of Lansing (acquired by the Acme Engine Company of Lansing), the Peerless Marine Motor Co. of Detroit/Buffalo and the Peerless Motor Car Co. of Cleveland is not known. In 1908 *Power Boating* reported on a 35 foot Elco Express that was equipped with a 6-cylinder 50 hp engine built by the Cleveland company.

Sources: Boating, 1907, p 55
Motor Boating, 1914
OME, 218
Power Boating Ad, 1908
The Motor Boat, 1907, p 44

Peninsular Auto Parts Co. of Detroit
Detroit
This company may have been successor to Peninsular Motor Co, Grand Rapids and/or the Morton Company of Detroit.

Trade name	R.P.M.	H.P.	Weight	Year	Notes
Morton		20		1918	

Source: OME, 219

Porto: See listing for Waterman Marine Motor Company

Premier: See listing for Whittmaak Machine Company

Pungs Finch Auto and Gas Engine Company,   See Sintz Gas Engine Company of
Detroit
Detroit
1524 Jefferson Ave
The company, incorporated on October 10, 1904 as the successor to the Sintz Gas Engine
Company and Michigan Yacht & Power Company.   William A. Pungs was the president
of the firm, D. C. Rexford, vice-president, and Edward B. Finch, secretary – treasurer
and chief engineer.   The company was organized to manufacture the Pungs-Finch
automobile and the Pungs-Sintz marine engine.

The first Pung-Finch automobile was introduced in 1904, the last in 1910. Reportedly
Henry Ford told Pungs that the 1906 "Finch Limited" was the finest car he had ever seen.
Due to difficulties with Pungs, Finch left sometime in 1906 and went to the Packard
Motor Car Company, first as assistant to the factory manager and later as head of the
technical department. Subsequently he joined the Chalmers Motor Car Company and
opened a Chalmers dealership in Cleveland about 1910. By that time he was married to
Mr. Pungs' daughter.

Continued presence in the marine engine business is indicated by a review of the 1908
Detroit Motor Boat Show that listed the Sintz Motor Company as one of the 42 exhibitors.

From 1906 to 1908 the United Manufacturing Company marketed a 2-cycle engine named
"Little Giant" that was licensed under the Sintz patent 509,255.

A fire in 1909 destroyed most of the facilities. Pungs-Finch Auto & Gas Engine Company
filed notice of it dissolution on May 9, 1911.

Trade Name	R.P.M.	H.P.	Weight	Year	Notes
Pungs-Finch				1905-09	Automobile
Pung-Sintz				1904-09	Marine Engines
Little Giant				1906-08	Marine Engines

Sources: MSG, 1905-1908
         MSA, 1899 – 1909
         SCAC, p 1252
         Szudarek, p 100

Racine Boat and Auto Company: See listing for Truscott Boat Company and Racine
in "Other Michigan Engine Builders"
Detroit
253 Jefferson Ave
This company was most likely affiliated with the Racine and Truscott boat and engine
enterprises in Muskegon and St. Joseph. In 1909 this company announced the production
of an automobile using one of their 4-cylinder, 4-cycle, 22.5 hp engines. Limited
production followed for about two years. W. Sidney Sumer was the manager.

Source: SCAC, p 1257

Reliance Gas Engine Company
Detroit
The company catalog noted that the engines could be switched form marine to stationary use and back to marine use again with little trouble.

Four Cycle.

Trade Name	R.P.M.	H.P.	Weight	Year	Notes
	150-700	2,4		1910	

Sources: AGE, p 419

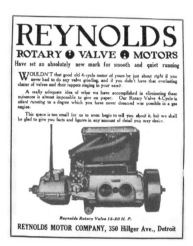

Reynolds Motor Company
Detroit
350 Hillger Ave
The company was incorporated on November 26, 1909 with Michael J. Murphy as president, Walter S. Russel as vice-president and A. Macomb Campau as secretary and treasurer. Regarding the three principals: Campau was secretary of A. M. Campau Realty Company; Murphy was president of Murphy Chair Company and Murphy-Potter Company (a brass foundry and machine shop that became Federal Brass and later part of Federal-Mogul); and Russel was president and manager of Russel Wheel & Foundry Company (railroad car manufacturers.)

The engine was displayed at the 1911 Boston Power Boat Show. The engine offered several unique features including a water-cooled exhaust pipe and a rotary valve system that proposed to combine the advantages of 2-cycle and 4-cycle engines. Cams, cam shafts and springs were completely eliminated to provide silent running and eliminate the trouble of grinding valves.

Four-Cycle

Trade name	cylinders	R.P.M.	H.P.	Weight	Year	Notes
Reynolds	4	1,000	15-20	405	1911	Rotary valves

Sources: Detroit City Directory, 1911
Motor Boat, December 10, 1911, pp. 200-202; 292-29.
Yachting Ad, 1912

Saint Clair Motor Company See Gray-Hawsley
Detroit
1907 advertising claimed that this was H. D. Baird's "Latest and Greatest" 2-cycle engine, "the first and only engine ever made that runs equally well on gasoline, kerosene, Blue Blaze, distillate oil or alcohol without changes or extra attachments." No information is available regarding any relationship with the W. J. Baird Company or the Baird Machine & Manufacturing Company.

In 1910 the Monarch Tool & Manufacturing Company, Cincinnati, Ohio, advertised a 2-cycle, single cylinder "Little Skipper," that looked very much like the one previously advertised by the Saint Clair Motor Company.

Two-Cycle

Trade name	R.P.M.	H.P.	Weight	Year	Notes
Little Skipper		2,4,6	49.5 -	1907	

Sources: Boating Ad, 1907; October 10, 1909. See Skipper Marine.
MotorBoat, 1910, p 140
The Motor Boat Ad, 1907

Scripps Motor Company
Detroit
604 Trumbull (1907)
647 Lincoln (1908)
William E. Scripps was a dynamic promoter of the gasoline marine engine business. His father founded the Detroit News, but he was not content to passively enjoy the certain wealth that would come his way. His first passion was power boating, but his many interests also led him to being a pioneer and leader in aviation and commercial radio. Reportedly he was "a kid in knee pants" when he persuaded his father to buy O. J. Mulford's first Sinz powered launch. Some ten years later, in 1906, Scripps and a few mechanics used the family shop to build the 4-cylinder 25 hp marine engine that became the foundation of the Scripps Motor Company in 1907. Oliver E. Barthel reportedly designed the first engines. By the Fall of 1907 *Power Boating* magazine was reporting that the company would soon be adding one and six cylinder models.

1908 was a year of impressive promotion of the Scripps engine. That year Scripps *acquired the race boat General formerly equipped with Smalley motors and a winning record. Renamed Scripps and re-equipped with his engines, it set a new 100 mile American speed record* at 27.36 statue mile per hour. Reviewing the 1908 Detroit Motor Boat Show for Power Boating, O. E. Sovereign stated that in general interest the Scripps Motor Company's exhibit probably drew the pennant. The company's speedboat, *Unome*, was exhibited along with six motors of 4 to 75 hp. That year Power Boating noted that Scripps reduced the 75-150 pounds per engine by using aluminum for the crankcases. That provided "a most pronounced advantage in racing craft."

Scripps believed that all-out speed alone, without long distance reliability, would not serve the company or industry in the long term. In 1908 Scripps sponsored the "Reliability Cruise," a race across Lake Erie that began in Detroit and ended in Buffalo. He said the purpose of the race was to place a penalty upon defective design material and workmanship and to promote the building of reliable boats and engines. In 1911, the annual Reliability Cruise crossed both Lake Erie and Lake Ontario, beginning in Detroit and ending at Hamilton, Ontario.

In 1912 Scripps provided a dramatic promotion of the safety and reliability of gasoline marine engines. He commissioned a custom 35-foot Mathews cruiser that he named *Detroit*. The boat was powered by a standard Scripps 2-cylinder, 16 hp production engine. For maximum publicity, the Editor of The Rudder, Thomas Fleming Day, was the skipper for the entire 6,000 mile journey from Detroit to St. Petersburg, Russia. The voyage of the little *Detroit* was completed at a time when the sinking of the *Titanic* was still fresh in everyone's mind.

For many years thereafter Scripps advertising carried the caption "The Motor That Crossed the Atlantic." (It was not the first but certainly the most well known crossing in a small gasoline powered boat up to that time.) The company prospered as a marine engine manufacturer until the early 1950's and then under a succession of owners the company has continued as a parts business. Most recently it has been located at Harsens Island, Michigan.

Four-Cycle

Trade Name	cylinders	R.P.M.	H.P.	Weight	Year	Notes
Scripps	2,4		8,15		1907	
	1-6	1,000+	4-100		1908	
	V-12	2,600	350	c. 1,500	1949	

Sources: Motor Boat Ad, 1908
Motor Boat, February 10, 1914, p. 34.
Motor Boating, December 1914
Popular Mechanic Ads, ca. 1910
Power Boating Ad, 1908
Power Boating, April 1908, pp 183-189

Shadow: See listing for Detroit Motor Car Supply Company

Sibley-Haufley Machine Company See listing for Peerless Marine Engine Company
Detroit
182 Brush
In 1908 the Sibley-Haufley Machine Company offered a one cylinder marine engine that they called the "Peerless." The next year the company ceased operation or changed its name.

Trade Name	cylinders	Weight	Year	Notes
Peerless	1		1908	

Sources: Motor Boat, July 10, 1908, p. 119.
   AGE, p 466

Simplex Engine Company
Detroit

Two-Cycle

Trade Name	cylinders	H.P.	Weight	Year	Notes
	2, 4			1915	

Sources: Motor Boating, January 1915, p. 53.

Sintz Gas Engine Company, See listing for Pungs Finch Auto and Gas Engine Co.
Grand Rapids/Detroit
242 Canal (Grand Rapids)
1524 E. Jefferson (Detroit)
The Sintz Gas Engine Company, incorporated December 21, 1892, in Grand Rapids, was perhaps the most important firm in the infancy of the gasoline engine era in Michigan, both for boats and horseless carriages. In November 1893 pioneer engine builder Clark Sintz received the patent that created the prototypical two-cycle gasoline engine, introducing the 3-port design that eliminated the intake valve required in the 2-port system. The oldest gasoline powered American automobile in the Collection of the Smithsonian was powered by a 3-hp Sintz engine that Elwood Haynes purchased at the 1893 Columbian Exhibition in Chicago. It was later upgraded, about 1896 with a 6-hp Sintz engine.

By 1894, Clark Sintz had left the company and the management of the firm passed on to A. A. Barber as president and Fred D. Hills as secretary. By 1897, F. C. Miller replaced Hills as secretary, and the firm moved to South Waterloo Street near Godfrey Avenue.

The firm was managed by H. A. Winter when the company became a subsidiary of the Michigan Yacht & Power Company in 1900. O. J. Mulford, president of MY&P, had for some years been the Detroit agent for Sintz with a sales office at 99 Woodward. After the acquisition, manufacturing operations of the company moved to the facilities of MY&P located on the Detroit River at the foot of Townsend Avenue.

On February 4, 1902, the company changed its name to Sintz Gas Engine Company of Detroit. Officers in 1903 included W. A. Pungs, president; H. A. Winter, treasurer and general manager; and Ora J. Mulford, secretary. Mulford left the organization in 1904 and organized the Gray Motor Company the next year.

Sintz Gas Engine Company of Detroit, Michigan, filed notice of its dissolution on May 8, 1905 The company's assets were merged with those of the former Michigan Yacht and Power Company, whose name had changed in October, 1904 to Pungs Finch Auto and Gas Engine Company.

Two-Cycle

Trade Name	R.P.M.	H.P.	Year	Notes
Sintz			1892	2-port
	600		1893	3-port; 0.1 gal per hp per hour
			1901	Relocated to Detroit

Sources: AGE, p 470
Beeson's Marine Directory, 1895 p 241; 1901, p 25
Catalog, Michigan Yacht & Power Company and the Sintz Gas Engine Company, 1901
Grayson, Stan, "Engines Afloat: Volume I The Gasoline Era, Deveroux Box, Marblehead, Ma,
1999, p 8 – 17
MSG, 1895-1906
Power Boating, April, 1908, p 189
The Rudder ad, February 1899

Skidoo: See listing for Belle Isle Motor Company

Smith & Baldridge Machine Company
Detroit
61-69 Amsterdam (1907)
In 1907 Boating reported that the company had taken possession of a new building that was said to "contain ample space for the production of their two cycle marine engine which has proven wonderfully successful."

Two Cycle

Trade Name	cylinders	R.P.M.	H.P.	Year	Notes
S & B	1	650	6	1907	3-port
	1,2,3,4		6+	1908	Also "Baldridge Reverse Gear"

Sources: Boating 1907, p 64,
           Motor Boat Ads, 1907, 1908
           Power Boating, 1908, p 158

Smith-Bosserdet Motor Company: See also
Bosserdet Yacht & Engine Company
Detroit
Foot of Holcomb Avenue
The Detroit city directory for 1909 lists Charles F.
Smith and Henry C. Bosserdet as operators of the
company, with Charles F. Smith, Jr. working as a clerk.
According to the 1909-1910 *Michigan State Gazetteer
and Business Directory*, owners of the firm were C. F.
Smith and R. H. Mitchell. The company may have been succeeded by the Bosserdet
Yacht & Engine Company that was incorporated in October 1910, after which the Smith-
Bosserdet name no longer appears.

Two-Cycle

Trade Name	H.P.	Weight	Years	Notes
	20		1908	

Sources: Detroit City Directory, 1909
           MSG, 1909-1910

The Chas. A. Strelinger Company, - 1907
Strelinger Marine Engine Co, 1907 -
Detroit
50 Fort St, E. (1907)
46 E. Lafayette (1908)
The Strelinger Company was organized as a hardware
and machine tool dealer in 1884. By 1900 they were
marketing marine engines that they contracted Leland
& Faulconer to design and build. In 1907 the Chas. A.
Strelinger Company marine engine business was
reorganized as a separate company, the Strelinger Marine
Engine Company.

In 1908 they bought the Detroit Gas Engine &
Machinery Co. At the 1908 Detroit Motor Boat Show
it was reported that Strelinger showed an unusually
complete line. Besides the "old reliable," one, two, three
and four cylinder, four cycle engines, they also exhibited
an electric lighting system with a 1.5 hp engine, a semi-
portable outfit for spraying and an outboard motor.

Two & Four-Cycle

Trade Name	cylinders	RPM	H.P.	Weight	Year	Notes
	.				1900	
	1-4		1.5-50		1908	offered a boat with a 1.5-hp, 2-cycle engine complete with electrical fittings for $48.50;
Little Giant	2				1910	2-cycle
Strelinger	1-,4	600	4-40	330-1608	1911	
Strelmotor	4		30-40		1915	4-cycle
					1924	

Sources: AGE, p 497
Leland, Mrs. Wilfred C. and Millbrook, "Master of Precision, Henry M. Leland," Wayne State
University Press, Detroit, MI, 1966, 1996, p 61.
Motor Boat Ad, 1908
Motor Boating, December, 1914
Power Boating, April 1908, pp 183-189
The Rudder ads, December, 1905: March, 1906: 1907

Simplex Engine Co.
Detroit
Trade Name: Simplex
Source: MotorBoating, December, 1915

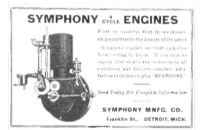

Symphony Manufacturing Co.
Detroit
Franklin St.

Four-cycle

Trade Name	H.P.	Weight	Year	Notes
			1908	

Source: Power Boating Ad, 1908

Superior Machine & Engineering Company
Detroit

Trade name	cylinders	H.P.	Weight	Year	Notes
Yale	1, 2			1913	

Sources: Motor Boating, January 1913.

Sweet Manufacturing Co.
Detroit

Trade name	cylinders	R.P.M.	H.P.	Weight	Year	Notes
Sweet					1914	

Source: The Motor Boat Ad, 1914
               MotorBoating, December, 1915

Tessmer Machine & Tool Co.
Detroit
285 Rivard St.

Trade Name	H.P.	Weight	Year	Notes
Ideal	1.5		1907	$35 complete

Source: Power Boating Ad, 1907

Thelma Motor Works
Detroit
Little is known about the company but, in the Detroit Motor Boat Regatta of 1907 a boat named "Thelma" made the fastest run over the course in the speedboat class.

Trade Name	H.P.	Weight	Year	Notes
Whirlwind			1911	

Sources: Motor Boating, April 1911, p. 91; December 1911, p. 83.

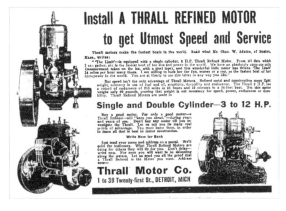

Thrall Motor Company, -1907)
Thrall-Fishback Motor Company, 1907
Thrall Motor Company, 1909:
 See also the Detroit Engine Works
37 Fort St, East (1909)
Detroit
In 1907 Thrall merged with the Fishback Motor Company. *Power Boating* reviewed the "refined" motor of the "new" Detroit Company in

1908. This was one of the many companies owned by Sherer and Wasdsworth in affiliation with the Detroit Engine Works.

Two-Cycle

Trade Name	R.P.M.	H.P.	Weight	Year	Notes
Thrall Refined		3	50	1908	3-port
		3-15		1909	2 & 3 port

Sources: Motor Boat, July 10, 1908.
MotorBoat, April 10, 1910
Powcr Boating, 1908
Power Boating, May, 1909

Togo: See listing for Ericsson & Moon Manufacturing Company

United Manufacturing Company
Detroit
171-175 West Woodbridge St.
A review of the exhibitions of the 1908 Detroit Motor Boat Show noted that the company had not changed their design for the last two seasons. Their "positive force" lubricating system was noted for its economy and effectiveness. A March 1906 advertisement in *The Rudder* magazine noted that the "Little Giant was licensed under the Sintz Patent 509,255. By 1916 Strelinger Marine Engine Company was marketing the "Little Giant."

Two-Cycle

Trade Name	H.P.	Weight	Years	Notes
Little Giant	1-4	11/2@53	1906	3-port
Little Giant	3-16		1907	"Dwarf in size Giant in Strength"
Little Giant			1908	

Sources: Motor Boat Ad, 1908
Power Boating, April 1908, pp 183-189
The Rudder, December 1905: March, 1906: 1907
The Motor Boat Ad, 1907

Van Blerck Motor Co. (1909)
J. V. B. Engine Co. (c. 1918 – 1921)
Joseph Van Blerck, Inc. (1927)
Van Blerck Motors Inc. (1928)
Van Blerck Marine Marine Engine Corp. (1932)
Detroit/Monroe/Ohio/New Jersey
137 Leib Street (1909)
35 Hibbard Ave (1912)
Joseph Van Blerck was a Dutch immigrant who settled in Monroe, Michigan in 1904 and became a pioneer manufacturer of high-performance marine engines, attaining fame

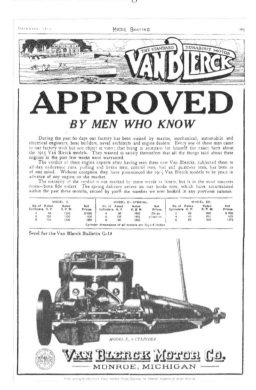

primarily through racing successes. Before building his own engines he worked at the Ford Motor Company with C. Harold Wills, chief engineer. About 1909, the firm was established in Detroit with Van Blerck as president and general manager and John S. Haggerty as the secretary and treasurer.

In December 1913 the company relocated to larger facilities in Monroe. About that time the management team had grown to include Charles B. Page, VP and Treasurer, A. G. Griese, Sales Manager, and John A. Masterman, Service and Production Manager. Mr. Masterman came from the Ferro engine company in Cleveland where he had been the service and production manager for the prior six years.

For a half dozen years before WWI Van Blerck engines combined with John Hacker and Chris Smith built hulls to dominate American power boat racing. During the war he developed the "J.V.B." four cylinder engine for the military's use in tanks and after the war converted the surplus engines to marine use under the name of the J.V.B. Engine Company in Akron, Ohio. In 1921 that company was acquired by Elco, a boat company in Bayonne, NJ.

About 1923 the Van Blerck Engine Corp was organized and built engines in Plainfield, NJ. By 1928 Van Blerck was in Red Bank, N. J. converting Continental engines for marine use until Gray Marine Motor Company became the exclusive converter.

Four-Cycle

Trade Name	cylinders	R.P.M.	H.P.	Weight	Year	Notes
					1909	(T-Head) Detroit
Van Blerck	2,4,6	1,000	12-80	400-900	1911	
	2,4,6	1,600	20-180		1914	Monroe
	4,6,8	1,700	40-220	1025-1640	1915	
	-12		-400		1916	
J.V.B.	4, 6, 8				1919	Akron, OH
			16-275		1923	Plainfield, NJ
Continental-Van Blerck					1928	Red Bank, NJ

Sources: Catalog, Pacific Net and Twine Company, 1918. pp. 1324-1326
Detroit City Directory, 1912
Motor Boating, December, 1914; December, 1915; April, 1916; November, 1919; March, 1920
OME, p 229.
Van Blerck Motor Company catalog, 1915, Library of Michigan, Rare Book Collection.
Yachting Ad, 1912

Victor: See R. S. Hill

Waterman Marine Motor Company
Detroit
1500 Fort St, 1907
Mt. Elliot, 1914

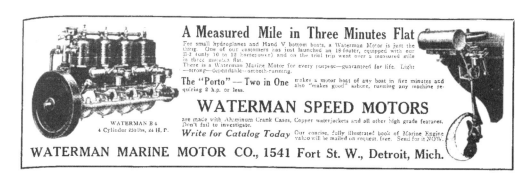

The company was incorporated on November 5, 1906 and has been credited with producing one of the first commercially successful outboard motors.   Cameron B. Waterman, the inventor and developer, served as president. Harvey Miller was the vice-president and treasurer and Lawrence K. Butler was the secretary.

By 1907 the company was marketing inboard canoe motors. In 1908 they acquired the Kowalsky Engine Company of Veron, Pa., and consolidated operations in Detroit.   In 1912 the company offered a unique outboard that converted to stationary use by removing the detachable engine and bolting it to a stationary base.

About 1917 the company was sold to Arrow Motor and Machine Co. of New York. Subsequently the company was acquired by Johnson Motor Company of Wisconsin.

Trade Name	R.P.M.	H.P.	Weight	Year	Notes
Waterman	750	2	36	1907	Outboard (40 lbs complete)
		4-10		1907	Canoe motors
Improved Kowalsky		6,10	150,200	1908	
Porto				1912	Outboard/stationary
				1915	Uni-lectric lighting outfits

Sources: Detroit City Directory, 1911
        MotorBoating, December, 1915
        Power Boating Ad, 1908
        The Motor Boat Ads, 1907 and 1908
        Yachting Ad, 1912

Wayne Motor Company
Detroit

Two-Cycle

Trade name	cylinders	R.P.M.	H.P.	Weight	Year	Notes
			4,8		1912	3-port

Sources: Motor Boating, January 1912, p. 84.

Whirlwind: See listing for Thelma Motor Works

Wilpen Company
Detroit,

Four-Cycle

Trade Name	cylinders	R.P.M.	H.P.	Weight	Year	Notes
Brushmarine	1-4	750	3-20	187-800	1911	
Oakland						

Sources: Homfeld, Max F, "753 Manufacturers of Inboard Marine Engines",   Max F. Homfeld, St. Michaels, MD, 1991, p. 14.

The Wittmaack Machine Co.
Detroit
Leib & Wight St.
This company's advertisement in 1908 claimed, "The first 2-cycle engine with mechanically controlled intake ports. Four-cycle operation with two-stroke simplicity." A mechanically operated disk valve on the crankshaft inside the base opened and closed the intake port that allowed the fuel to enter the crankcase. This replaced the one-way valve that was the weak link of the typical on a 2-port design.

Two-Cycle

Trade name	R.P.M.	H.P.	Weight	Years	Notes
Premier	700	2 - 60		1908	2-port

Source: Power Boating, 1908, pp 9, 158

Yale: See listing for Baird & Henselwood Company (1908) and
Superior Machine & Engineering (1913)

Appendix B — Other Michigan Marine Engine Builders

Aristox: See Lake Shore Engine Works

Ayres Gasoline Engine Works 1904
Ayres Gasoline Engine and Automobile Works 1906
Ayres Engine & Motor Company 1911
Saginaw/Rochester
This firm was organized by 1904 and at one time offered both 2 & 4 cycle engines. In 1906 the company was known as Ayres Gasoline Engine and Automobile Works. William F. Ayres was president and manager of the company. The company moved to Rochester in 1907. By 1911 all listings are for "Ayres Engine & Motor Co."

Four-Cycle

Trade Name	Model(s)	cylinders	R.P.M.	H.P.	Weight	Year	Notes
	5	1,2,3,4,6	5-800	1.5-30	43-650	1911	

Sources: AGE, p 41
         Saginaw Directory, 1906

Bates and Edmunds Gas Engine Co. 1899
Hill Diesel Engine Co. c.1926
Lansing
In 1899 Madison Bates and James P. Edmunds became the first Olds alumni to strike out on their own. Bates had been largely responsible for some of the early Olds patents on gasoline engines. This company sold many of its gasoline engines through the Eastern Fairbanks Company, a large supplier to railroads, mills and factories.. By 1924 Harry Hill had a controlling interest in the company and Ransom Olds bought the remainder. About 1926 the company reorganized as the Hill Diesel Engine Co. Olds personally spent much time working on the diesel development and used the engines in his yachts. He was unable to persuade the other Directors of the REO Company to get involved.

Trade Name	cylinders	H.P.	Weight	Year	Notes
Bull Dog				1900	Gasoline Engines
Hill Diesel	2, 4, 6	6-25, 60, 90		1926	Diesel Engines

Source: AGE, p 231
        AMUM, p 58
        Motor Boating, February 1926, p 372
        REO, p 333, 362-364

The Beilfuss Motor Company
Detroit/Lansing
701 E. Saginaw (Lansing)

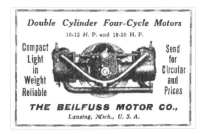

Richard A. Beilfuss organized the company in Detroit by 1902 and relocated to Lansing by 1904. In 1912, the officers of the company consisted of Dr. C. M. Watson as president; Edward M. Reitz as secretary and treasurer; and Richard A. F. Beilfuss as superintendent.

Four-Cycle

Trade Name	R.P.M.	H.P.	Weight	Year	Notes
Beilfuss	1,000	1-20	300	1908	Horizontal Dual-opposed
Beilfuss	8-1,000	7.5-18	265	1911	Horizontal Dual-opposed

Sources: AGE, p 51
Lansing City Directory, 1911-12
Power Boating ad, 1908

Beiver Gas Engine Company
Kalamazoo, Michigan

Trade name	R.P.M.	H.P.	Weight	Year	Notes
				1911	

Sources: Motor Boat, December 1911, p. 74.

Blakely Engine Company
Muskegon
Nims St.
E. B. Blakely was the manager of this firm and the manager of Lyons Machine & Manufacturing Company. In 1915 Blakely advertised a flexible shaft outboard that looked identical to the Gray Motor Co product, except, unlike the Gray, it did not have its name cast on the flywheel.

Trade Name	No. of cylinders	H.P.	Weight	Year	Notes
	1			1915	outboard

Sources: Motor Boating, March 10, 1915, p. 88.
MSG, 1915 - 1917

Brooks Boat Company, Inc
Saginaw
2310 Ship Street
The company claimed to be the originators of the "Pattern System" of boat-building and was a leading manufacturer of kit boats. The company may also have manufactured a line of engines at one time. The attached advertisement includes a "Special Engine Offer." "The Brooks Special," was offered with a launch frame and engine for a combined price of $62.00 in 1908. The ad encouraged the reader to order their engine catalog. However, the engines sold with the kit boats may have been re-branded engines manufactured by others. Reportedly Stork Motor Company had an arrangement with Brooks.

Trade Name	cylinders	H.P.	Weight	Year	Notes
Brooks	1	3, 6		1908	

Sources: Motor Boat, July 10, 1908, p. 53.

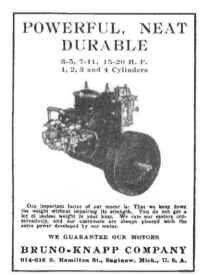

Bruno-Knapp Company
Saginaw
614 Hamilton St.

Trade Name	cylinders	R.P.M.	H.P.	Weight	Year	Notes
	1-4		3 - 30		1907	

Source: The Motor Boat Ad, 1907

Bull Dog: See Bates and Edmunds Gas Engine Co.

Burtt Manufacturing Company
Kalamazoo

Trade Name	R.P.M.	H.P.	Weight	Year	Notes
				1904	

Sources: 1904 Marine Buyers' Guide.

Charlevoix Boat and Motor Company
Charlevoix
The Company was owned by Theodore and John Erickson with Louis J. Mercier, and is known to have operated between 1903 and 1905.   An advertisement in the 1903-1904 *Michigan State Gazetteer and Business Directory* listed their services and products as: "Designers and Builders of High-Grade Pleasure Boats, Steam,/Gas and Electric Launches,/Sail Yachts, Row Boats, Working Boats, St. Lawrence River/Skiffs. Hand-Made Spoon Oars and Paddles a Specialty./Charlevoix, Mich."

In 1905, Louis J. Mercier was the only proprietor noted, and the business was listed only as builders of engines.

Trade name	R.P.M.	H.P.	Weight	Year	Notes
				1905	

Sources: MSG, 1903-1906

Chippewa Gas Engines and Boat Company 1903
Chippewa Engine Works, Inc. 1904
Sault Ste. Marie
Perry Ave

Chippewa Gas Engines and Boat Company incorporated on January 19, 1903. Presumably, as the result of a reorganization, the Chippewa Engine Works was incorporated on July 9, 1904 as a foundry, machine shop, boat builder and engine manufacturing firm.

In an advertisement in the 1905 *Michigan State Gazetteer and Business Directory*, the company advertised: "Cyrus W. Baldwin, President/Geo. P. McCallum, Vice-President/ Charles W. Given, Secretary and Treasurer/Frank H. Hoard, General Manager/Chippewa Engine Works/(Incorporated.)/Founders and Machinists/Boats and Launches./Heavy Forgings and Marine Repairs. Gasoline Engines and Repairs a Specialty/Office and Shops, Perry Avenue./Sault Ste. Marie, - Michigan/Telephone 260."

Chippewa Engine Works forfeited its Michigan charter and filed for dissolution on June 11, 1907.

Trade Name	cylinders	R.P.M.	H.P.	Weight	Year	Notes
					1905	

Sources: MSA, 1899-1909
         MSG, 1905-1906

218

Church Manufacturing Company
Adrian
The company was set up by a group of former Oldsmobile employees. Reportedly they marketed some engines for stationary and marine use but the primary business at the beginning was building automobiles and engines. Between 1902 and 1903 they built about 1,000 "Murray" automobiles and in 1903 introduced the "Lenawee."

In 1905 the company was acquired by the Page Fence and Gas Engine Co. of Adrian. It was then reported that they intended to market their engine through the Page Fence dealer network that was selling woven wire fence in many parts of the country.

Trade Name	R.P.M.	H.P.	Weight	Year	Notes
		3-20		1905	hot-tube ignition

Source: AGE, pp 97, 376

Continental Motor Manufacturing Co.
Muskegon/Detroit
The company was founded in Muskegon in 1905 to manufacture automobile engines. Manufacturing operationscontinued there until 1980. Later the company's headquarters moved to Detroit.

It is known that they marketed their own marine engines in 1908, but most other years they provided their basic engine to other companies that converted them to marine use. In 1969 the company was acquired by Teledyne Technologies.
See more details in Metro Detroit listing.

Trade Name	cylinders	H.P.	Weight	Year	Notes
Continental	4	4		1908	Exhibited at Chicago Boat Show

Cook Manufacturing Company
Albion
The Company manufactured gasoline engines and engine supplies. I. L. Sibley was president of the company and P. M. Dearing served as secretary and treasurer. *The Michigan State Gazetter and Business Directory* indicated that they marketed some engines for marine use.

Trade Name	R.P.M.	H.P.	Weight	Year	Notes
				1903	

Sources: MSG, 1903-1904

Defoe Boat & Motor Works - See Stork Motor Company
Bay City

Duryea Motor Company
Saginaw

Charles and Frank Duryea built their first gasoline powered automobile in 1893 and in 1895 won a notable race in Chicago, after which they organized a short lived company to manufacturer automobiles. The brothers later went their separate ways. Charles organized this company in 1911 to build automobiles. From December 1912 through 1925 they also advertised engines intended for marine use.

Trade Name	R.P.M.	H.P.	Weight	Years Produced	Notes
				1912	.

Sources: Motor Boating, December 1912, p. 20.
          OME, 198

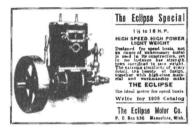

Eclipse Motor & Boat Company, 1901
Eclipse Motor Company, 1903
Traverse City Iron Works, 1913
Traverse City / Mancelona / Traverse City
364 Ming St. (1908)

The company was organized by William M. Fetterley and Brownlow Starbuck in 1901. In the beginning the company was located in Traverse City. Brownlow Starbuck managed the company and he was probably responsible for moving the company to Mancelona and reorganizing as Eclipse Motor Company. In March 1901 Starbuck had a new 24' X 40' shop near his residence in Mancelona and the Eclipse Motor Company was located there in 1903. The Eclipse Boat Company, owned by Ransom T. Merrill was located nearby on Walloon Lake. Presumably the two were successor to the Eclipse Boat and Motor Company.

An order for six launch engines from New Smyrna, Florida, was received in May 1903. In March 1905 they provided an engine to Mathews Boat Company for a boat to be shipped to St. Petersburg, for the Russian navy.

Patterns for a new five-horsepower, double-cylinder, two-cycle engine to be used in both automobiles and launches were completed by Starbuck in January 1904.

By October 1906 the company made plans and patterns for a new model, and the motors were to be cast in Grand Rapids. In 1908 *Power Boating* reported that the company could not meet demand the previous year and had recently doubled the size of its factory. Mathews Boat Co. of Port Clinton, Ohio, had selected a 10 hp No. 8 Eclipse Special for their new 22-foot speed model.

By 1913 the "Eclipse" engines were being offered by the Traverse City Iron Works, believed to be a successor firm.

Two-Cycle

Trade Name	cylinders	H.P.	Weight	Year	Notes
Eclipse				1901	Traverse City
Eclipse	1,2,3	1.5-16		1908	Mancelona
Eclipse				1913	Traverse City Iron Works

Sources: Motor Boat, July 10, 1908, p. 103.
Motor Boating, December 1913, p 58
Mancelona Area Historical Society. First Hand Account of Life in Mancelona in the 20th Century (Mancelona, MI: Mancelona Area Historical Society, 2002.) pp. 164-166.
MSG, 1901, 1903-1904
Power Boating Ad, 1908

Erd Machine Co., 1905
Erd Motor Company Co., 1906
Erd Motor Company, Ltd., 1909
Saginaw

1357-1363 N. Niagara
The origins of the Erd Machine Company are not known but an article in *Motor Boat* in December 1905 stated that the company would be building motors ranging in size from 1 to 20 horsepower, using jigs and templates to assure the interchangeability of parts. By 1906 The Erd Motor Company was in the process of increasing the size of its plant and was installing new machine tools. At the same time, the company advertised a 16-foot launch equipped with a 1.5- h.p. motor for $125. The motor weighed 65 lbs and sold separately for $50.00.

The Erd Motor Company, Ltd., was incorporated in March 1909 with a capital of $25,000. Officers of the firm in 1910 included J. G. Erd as president and general manager; R. H. Knapp, vice-president; and Harry S. Erd, secretary and treasurer.

The company reportedly also built lightweight racing engines in 1912. At some time company also supplied engines for tractors. The assets of the company were sold in a Receiver's Sale April 5, 1929.

Two-Cycle

Trade Name	cylinders	R.P.M.	H.P.	Weight	Year	Notes
			1 - 20		1906	16-ft launch 1.5 hp, $125
	1-4		2-30		1907	
Erd	1-4, 6	800	3.5-60	95-800	1911	

Four-Cycle

Trade Name	cylinders	R.P.M.	H.P.	Weight	Year	Notes
Erd	2,3,4	500	12-40	610-2,100	1911	
	4		25		1914	Built in two types: Standard (Iron), High Speed (Aluminum)

Sources: AGE, p 154
            Boating Ad, 1906
            Gas Power ad, 1906
            Motor Boat, Vol. 2, No. 23, December 10, 1905. p. 30; Ad, 1907
            Motor Boating, December 1914; December, 1915; July, 1924
            Saginaw Directory, 1910

General Machinery Company - See Smalley Motor Company

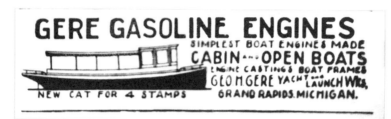

George M. Gere Yacht and Launch Works, - 1895 Grand Rapids This advertisement from a national publication, *Scientific American*, in 1895 indicates that there was some substance to the organization. However little is known of the company. George Gere became a founding partner in the Monitor Vapor Engine and Power Company that same year. See that company for additional detail.

Gile Boat and Engine Company
Ludington
The company was incorporated on March 8, 1909 with a capital stock of $50,000. Its management consisted of J. S. Stearn, President; William L. Mercereau, Secretary and Treasurer, and W. L. Gile, General Manager. Stearn was also president of Stearns Salt and Lumber Company and the Stearns Hotel Company. Mercereau was Superintendent of steam ships for the Pere Marquette Rail Road.
Gile Boat & Engine Company was listed in the 1911 *Michigan State Gazetteer and Business Directory* as: "Manufacturers of/High Grade Launches and/Marine and Stationary Engines/Office and Works at - - - Ludington, Mich." A similar advertisement appears in the 1913 edition. In 1915 the advertisement included the introduction of Gile Agricultural Tractors.

In 1918 the company was acquired by the Stearn Motor Company, also known as a manufacturer of tractors and stationary engine business.

Trade Name	R.P.M.	H.P.	Weight	Year	Notes
Gile				1909	
Stearn				1918	

Sources: AGE p 206, 481
    Michigan State Archives, RG 61-11, Abstracts of Reports of Corporations, Lot
        3, Vol. 4 (1903-1909). p. 227.
    MSG, 1911-1912
    OME, p 226

The Unrivalled Monarch.

The standard of excellence in Pleasure Craft and Marine Engines.
Standard sizes in Hulls 17 to 30 ft. carried in stock.
Special sizes in Hulls built to order.

Engines all our own make.
Hulls all our own make.

Assuring absolute satisfaction and fulfilling in detail in specifications.

Prompt deliveries guaranteed.
Write for illustrated catalogue and price list.

Grand Rapids Yacht & Gas Engine Co.
92 Front Street,
Grand Rapids, Michigan.

Grand Rapids Gas Engine and Yacht Company
Grand Rapids
60-132 N. Front St.
The company's 1899 catalog detailed the specifications of their marine and stationary engines from 1-45 hp. The 1-hp marine engine weighed 110 pounds and the stationary engine weighed 200 pounds. The marine engine cost $200 and the stationary cost $190.) They offered a 16-ft launch with the 1 hp engine for $330 and a 30-footer with a 10 hp engine for $1,255.

The company was founded in 1895 by industrialist Willis J. Perkins. Mr. Perkins also owned Perkins & Company, a manufacturer of shingle machines organized in 1874. Both firms shared a common building and Mr. Perkins lived across the street at 95 N. Front St. GRGE&Y primarily made gas and gasoline engines for stationary, electric lighting and marine purposes. They also produced pleasure launches as a specialty.

In 1907 *Boating* magazine reviewed the 4-cylinder, 4-cycle, 20-hp engine with removable heads and a choice of make and break or jump spark ignition. The review noted that the company also built stock boats from 17 to 30 feet and special sizes to order.

In 1908 *Power Boating* magazine reported on the 4-cylinder Monarch Kerosene Motor noting that the motors were generally accepted by fishermen for their economy and dependability. It was especially noted that conversions to kerosene by others had been only partial success but, it appeared the Monarch had overcome the difficulties.

Note: A man named Mr. Perkins was in charge of the Michigan Wheel Company of Grand Rapids and a relationship can be presumed.

Trade Name	cylinders	R.P.M.	H.P.	Year	Notes
				1895	
Monarch	1,2,3	300-450	¾-45	1899	1 hp @ 110 lbs
	1,2,3,4,6		1.5-120	1907	
				1908	
				1914	
	6			1916	

Sources: Catalog, Grand Rapids Gas Engine & Yacht Company, 1899
    The Motor Boat Ad, 1907
    Motor Boat Ad, 1908

Motor Boating December 1914

MSG and Business Directory, 1895-1896; 1911-1912

"They Make the Round Trip"

HILDRETH MARINE MOTORS

Eliminate Your Troubles When You Make Your Purchase

SINGLE AND MULTIPLE

What's the Use of Going If you can't Get Back?

Buy a HILDRETH, and tow your Friends Back.

2 to 22 H. P.

THE HILDRETH MFG. CO.

6 Race St., Lansing, Mich., U. S. A.

Hegeman Machine Works

Grand Rapids

Trade Name: Hegeman

Source: MotorBoating, December, 1915

Hildreth Motor and Pump Company

Hildreth Manufacturing Company, 1907

Novo Engine Co., 1912

Lansing

6 Race St (1907)

3-17 Waterside (1908)

In 1902, Ned E. Hildreth filed a patent for a low tension igniter, but it is not known when they began manufacturing engines. In 1907 they were marketing the Hildreth marine engines and by 1908 introduced the "Novo gas engine built by Hildreth." In 1912 the company was reorganized as the Novo Engine Co. By 1911 Hildreth had left the company and was known to be working in Kansas City.

Trade Name	R.P.M.	H.P.	Weight	Year	Notes
Hildreth		2-22		1907	"They Make the Round Trip"
Novo				1908	"Novo…built by Hildreth"

Sources: AGE, p 231

AMUM, p 58

Gas Power Ads 1904 and 1908

Motor Boat Ad, 1907

Power Boating Ad, 1908

Hill Diesel Engine Co. – See listing for Bates and Edmunds Gas Engine Co.

H. E. Hines Motor Company

Traverse City

Trade Name	R.P.M.	H.P.	Weight	Year	Notes
				1912	

Sources: Motor Boating, December 1912, p. 22; December 1913, p. 58.

Holland Launch and Engine Company

Holland

There is little information about the company except that it was incorporated on January 2, 1907 and appeared in the 1907 *Michigan State Gazetteer and Business Directory*.

Two and Four-Cycle

Trade name	R.P.M.	H.P.	Weight	Year	Notes
		1.5-100		1907	Launches & Cabin boats 16-75 feet.
					16 ft launch w/1.5 hp complete $125

Sources: MSG, 1907-1908

Jackson Machine Works

Traverse City

Two-Cycle

Trade name	R.P.M.	H.P.	Weight	Year	Notes
		1-7		1907	

Source: The Motor Boat, 1907, p 125

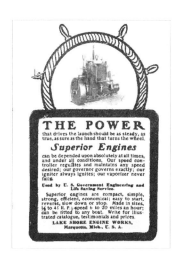

Lake Shore Engine Works

Marquette

The company was owned by the Kaufman family that also owned the community bank. Carl H. Blomstrom was associated with this engine manufacturer from 1896-1901 when he received a patent covering the design of the Lake Shore engine.

Two-Cycle

Trade name	cylinders	H.P.	Weight	Year	Notes
Lake Shore	1,2,3,4	½-45		1902	

Sources: AGE, p 285

Homfeld, Max F., "753 Manufacturers of Inboard Marine Engines", Max F. Homfeld, St. Michaels, MD, 1991, p. 7.

Sail and Sweep, The Illustrated American Magazine of Aquatic Sports, April, 1903

Lauth Auto & Engine Company
Port Huron

Trade Name	R.P.M.	H.P.	Weight	Years Produced	Notes
				1911	

Sources: Motor Boating, December 1911, p. 83.

The Leader: See listing for Sintz, Claude

Lockwood-Ash Motor Company
Lansing, 1906
Jackson, 1908
Fred Lockwood, A. L. Lockwood and W. L. Ash organized the company about 1904. In addition to building in-board marine engines the Company was also an early manufacturer of outboard motors.

Two-Cycle

Trade Name	cylinders	R.P.M.	H.P.	Weight	Year	Notes
			2		1906	
	1,2		2-6		1907	Lansing
	1-4		2-24		1908	Jackson
Lockwood-Ash	1,2,3,4	7-800	2.5-25	110-500	1911	
L-A					1914	

Sources   AGE, p 285
      The Motor Boat Ads 1907, 1908
      Motor Boat, April 10, 1924, pp. 53 and 98.
      Motor Boating, December 1914; December, 1915

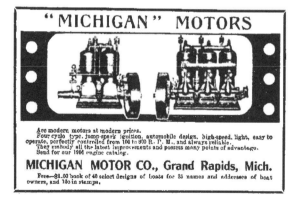

Michigan Motor Co. 1904
Michigan Wheel Co. 1908
Grand Rapids
In 1904 the Michigan Motor Company began manufacturing a 2-cycle marine motor and two blade reversible propeller wheels. In December 1905 they advertised "automobile design four-cycle marine engines." Due to great demand for their propeller wheels, by 1907 they were devoting their entire efforts to their manufacture along with reverse gears and other marine accessories. During 1907 they supplied propellers to over 750 engine builders in the US and foreign markets. Their 1908 catalog contained 32 color pages describing their 12 types of speed wheels, reverse gears, universal joints and numerous accessories.

According to a listing of American marine engine manufacturers in Motor Boating magazine, the company appeared to be a marine engine manufacturer again in 1914

Trade Name	R.P.M.	H.P.	Weight	Year	Notes
				1904	
				1915	

Sources: Boating, 1907, p 45
Power Boating, 1908
Motor Boating, December, 1914; December, 1915
The Rudder, December 1905; March 1906

McCormick Motor Company
Saginaw
223 N. Niagara
The company was formed by Edwin W. McCormick in 1909. It is unclear whether this company was a manufacturer or a boat and marine engine sales firm. McCormick was also active with the E. W. McCormick & Company, a grocery business.

Trade Name	R.P.M.	H.P.	Weight	Year	Notes
				1909	

Sources: Saginaw City Directory 1909

Monarch: See listing for Grand Rapids Gas Engine and Yacht Company

Monitor Vapor Engine and Power Company
Grand Rapids/Detroit
6-8 Erie St. (1896)
15 Mill St. (1899)
The "Monitor Launch Engine" has the distinction of receiving the first feature review of any "gasoline vapor" engine to be published in *The Rudder*, December 1895. At that time they said it had been on the market for two seasons, however, the Company was not incorporated until October 15, 1894. Officers of the firm included Thomas Stewart White, president, also president of White & Friant Lumber Co.; William S. McCay, vice-president, also president of Union Foundry Co. and W. S. McCay & Co. (special machinery manufacturers); and George M. Gere, secretary and treasurer. Of the three men in the management team, Gere may have been the only one with previous experience in the business. For some time he had been a yacht manufacturer in Grand Rapids (see listing for George M. Gere). The company's patented 1895 engine was designed by Leonida G. Wooley, later associated with the Wooley Foundry & Machine

227

Company of Anderson Indiana. Patents from 1898 were the work of Ralph B. Hain, a mechanical engineer and later superintendent of the firm. His brother Philip was a carpenter for the company.

The engines all appeared to have exhaust stacks similar to the popular "Naphtha Engines," perhaps to visually assure prospective buyers that the gasoline engine was a familiar and proven technology. From the beginning the company equipped the engines with 2-blade reversible propeller wheels.

When Thomas White left the firm in 1896, William McCay assumed the presidency and Maurice Shanahan (treasurer of the Bissell Carpet Sweeper Company) became vice-president of the firm. The company also added an eastern sales office at No. 2 Sunny Side Drive in Yonkers, New York.

When the company was inspected by the Michigan Bureau of Labor in January 1896 the firm had nine employees and an average monthly payroll of $835. At the time of the 1897 inspection the factory employed 24 and had an average monthly payroll of $1,145.

Despite apparent growth, the company either ceased operations or relocated to Detroit as it no longer appeared in the Grand Rapids directory after 1899. That year Ralph Hain co-owned the short lived Western Gas Engine Works of Grand Rapids. The Monitor Vapor Engine & Power Company of Detroit, Michigan, filed notice of its dissolution on December 5, 1903.

Reportedly George Gere moved to Newark, New Jersey where he established a similar firm.

Two Cycle

Trade Name	R.P.M.	H.P.	Weight	Year	Notes
Monitor		¾ - 10	90 -	1894	Stock launches built from 16 to 40-feet
Monitor				1914	Motor Boat & Engine Co, Newark, N.J.

Sources: MSG, 1895-96
MSA, Lot 3, Vol. 3 (1899-1904), p. 155.
Motor Boating, December 1914
The Rudder, December, 1895, p. 304-306

Novo Engine Co. – See Hildreth Manufacturing Co.

P. F. Olds & Son, 1880
Olds Gasoline Engine Works, 1897
Seager Engine Works, 1904
Lansing
Originally organized in September 1880 as a repair shop, by 1885 they were making steam engines. At that time Ransom E. Olds purchased most of the stock owned by his older brother Wallace and thus became the "Son" and his father's partner. About the same time they introduced a gasoline-steam engine designed by Ransom. The innovation was that it used a gasoline burner to heat the boiler. The 1 and 2-hp engines were well

received and sold throughout the country. By 1897 Ransom held 2,600 shares, his father, Pliny, held 15, his brother Wallace held 200 and an employee, Madison F. Bates, held 150 (See Bates & Edmunds Gas Engine Co). By that time the Olds Steam and Olds Safety and Vapor Engines enjoyed a national reputation as stationary and marine engine builders. On November 22, 1897 the company name was changed to the Olds Gasoline Engine Works. In 1901 the marine engine division was sold to Michigan Yacht and Power Company and the stationary division was subsequently reorganized as Seager Engine Works.

Trade Name	R.P.M.	H.P.	Weight	Year	Notes
Olds		1 to 50		1885	

Sources: AMUM, pp 51-58

Original Gas Engine Company
Lansing
Founded by Wallace Olds, brother of Ransom Olds

Trade Name	R.P.M.	H.P.	Weight	Year	Notes
				1915	

Sources: Motor Boating, February 1915, p. 40.

Fred J. Pease Company
Grand Rapids
36 Court St.

Four-Cycle

Trade Name	cylinders	H.P.	Weight	Year	Notes
The Pease				1908	
The Pease	3	9		1915	

Sources: Motor Boat, March 10, 1915, p. 155.
Power Boating Ad 1908

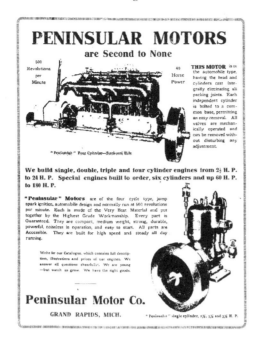

Peninsular Motor Company
Grand Rapids
A 1907 advertisement claimed their engines were the result of 20 years experience (without specifically saying whether it was the company or the engine designer that had the experience)

Trade Name	cylinders	R.P.M.	H.P.	Year	Notes
Peninsular	1,2,3,4	1-600	2 1/2-40	1907	special order 6 cylinder, 60-180 hp

Sources: Boating Ad, 1906; 1907

Pierce, Nye & Budd Company,-1909
Pierce-Budd Company, 1910 -
Pierce-Boutin Motors Inc. - 1923
Truscott-Pierce Engine Co., -1930
205-209 Saginaw St., Bay City (1910)
N. Walnut and Vermont Avenue, Bay City, (1914)
Merrill, Michigan (1923)
St. Joseph, Michigan (1930)
By 1909 James H. Pierce, formerly the plant superintendent and designer for the Smalley Motor Company, struck out on his own and formed a new firm with James H. Nye and James H. Budd. The company advertised engines ranging from six to sixty horsepower that year.

Powerboat, April, 1909, credited the company with being the first to suggest mixing oil in the gasoline to lubricate two-cycle engines.

By 1910 James Nye moved to Detroit. James Budd resided in Wilmington, Delaware, and later Philadelphia, Pennsylvania. When Nye left, the firm was reorganized as the Pierce-Budd Company. James H. Pierce was president of the firm. In 1913 Reuben Bastow was vice-president, F. H. Newcomer was the secretary, and Mrs. Anna S. Pierce was the treasurer. In 1914 Bastow was the secretary and treasurer and Budd was listed as the vice-president while James Pierce remained as president.

230

Two Cycle

Trade Name	cylinders	R.P.M.	H.P.	Weight	Year	Notes
Pierce-Budd			6-60		1909	
	1,2,3,6	1,800	4-200	118-800	1911	
					1923	

Sources: Catalog, Pierce-Boutin Motors, Inc., 1923
    Motor Boat, December 10, 1911, pp. 326-327.
    Motor Boating December 1914; December, 1915
    R. L. Polk & Co.'s Bay City Directory 1910
    Powerboat, April 1909

Racine: See T..H. Truscott

Regal Gasoline Engine Company
Coldwater
Pearl & Monroe St. (1907)
In 1901 Shuger Gasoline Engine Works was reorganized as the Regal Gasoline Engine Company. Their earliest products appear to have been marine engines. In 1914 they added generator units to the line. After 1929 the company ceased to operate or was renamed.

Four-Cycle

Trade Name	cylinders	R.P.M.	H.P.	Weight	Years	Notes
	1-4		3-24		1901	
	1,2,4		3-45	800-4,300	1908	"For Fishermen & All Cruising Launches"
Regal	1,2,4	700	3-45	225 –4,300	1911	
					1914	

Sources: AGE, p 414
    Motor Boating December 1914
    The Motor Boat Ads, 1907 and 1908
    The Rudder Ad, 1907

Schroeder Engine and Boat Manufacturing Works
Bay City
foot of E. Jane Street
The company appears to have been a small, short-lived boat-building firm owned by
Louis C. Schroeder in 1909.

Trade Name	R.P.M.	H.P.	Weight	Years Produced	Notes
				1909	

Sources: MSG, 1909-1910

Seager Engine Works   See the listing for P. L. Olds & Son

Shruger Gasoline Engine Works   See listing for Regal Gasoline Engine Co.

THE SINTZ MARINE ENGINE.

Sintz Gas Engine Company
Grand Rapids/Detroit
Clark Sintz was a pioneer gas engine manufacturer.
In the 1880's he built engines on his own and organized
a gasoline engine business with John Foos in
Springfield, Ohio. Grand Rapids industrialist A. L.
Barber purchased one of his marine engines and was
so impressed that he provided inducement for Sintz to
move to Grand Rapids. ISintz relocated and the
company bearing his name was organized in 1892. It
soon had a national reputation. The accompanying
illustration is from a review in *Scientific American*. In
1893 and the company's exhibit at the Columbian World Exhibition in 1893 attracted much
attention. Clark and his sons left the company in 1894 and organized the Wolverine Motor
Works. In 1900 the Sintz Gas Engine Company became a subsidiary of Michigan Yacht &
Power Co., and relocated to Detroit. (The Foos Gas Engine Company continued to prosper as
a stationary engine manufacturer in Springfield into the
1920's.) See the Detroit listing for additional details.

**DOUBLE OPPOSED FOUR
CYCLE MARINE ENGINE**

Noiseless, Compact, Powerful, Economical,
Reliable, Perfect Control, Beautiful Finish

¶ The same efficiency as a four cylinder vertical engine
with half the moving parts. ¶ If you contemplate purchasing an engine for a speed boat, family launch, hunting launch
or auxiliary power in sailing yacht do not fail to investigate
the merits of this engine. ¶ CATALOG FREE ON REQUEST.

SINTZ-WALLIN CO., Successors to CLAUDE SINTZ
SOUTH FRONT STREET, GRAND RAPIDS, MICH.

AGENCIES

F. H. BALLOU, 329 Main Street, Buffalo, N.Y.
CHAS. R. HALL, 410 Pine Street, Seattle, Wash.
CHAS. K. PUTKI, 104 Hancock Street, Brooklyn, N.Y.
ARTHUR LITHGOW, 39 G Street, N. E., Washington, D. C.

Claude Sintz Manufacturer (1905)
Sintz-Wallin Company   (1907)
Grand Rapids
Claude was the youngest son of Clark Sintz.
Advertisements in 1905 and 1906 for Claude Sintz,
Manufacturer, noted 20 years of practical experience.
In 1907 the Sintz-Wallin Company advertised as the
successor to Claude Sintz and for some time Claude's
name got the larger print. In a full page ad in Power
Boating, 1908, Claude Sintz claimed four years of
building the Horizontal Opposed 4-cycle marine gasoline
engine and 22 years building gasoline marine engines.

In 1908 Wilmarth & Morman, Grand Rapids, purchased from Sintz-Wallin all the patents and manufacturing rights of the well known Sintz reversing propeller. By 1913 the Sintz-Wallin Company reorganized or renamed itself as the Leader Gas Engine Co of Grand Rapids. By 1914 the company ceased operations or changed names again.

Two Cycle

Trade Name	cylinders	H.P.	Weight	Years	Notes
The Leader	2	1.5 - 3		1905	The 3hp single cylinder sold for $150 complete and ready to install
The Leader	2,4	6 - 30		1908	Opposed heads – "the only non-vibrating marine engine
Sintz-Wallin					

Sources: Power Boating Ad, 1908
        The Rudder, December, 1905; March, 1906, 1907

Guy L. Sintz Company
Marshall
Guy Sintz was Claude's brother and Clark's son.

Trade Name	cylinders	Year	Notes
Sintz	2	1907	Opposed Horizontal, "Non Vibrating"

Sources: Power Boating Ad, 1908

Smalley Brothers Company
Smalley Motor Company, Ltd. 1903
General Machinery Co. 1907
Smalley General Co.
Bay City
205-211 Saginaw (1903)
47 Trumbull (1908)
Smalley Brothers Company began as a general foundry and machine shop. In 1903 the company reorganized as the Smalley Motor Company, Ltd. The company made a point in their catalog that they served Bay City's growing knock-down, kit boat industry, by

helping purchasers of those boats to match Smalley engines to their home-made craft.

Initially William Smalley was chairman of the firm, with M. B. Smalley as secretary and J. B. Smalley as treasurer. By 1906 the management of the company was taken over by the Eddy family. The Eddy family had a long background in the lumber business. The new officers consisted of Newell A. Eddy, chairman; James B. Smalley, treasurer and general manager; and Newell A. Eddy, Jr. as secretary. By 1907 the Smalley Motor Company was in receivership and was reorganized as the General Machinery Company.

In 1908 the General Machinery Company's advertising promoted the racing success of *General II* powered by a M-3B Smalley engine. It was claimed to be the fastest boat in the world of her size (30'x4'3") and hp (15-20).

James H. Pierce designed the company's engines from the beginning and served as the plant superintendent before organizing the Pierce, Nye & Budd Company in 1909.

Two-Cycle

Trade Name	cylinders	H.P.	Year	Notes
Smalley	1-4	2-35	.1905	3 port
			1907	"From Foundry to Finish" all major components were made in house
	1-6	4-70	1908	

Sources: AGE, p 470
        Bay City Directory, Year Ending November 1st, 1907
        MSG, 1903-1904
        Smalley Motor Company, Ltd. Smalley Marine Gas Engines, Catalog No. 17,
            c.1905. Library of Michigan, Rare Book Collection.
        The Motor Boat Ad, 1907
        Power Boating Ad, 1908

Spaulding Gas Engine Works (c 1903)
Spaulding Engine Company (1905)
St. Joseph
Reportedly the company was manufacturing both 2 & 4-cycle marine engines by 1903. In 1905 the company offered both "Jump Spark" and "Make and Break" ignition systems and, upon special request, furnished aluminum crankcases for light racing boats.
Little else is known about the company except that it was still in business in 1908

Trade Name	cylinders	H.P.	Weight	Year	Notes
	1,2,3	4-32		1907	

Sources: AGE, p 441
Catalog, Spaulding Engine Co., 1905
Motor Boat Ad, 1908
The Motor Boat Ad, 1907

Stern: See listing for Gile Boat and Engine Co.

Stork Motor Company
Saginaw
Reportedly the company primarily sold their engines through the Defoe Boat & Motor Works as standard equipment for their line of kit boats.

Two-Cycle

Trade Name	cylinders	H.P.	Weight	Year	Notes
				1908	
Stork	1, 2 & 3			1919	

Sources: Power Boating Ad, 1908

T. H. Truscott Shipyard, 1870
T. H. Truscott & Sons, 1887
Truscott Boat Manufacturing Company, 1892
Racine Boat Manufacturing Company (Racine-Truscott-Shell Lake Boat Company), 1911
Truscott-Pierce Engine Company, 1930

Grand Rapids/St. Joseph / Muskegon / St. Joseph

When the first Truscott shipyard was wiped out by the Chicago fire of 1871 the family moved to Grand Rapids. In 1892 the business relocated to St. Joseph and incorporated as Truscott Boat Manufacturing Company.

In 1893 they had a marketing relationship with the Sintz Gas Engine Company and provided space for them to exhibit at the World's Columbian Exhibition in Chicago that year. Later the company is know to have used many Monitor Vapor Engines. By 1898 they began building engines designed by Edward E. Truscott. By 1905 they offered both 2 & 4-cycle engines with 1,2 & 3 cylinders.

The July 1907 issue of *The Launch*, a quarterly publication of the Truscott Boat Manufacturing Company, listed the principal sales agencies, including the major cities in the US and 13 other major cities in Europe, Asia, Latin America and Australia.

The company's transition from 1907 to 1930 is not well known. However, in 1930 Truscott-Pierce Engine Company of St. Joseph was the successor of the Racine-Truscott-Shell Lake Boat Company. E. E. Truscott was president of the firm, with J. M. Truscott as secretary-treasurer.

Two and Four-Cycle

Trade Name	cylinders	R.P.M.	H.P.	Weight	Year	Notes
Truscott					1898	
	1,2		2-100		1900	
	1,2,3				1908	
Racine	1,2	600	2-12	175-900	1911	
Racine	2,4	450	12-24	950-1,350	1911	

Sources   AGE, p 515
          Motor Boating, December 1911, p. 30
          MSG, 1931-1934
          Truscott, James M., "The Boat Building Truscott Family," The Rudder, January
             1945

Weco: See listing for C. T. Wright Engine Co.

Western Gas Engine Works

Grand Rapids
184 N. Front St
The company appears to have been a short-lived engine manufacturer and boat builder owned and operated by A. H. Sherwood and Ralph B. Hain. Hain had previously been the mechanical engineer and superintendent of the Monitor Vapor and Power Company of Grand Rapids.

Sources: MSG, 1899

Wolverine Motor Works
Grand Rapids, 1894, Bridgeport, Connecticut, 1907 (12 Huron St.) (Grand Rapids) (35 Union Ave.)

In 1894 Clark Sintz left the Sintz Gas Engine Company ahd backed his son Claude in the organization of this company. The company was primarily a builder of marine engines but, they also built boats for their products, employing boat builders such as Charles L. Greene and George E. Clark.

In 1899, the Snyder family made a fortune selling their banana business. In 1894 Charles R. Snyder ordered two Wolverine engines to power launches hauling bananas along the rivers linking his plantations and the shipping ports. In 1895 he visited Grand Rapids and spent several months there working closely with Clark Sintz to design and build a narrow gauge railway powered by Wolverine engines to connect the plantations with each other and the ports. The next year they purchased this company.

In 1901 the president and treasurer of the firm was C. L. Snyder, with A. C. Denison as vice-president and Claude Sintz as secretary. An advertisement in the 1903 *Michigan State Gazetteer and Business Directory* stated:

> "*Wolverine Gasoline Marine Engines/and Launches./[illustration of a canopied launch]/The "Wolverine" is the only Reversing and Self-Starting /Gasoline Engine on the Market./Lightest Engine for the Power Built./Practically no vibration. Absolutely safe. Single, double and triple/marine and stationary motors from 2 to 85 H. P. Write for Catalogue./Wolverine Motor Works,/128 S. Front Street,—Grand Rapids, Mich.*"

Between 1901 and 1903, the company also had a plant located at Holland, Michigan. The superintendent of that plant, George E. Clark was previously a boat builder on his own in Holland.

By 1905 Charles L. Snyder assumed daily management of the firm. He was the president and treasurer and Louis I. Snyder was vice-president and secretary. M. T. Snyder was listed as vice-president in 1907.

In 1907 the firm moved to Bridgeport, Connecticut, where production continued until 1955. Parts continued to be offered by a successor company until the early 1970's.

Four-cycle Gas and Diesel

Trade Name	cylinders	R.P.M.	H.P.	Weight	Years	Notes
					1894	Grand Rapids
			18-100		1907	Bridgeport, CN
Wolverine	1,2,3	500	5-100	380- 10,277	1911	
					1914	

Sources: Grayson, Stan, "Beautiful Engines," Devereux Books, Marblehead, Ma, 2001
MSG, 1897, 1907-1908
Motor Boating December 1914

C. T. Wright Engine Company
Greenville, Michigan.
Chicago, Illinois
The company was founded prior to 1909 by Cass T. Wright and may have been in business as early as 1896. By 1914 the company relocated to Chicago.

Two-Cycle

Trade Name	cylinders	R.P.M.	H.P.	Weight	Year	Notes
Weco	1,3,4	700 -775	3 -15	86 – 160	1911	Detroit
					1914	Chicago

Sources: Gas Engine Magazine, Photo, December 1909, p. 6.
Motor Boating, December 1914